Collective Bargaining and the Battle of Ohio

Also by John T. McNay

Acheson and Empire: The British Accent in American Foreign Policy
The Memoirs of Ambassador Henry F. Grady: From the Great War to the Cold War

Collective Bargaining and the Battle of Ohio

The Defeat of Senate Bill 5 and the Struggle to Defend the Middle Class

John T. McNay

palgrave
macmillan

COLLECTIVE BARGAINING AND THE BATTLE OF OHIO

First published in 2013 by PALGRAVE MACMILLAN® in the United States—a division of St. Martin's Press LLC, 175 Fifth Avenue, New York, NY 10010.

Where this book is distributed in the UK, Europe and the rest of the world, this is by Palgrave Macmillan, a division of Macmillan Publishers Limited, registered in England, company number 785998, of Houndmills, Basingstoke, Hampshire RG21 6XS.

Palgrave Macmillan is the global academic imprint of the above companies and has companies and representatives throughout the world.

Palgrave® and Macmillan® are registered trademarks in the United States, the United Kingdom, Europe and other countries.

ISBN 978-1-137-33917-1

Library of Congress Cataloging-in-Publication Data

McNay, John T., 1957-

Collective bargaining and the battle of Ohio : the defeat of Senate Bill 5 and the struggle to defend the middle class / John T. McNay.

pages cm.

Includes bibliographical references and index.

ISBN 978-1-137-33917-1

1. Collective bargaining—Government employees—Ohio. 2. Collective bargaining—Law and legislation—Ohio. 3. Labor unions—Law and legislation—Ohio. 4. Labor laws and legislation—Ohio. 5. Ohio—Politics and government—1951- I. Title.

HD8005.6.U53O353 2013

331.8909771—dc23

2013005543

A catalogue record of the book is available from the British Library.

Design by Amnet

First edition: August 2013

10 9 8 7 6 5 4 3 2 1

To the People of Ohio,

For defending their neighbors, the labor movement, and the middle class.

Contents

Foreword

Ohio's Secretary of State had never seen anything like it. Volunteers toted hundreds of boxes with hundreds of thousands of signatures into his office. The 1.3 million signatures—only about 230,000 were required—were so heavy that the Secretary of State had to call in a structural engineer to make sure that the floor could support the weight.

Issue 2—the ballot initiative to repeal Ohio Senate Bill 5, the anti–collective bargaining law—brought together a coalition of seasoned activists and regular working people who had never before been so engaged in the political process.

Some months before, I convened a roundtable of Ohioans at Trinity Episcopal Church across the street from the statehouse to listen to what collective bargaining meant for workers. A teacher said that she negotiates not only for wages and benefits, but also for class size. A police officer explained how he negotiates not just for materials, but for safety equipment. A nurse negotiated for better patient safety.

As new threats to organized labor emerge in statehouses throughout the nation, *Collective Bargaining and the Battle of Ohio* traces the victory over Ohio SB 5 and explains why it is a twenty-first-century turning point in Ohio politics.

Some time ago, I met with a group of janitors working in downtown Cincinnati who just that day had signed their first union contract. I asked one of them what being in a union meant to her. "At the age of 51," she said, "this is the first time in my life I will have a paid vacation." These custodians understood—as people all over my state understand—that collective bargaining is the ticket to the middle class.

This was the first time in American history that a ballot initiative defended collective bargaining. Never before have we witnessed this kind of organized, well-financed effort to destroy gains made by American workers.

This resounding 22-point win to preserve collective bargaining rights was a triumph for hotel workers and firefighters, for small business owners and police officers. It was a victory for middle-class workers—and for those who aspire to join the middle class.

Sherrod Brown
United States Senator

Acknowledgments

Any book has many contributors in addition to the person who actually does the writing. This book has more than most, because it is about a joint endeavor of the most serious kind, involving the careers and education of thousands of faculty and students, as well as the lives and livelihoods of middle-class working people in many different occupations across Ohio.

My colleagues at the University of Cincinnati have been wonderfully supportive and intellectually challenging. My colleagues with the AAUP across the state and the nation always have our backs. My local chapter of the AAUP is a remarkable organization because of the people who contribute their time to make it so. The energy and optimism of our students is a constant inspiration. My family has been invaluable. I wish to thank those people, as well, who directly helped me with this book. Because they are many and helped in different ways, I hesitate to name them, but I will try to name a few. They include Andrea Tuttle Kornbluh, Sara Kilpatrick, Ionas Rus, Debby Herman, Marty Kich, and Evan Barrett. The great staff at Palgrave have helped enormously, among them Matthew Kopel, Brian O'Connor, and Scarlet Neath.

Nevertheless, this book and any mistakes it may contain or opinions it expresses are mine and mine alone.

This book is dedicated to the people of Ohio. It is often said that the hottest places in hell are reserved for those who, in times of great moral crisis, fail to take a stand. In this time of great moral crisis in our battle against Senate Bill 5, the people of Ohio stood up for the middle class and did what was right. We will always be grateful.

Introduction

The Battle of Ohio

On the evening of November 8, 2011, Ohio Gov. John Kasich stepped before microphones to admit that the centerpiece legislation of his administration, Senate Bill 5, had been heavily defeated in a referendum by the people of his state.

"When you get beat," an at least temporarily chastened Kasich said, "you've got to admit it. It is clear the people have spoken."[1]

On Election Day 2011, with voter turnout unusually high for an off-year ballot, Ohio voters defeated Senate Bill 5, or Issue 2, as it was known on the ballot, by a margin of nearly 62 percent to 38 percent (2.2 million votes to 1.3 million).

Senate Bill 5, or SB 5, launched with great fanfare by its right-wing Republican Party supporters early in the year, had been decisively defeated by Ohioans—Democrats, those increasingly rare moderate Republicans, and independents—who didn't believe in scapegoating public employees for the recession or the state's budgetary woes.

For me, a university professor and union member, as for so many others, this fight had become very personal. It said a great deal about two different views of Ohio and two different views of America. On the one hand, the proponents of SB 5 suggested that the world was one where, if only individuals would offer themselves up to the benevolent corporate forces of the free market and conservative political officials, then the state's budget and economic problems would be solved. Backed by corporate titans, conservative think tanks, and right-wing politicians, supporters of SB 5 promised they were only trying to do what was necessary and best for Ohio. In reality, they represented an ideology that, despite borrowing from some of the worst strands of American history, is actually quite foreign to American traditions.

The United States had never been a place, until recently, where any significant portion of the population believed that submission of individual freedom to corporate power was a necessity.

On the other hand, like many others, my life experience had suggested a very different world. In my world, ordinary people needed some protection from the rapacious corporate and political forces that saw their labor as only another commodity to buy and sell. Empowered by shared interests and goals, people could craft lives that were both successful and satisfying. There was no need to sacrifice individual freedom to market forces. More than that, my experience had shown to me how essential it is that the people who actually do the work and produce value also have a say in the workplace.

For me, part of this view was generated by growing up in a small town in the Rocky Mountain West. Anaconda, Montana, was created and dominated by a huge multinational mining corporation, the Anaconda Copper Mining Company. The fabulously rich copper mines in nearby Butte, and the rumbling of the world's largest copper smelter in Anaconda, kept generations employed while creating a unique urban industrial world in the agrarian vastness of Montana. Meanwhile, the famous Copper Kings used their enormous fortunes to play with the state's political system like a toy. The opportunity for real political freedom for Montanans came only in 1912, when by public referendum the people passed the Montana Corrupt Practices Act, which barred corporate contributions to political campaigns, one of the toughest such laws in the nation. Without the powerful unions that had developed to provide some balance and protection, the mighty Anaconda Company would have left nothing behind when it was done depleting the area's resource. These were truths learned in Montana through hard experience. The Montana Corrupt Practices Act has now been undermined by the Supreme Court's Citizens United case, making unconstitutional any reasonable limits on corporate ability to buy elections. To paraphrase a *New Yorker* article on this situation, conservatives have proven to be peculiarly indifferent to the hard-learned lessons of history.[2]

A further aspect of my background that informs my understanding of the SB 5 battle is my decade-long career as a newspaper reporter and editor in Montana and Idaho, including eight years at *The Montana Standard* in Butte, before I chose to return to academia. My work in newspapers made me keenly aware of economic issues, the motivations of elected officials, and the need for openness in government. It also highlighted the value of a free and accurate press, as well as the dangers of allowing corporate interests too much control over public money and public policy.

In 2011, as a professor at the university, this need to provide some balance and protection was met by the American Association of University Professors (AAUP), a faculty union at the University of Cincinnati (UC). Certainly, the AAUP is not the kind of industrial union that I had been familiar with in my youth. But with the increasing corporatization of higher education in Ohio and elsewhere in the country, where many university presidents see themselves as CEOs and administrations tend to behave like property management firms, the AAUP has been a valued voice for students, the classroom, and the faculty. I happened to be president of the AAUP at UC in 2011.

Founded in 1915 by John Dewey, a philosopher, psychologist, and educational reformer, and Arthur Lovejoy, a philosopher and historian, the AAUP's original and longstanding objective is to protect faculty from unwarranted intimidation or removal from their positions because of holding unpopular views. This conception of "academic freedom" is essential to the life of higher education and was introduced into academia by the AAUP. In addition to promoting academic freedom, the AAUP also has strongly endorsed the practice of shared governance at colleges and universities. "Shared governance" means that on issues affecting the operation of their institutions, especially on education, curriculum, hiring, reappointment, and tenure, the faculty should have an important role in contributing to decisions. The AAUP's "Statement of Principles on Academic Freedom and Tenure" is the definitive articulation of these principles and practices; it is widely accepted throughout the academic community and known as the "Red Book." In Ohio, the AAUP has a dozen collective bargaining chapters and 11 advocacy chapters, and it represents more than 6,000 faculty members in bargaining units across the state.

The University of Cincinnati has historic roots in the city dating back to 1819. With more than 42,000 students, UC is second in size only to Ohio State University, the behemoth in Columbus.[3] Combining a large and complex research-intensive institution with open-access regional campuses, UC can provide students with the kind of opportunities that change lives.

The UC Chapter of the AAUP, which was founded in 1933 but negotiated its first contract in 1975, is the oldest and largest chapter in Ohio. In nearly 40 years of collective bargaining, it has only resorted to a strike twice and has been successful in defending faculty rights, shared governance, and academic freedom. Despite the stormy periods, most of the time a sense of partnership in a joint endeavor of building a great university informs the AAUP's relationship with the UC administration. Unlike many traditional labor unions, AAUP chapters operate independently of the national office in Washington and the state office in Columbus. It is a grassroots professional organization.

Over the decades, the AAUP—including both its collective bargaining and advocacy chapters in Ohio—had remained studiously nonpolitical. This is especially true of our chapter in Cincinnati. Given UC's size and complexity, and with more than 1,700 full-time faculty members in the bargaining unit, the chapter had chosen to avoid the controversy that might have come with routine political partisanship.

John Kasich, however, by his campaign promises, worked just as hard to change our stance. Over the course of the campaign for governor in 2010, we gradually became aware that Kasich had in mind a sweeping attack on public education and that we in the state's colleges and universities would be targeted as well. Professor Steve Howe, chair of the Psychology Department and then president of the chapter, began to bring these issues to our attention during the summer of 2010, and by September we were ready to break new ground in trying to defend our faculty and the university from this anticipated broad-based attack.

First, our executive council considered, with great gravity, the choice to make our first-ever political campaign donation. Democratic Gov. Ted Strickland had introduced a series of innovative strategies for higher education and had used some federal stimulus funds to help protect education in Ohio from severe cutbacks. He had emphasized the importance of higher education in Ohio in building an economy of the future. Many of the state's budget problems, as will be explained later in this book, were not because of the economic downturn but because of ideologically driven tax cuts that drastically reduced state revenue. Candidate Kasich was evidently going to use the manufactured crisis to attack all of the public unions in Ohio, including the AAUP. Certainly, the next step would be to attack the private unions. Over the decades, the AAUP had created a positive environment at UC, where faculty had respect and influence over the quality of education our students received. Now we were looking at losing all of that. In the face of this crisis, we chose to make a major contribution to the Strickland campaign—the UC chapter of AAUP's first-ever political contribution.

Second, President Howe and I, as vice president at the time, wrote a letter dated October 1, 2010, that was mailed to the homes of our faculty members, outlining why it was of paramount importance that we do what we could to see that Strickland was reelected. The difference between the two candidates, we wrote, was "so stark" and the "implications for higher education and collective bargaining rights" so great that we needed to take a stand. "John Kasich," we wrote, "has publicly expressed on numerous occasions, his belief that professors and Ohio's public universities are obstacles to a better future for Ohio, not assets. Mr. Kasich has also repeatedly stated that Ohio's public employees, and collective bargaining rights currently held by public employees, are 'the problem' in Ohio." We went on to cite statements made by Kasich during the campaign, such as "We need to break the back of organized labor in the schools."

"We believe," we wrote in conclusion, "that we will be far better off in these tough times with a governor in Columbus who believes public universities and colleges are an asset to Ohio and the basis for a better future, rather than a governor who sees them—and us—as either an obstacle or irrelevant." We then encouraged the faculty to review the enclosed flyers that listed the opposing positions on educational issues and asked our faculty to make up their own minds and be sure to vote.

This may have all been too little too late, and certainly many public and private unions, as well as many ordinary Ohioans, did not anticipate the ruthlessness of the attack that did come and thus did not mobilize in time to keep Gov. Strickland in office, where he could have served as a firewall against radical and destructive policies. Kasich won the election by the narrowest of margins, with 49 percent of the vote to Strickland's 47 percent; a mere 77,000 votes out of 3.6 million cast separated the two candidates.[4]

When Senate Bill 5 was rapidly signed into law by Gov. Kasich just a few months later, it contained language that singled out university faculty unions for virtual elimination, alone out of all the other public unions in Ohio. At that point, we knew that our effort to avoid a Kasich governorship, and to defend our university and higher education in Ohio, had been the correct course of action.

Over the next several months, a titanic political struggle ensued, pitting a formerly moribund labor movement in a rust-belt state against right-wing extremists who wanted to remake the state in their own corporate-friendly image. In the process, a historic labor coalition brought together professors, teamsters, secretaries, food service workers, police officers, schoolteachers, firemen, nurses, and janitors to fight for the continuation of the middle class in Ohio and to help the state continue to be the place of opportunity it has always strived to be.

This book is one story of that battle for Ohio—and perhaps for the soul of America.

Chapter 1

The Storm Comes

"Here we go." That was the subject line of an email I received early Tuesday morning, February 1, 2011, sent by Stephanie Spanja, one of the University of Cincinnati American Association of University Professors (UC-AAUP) staffers who had been monitoring Ohio legislative activity for the UC faculty. Senate Bill 5 had been introduced by Sen. Shannon Jones, a Republican legislator from the Cincinnati area.

"As it stands," Spanja wrote, "it is now a statement of intent, but far more sweeping in scope than what most Republicans have been talking about." Senate Bill 5 was designed to repeal Senate Bill 133, passed in 1983, which had allowed for public employees' collective bargaining.

This was the beginning of a long and difficult fight to defend workers' rights in the face of ruthless attacks from right-wing political forces. However, the struggle really began with the Republican sweep of Ohio's legislature and state offices in the November 2010 election. The GOP had been buoyed by the stagnant state economy and by loud and consistent attacks on Gov. Ted Strickland and other Democratic office holders by the Tea Party and other conservative extremists.

Despite Gov. Strickland's largely positive record and initial popularity, his administration was undermined by the Great Recession that had engulfed the nation and Ohio. Job losses in the state had soared, and the unemployment rate in Ohio, which had been 5.4 percent in 2007, had topped out at 10.6 percent in late 2009. Although Strickland worked diligently on remedies, Ohio's economy is so completely entwined with the national market that there is very little that a governor can do in the face of such a systemic crisis. Into this situation walked an opportunist by the name of John Kasich.[1]

Coming into the race with a close association with the failed Lehman Brothers investment bank, Kasich nevertheless portrayed himself as a kind of financial wizard, endowed with the know-how to solve Ohio's economic problems. Kasich was born in McKee's Rocks, Pennsylvania, a small Ohio River town not far from Pittsburgh, and his father was a U.S. Post Office employee, making his son's animosity toward public unions a bit odd. Moving to Ohio in 1970 to attend Ohio State University, Kasich earned a bachelor's degree in business administration in 1974. He served from 1975 to 1978 as an administrative assistant to then-senator Donald "Buz" Lukens.[2]

With his election to the Ohio Senate in 1978 at age 26, Kasich became the youngest person ever elected to that body. He won election to Congress in 1982 from Ohio's Twelfth Congressional District. He rose to chair the House Budget Committee, where he was known as a chief architect behind the Balanced Budget Act of 1997. Like President Bill Clinton, Kasich has routinely claimed credit for the government surplus that developed in the 1990s. This claim, however, earned three "Pinocchios" from *The Washington Post*'s fact-check of the speech Kasich gave the 2012 Republican National Convention. The *Post* pointed out that no Republicans voted for the 1993 budget bill, which included tax increases that provided the revenue for the surplus. Further, the *Post* noted, "two of the seven budgets Kasich helped craft as chair of the Budget Committee from January 1995 until January 2001 ended up running deficits, so the former congressman can't claim to be so horrified by a growing national debt."[3]

Kasich chose not to run for Congress in 2000; instead he opened an exploratory effort for the presidency. His campaign soon foundered on a lack of money and a lack of support from voters in Iowa and New Hampshire. Kasich abandoned his effort and announced his support for George W. Bush. Kasich then launched a brief career on Fox News, co-hosting Bill O'Reilly's show as well as debuting his own, *From the Heartland with John Kasich.*

Gov. Kasich has authored a couple of books that give us a window into his thinking. In 1998, he published a series of essays entitled *Courage Is Contagious: Ordinary People Doing Extraordinary Things to Change the Face of America*. This seemed a rather heavy-handed attempt at modeling his book after John F. Kennedy's *Profiles in Courage*, but in actuality, the book follows much more closely the ideas on volunteerism expressed by another president, Herbert Hoover.

In books and speeches, Hoover was an enthusiastic supporter of people volunteering to provide services individually, rather than having government resources used to provide necessary public services.

Hoover, much like Kasich and other very conservative Republicans, was a great critic of Franklin D. Roosevelt and the New Deal. In a speech at Madison Square Garden in New York on October 21, 1932, Hoover argued that the New Deal threatened a change that had come to America. This change was widespread volunteerism.

"There has thus grown within us, to gigantic importance, a new conception," Hoover said. This new development was "voluntary co-operation within the community," and it was sweeping and comprehensive. He enumerated the details: "Co-operation to perfect the social organizations; co-operation for the care of those in distress; co-operation for the advancement of knowledge, of scientific research, of education; for co-operative action in the advancement of many phases of economic life." This was, he said, "self-government by the people outside of Government; it is the most powerful development of individual freedom and equal opportunity that has taken place in the century and a half since our fundamental institutions were founded." So important was this "co-operation," Hoover maintained, that it was the "greatest function of government" to "build up that co-operation, and its most resolute action should be to deny the extension of bureaucracy." Similarly, Hoover told the Republican National Convention in 1936, "Government must either release the powers of the individual for honest achievement or the very forces it creates will drive it inexorably to lay its paralyzing hand more and more heavily upon individual effort."[4]

Of course, an enormous amount of time and vast changes in American society separate Kasich and Hoover. And yet, one can hear Hoover in the pages of *Courage Is Contagious*:

> My dad delivered mail and often told me how much the New Deal meant to working people in the 1930s. Later, in the 1960s, we needed civil rights legislation and Medicare. But now it is time for the pendulum to swing back. Government has an important role to play but it must be limited. Instead government has gotten too big, has become too intrusive into people's lives. Too often now, it's part of the problem instead of part of the solution. Too often, instead of helping the heroes I celebrated in this book, it hobbles them with heavy-handed regulations, red tape and boneheaded tax policies.[5]

All of this, even including Kasich's actions in the early 1990s, reflects typical and familiar Tea Party perspectives and rhetoric. In the real world, problems do exist with the delivery of government services. But most of the heroes in Kasich's book are driven to action because government services were crippled by being starved for resources. When the "government" acts on its responsibility to serve people in need, it is not some inanimate third party, as is so often portrayed in conservative circles. The government is the collective arm of the taxpayers, the people.

Furthermore, it should be recognized that Hoover's ideology of volunteerism is manifestly inadequate for dealing with the problems of the modern United States. Hoover's excuse may be that he spent a great deal of time out of the country building a fortune as an engineer, and it is possible that he failed to appreciate that the America of the 1930s was not the America of his small-town Iowa youth.[6] Kasich, by contrast, has been not so much naïve as calculating. In being extraordinarily consistent with what Mitt Romney would call an "extremely conservative" approach that views government as an opponent and a threat to "freedom," Kasich wants simple answers that will create simple solutions. In Ohio, Kasich thus adopted a governing strategy that vilified public servants and public institutions, including universities and schools, and suggested that the very paying of taxes was illegitimate, proposing even to do away with the state income tax, the only progressive tax left after continuous Republican tax "reform" strategies shifted the tax burden to the middle class. Rather than solving problems, Kasich's approach of privatizing services would instead funnel taxpayers' money directly to deep corporate pockets.[7]

Another prominent figure in the fight over SB 5 was state Sen. Shannon Jones. Her early political work began in Cincinnati with the Hamilton County Republican Party and the campaigns of conservative Congressman Steve Chabot. A graduate of the University of Cincinnati in Communications, Jones first ran for a House seat in 2006 in her heavily Republican district in Warren County to replace Tom Raga, who had been chosen to be Ken Blackwell's lieutenant governor in that ill-fated gubernatorial campaign. Jones was reelected easily in 2008.[8]

The death of state Sen. Bob Schuler in June 2009 set up an intriguing situation. Both Jones and former House member Michelle Schneider were looking to replace him. But now they vied with each other to be appointed to fill the post until the 2010 election. Jones was able to work her connections better than Schneider and was named to fill out the term. Thus, in the 2010 primary battle against Schneider, Jones became the incumbent.

Jones revealed several aspects of her personal ambition in this race. Jones and Schneider had once been friends, even roommates, but that was no longer the case. "Tempted by the prospect of an open state Senate seat, Jones elbowed her way past her political mentor and Columbus roommate, former Rep. Michelle Schneider of Madeira," *The Cincinnati Enquirer* reported, "despite what Schneider insists were Jones' repeated assurances to 'never, never run against'" her. "She stabbed me in the back," Schneider said. "Some friend."[9]

Jones had shown similar determination early in her political career. In her first race, in 1992, she ran against Rep. William Mallory, Sr., a member of a prominent African American political family in Cincinnati and, at the time, the Democrats' majority leader in Columbus. Because Jones had once taken a state government and politics course from Mallory at the University of Cincinnati, the election was billed as "the professor versus the pupil." And Mallory schooled Jones, defeating her by 68 percent to 32 percent.[10]

Jones's friends and allies said that what was memorable about her defeat was that Jones maintained her enthusiasm and commitment to staying in politics. Perhaps the genesis of her sponsorship of Senate Bill 5 can be found in the determination that she demonstrated to do whatever was necessary to further her own political career.

Two other important figures in the Senate Bill 5 battle were the Senate majority leader, Tom Niehaus, and the Speaker of the House, William Batchelder. Like Jones, they are both members of the American Legislative Exchange Council (ALEC), the radical conservative organization that has proposed many model bills that undermine the rights of ordinary Americans, including House Bill 194—a voter suppression bill—and the "stand-your-ground" laws that have proliferated around the country.

Niehaus, a Republican from New Richmond, was first elected to the Ohio Senate in 2005 after having served two terms in the House. Upon his election to Senate president, he said that he looked forward to working with Gov. Kasich and Speaker Batchelder "to pass a balanced state budget, get our state economy back on track, and create an optimal environment to create good paying jobs in Ohio." In retrospect, one can detect in that language the union-busting legislation that was in the future—an "optimal environment" for corporations being one where workers have no rights—but at the time Niehaus certainly did not claim that as his objective.[11]

Niehaus earned a bachelor's degree in journalism from Ohio State University in 1973 and an MBA from Cincinnati's Xavier University in 1986. He worked for 25 years with small newspaper companies in Ohio as an editor and publisher. Before the battle over Senate Bill 5, Niehaus was not viewed as a politician driven by ideology. "He is very pragmatic," Clermont County Commissioner Bob Proud told Rory

Ryan, publisher and editor of *The Highland County Press*, in January 2011. "Tom is very upfront with you . . . about whether something can be done."[12] Those statements would be called into doubt by Niehaus's own actions in the SB 5 fight.

Jones was named majority whip. It did raise eyebrows among many in the Cincinnati labor community that Niehaus, who was no friend of labor, as well as Shannon Jones, who had been hostile to unions—particularly toward the public school teachers' union, in earlier sessions—would both be in leadership positions. Ironically, as things would turn out, when he opened the Senate, Niehaus promised in his address that he would preside over a "deliberative body where all voices will be heard."[13]

William Batchelder, who had a legal career focusing on corporate law and personal injury defense, was appointed by Republican Gov. Bob Taft to Ohio's Ninth District Court of Appeals from 2000 to 2005. He then gained reelection to the Ohio House in 2006 (he had had a lengthy term in the House before becoming a judge). During Batchelder's time in the House, he has been hostile to unions and, especially, to public schools. Under his tenure, the corporate school entrepreneur David Brennan, head of White Hat Management, Ohio's largest operator of charter schools, and a major contributor to GOP candidates, had special access to the Legislative Service Commission (LSC) with no lawmakers present. The LSC, which offers assistance drafting bills, is supposed to be a service for the legislators, not corporate interests. According to *The Columbus Dispatch*, 10 of the 29 "concepts" proposed in private meetings with the LSC by White Hat to direct more public monies to private charter schools—like those operated by White Hat—were in the final House legislation. Not surprisingly, David Brennan and his wife, Ann, gave a combined $40,000 to Batchelder in 2008 and $33,000 in 2010, according to financial reports. In 2007, the Brennans gave a combined $733,000 to state candidates and Republican organizations, including $400,000 to the Republican Party. As a further window into the Speaker's political attitudes, Batchelder made national news in February 2012 when, at a Summit County Lincoln Day Dinner, he joked that "The liberals are asking us to give Obama more time. I think 25 to life would be a good start."[14]

While many others were involved in the conception, creation, and passage of Senate Bill 5, Kasich, Jones, Niehaus, and Batchelder were the very public proponents in the drama that unfolded in 2011 in Ohio. But had it not been for John Kasich's election, it is unlikely that the fight over Senate Bill 5 would have happened, so it is useful to examine the political situation in Ohio prior to the 2010 election and Gov. Strickland's place in it.

Gov. Strickland was born on August 4, 1941, in Lucasville, Ohio, where his father was a steelworker. He graduated from Asbury College in Kentucky in 1963 with a bachelor's degree in history. Strickland earned a master's degree in guidance counseling from the University of Kentucky in 1966 and a master's degree in divinity from Asbury in 1967. Later, in 1980, Strickland completed his doctorate in counseling psychology at the University of Kentucky and in 1982 became a licensed psychologist. Strickland worked at the Southern Ohio Correctional Facility as a counselor and taught psychology at Shawnee State University. He served briefly as a minister at United Methodist Church in Portsmouth, Ohio.

After several unsuccessful attempts at running for Congress, Strickland defeated incumbent Bob McEwen in 1992 by a narrow margin. The Republican wave in 1994 swept Strickland out of office, but he won the seat again in 1996 and held it until he left Congress in 2006 to enter the Ohio gubernatorial race.

Strickland easily defeated the Republican nominee for governor, Ken Blackwell, winning 60 percent of the vote. Blackwell had been tainted by having served as Ohio's secretary of state during the presidential election of 2004, when many "irregularities" in the voting process in Ohio contributed to George W. Bush winning the state and thus a second term in the Oval Office.[15]

As governor, Strickland introduced a series of important reforms, and those for higher education were particularly significant. Under Republican Gov. Taft and a conservative-dominated legislature, Ohio's colleges and universities had often been targeted for cutbacks, despite the relatively prosperous times. Prior to Strickland's election, Ohio's state colleges and universities had seen funding reduced for five consecutive years. Strickland turned this around with a new vision for higher education as a driver for economic development in Ohio and as a key tool in making the state economically competitive with other regions of the country. Ohio's universities were encouraged to freeze tuition in exchange for increased funding from the state, thereby making college more affordable to Ohioans. Strickland introduced an innovative concept known as the University System of Ohio, which was designed to create a more seamless transfer of students and credits among Ohio universities and increase cooperation while boosting enrollments and graduation rates. In 2007, Strickland's approval rating was 61 percent according to Quinnipiac polling. A conservative Democrat, Strickland reduced government regulation of businesses and was a moderate on abortion issues. A defender of public education, he boosted funding, increased graduation rates, and blocked school vouchers. Strickland's efforts brought Ohio's public schools from a spot low on the ratings lists to a ranking of fifth-best school system in the country in *Education Week*'s widely respected Quality Counts report of 2010.[16]

An unprecedented cut to the state income tax created the context in which the battle for Ohio would take place. The destruction this tax cut inflicted on state priorities, while enriching the wealthiest Ohioans, is a story of immense importance because the reduction was such a central part of conservative strategy. The dull numbers and percentages of this story provide a rich resource for understanding the manufactured crisis that Republican policy makers attempted to take advantage of in 2011.

In 2005, in House Bill 66, the GOP enacted a sweeping tax reduction plan that has since cut the state's income tax by 21 percent. The final 4.2 percent of the reduction was put in place by Senate Bill 5 proponents in early 2011. Each year, the tax reduction plan cost Ohio more than $2 billion in annual revenue; the accumulated deficit was roughly equal to Ohio's budget deficit in 2011 (about $6 billion, not the exaggerated $8 billion the Kasich administration claimed). In 2005, a number of groups and legislators tried to convince Gov. Taft and his Republican allies that gutting the state budget in such a way was a very flawed approach.

The think tank Policy Matters Ohio issued a series of reports about the impact of this kind of regressive tax policy, and their economists testified before the legislature.[17] Policy Matters reports argued accurately that the income tax cuts would create more budget problems, rather than solve them. The income tax cut would reduce state revenues by nearly $1 billion during the fiscal year 2006–2007 biennium, and by $2 billion a year when fully implemented in 2010. Policy Matters correctly predicted that this would make it difficult for Ohio to pay for crucial services and investments and would increase the chances of another state budget shortfall in the future. Policy Matters also accurately pointed out that the tax cut would lead to higher local taxes as local governments attempted to make up for reduced state support.[18] Policy Matters also warned that about one-seventh of the tax cut would leave Ohio because taxpayers who itemize would have lower state income tax to deduct on their federal taxes, probably totaling about $280 million a year by the time the cuts are fully implemented.[19]

Further, while the Republicans were elected in 2010 largely on a platform of creating jobs, Policy Matters pointed out that there is no evidence that cutting income tax creates jobs. California and North Carolina have among the highest individual income tax rates in the country (top rates of 9.3 percent and 8.25 percent, respectively), and yet Silicon Valley and the Research Triangle area are two of the world's leading high-technology centers. States with lower taxes, like the southern states, also have lower average incomes than those with higher taxes, according to the Center for Community Solutions. Further, the extreme tax cut was unnecessary because Ohio already had a mechanism in place, the Income Tax Reduction Fund, which automatically reduces income tax rates when the state has enough of a surplus and can afford it.

According to a study conducted by the Institute on Taxation and Economic Policy (ITEP), Ohio residents who made more than $274,000 would be part of the 1 percent of Ohioans who, on average, would see their tax bill decline by more than $8,000 each from the reduction. This small wealthy group would receive almost a quarter of the benefit from the income tax rate cut. On the other hand, the 60 percent who made less than $43,000 a year would get just 14 percent of the reduction. Ohioans making less than $16,000 a year—a fifth of all taxpayers, on average—would see a reduction of just $19 a year.[20]

The cumulative effect of cutting income tax rates and raising regressive taxes, such as the sales tax, was a shift in the tax burden from wealthy individuals to the poor and middle class. Policy Matters correctly argued that keeping the top rate of 7.5 percent would have been important for future state revenue growth because much of Ohio's income growth in recent decades, like the growing inequality that has occurred nationwide, has been concentrated in the uppermost income strata. The bottom 60 percent of Ohio workers have seen little or no increase in real hourly pay over the past 25 years, paralleling the decline of union membership. In contrast, the top 10 percent experienced a 19 percent increase in real hourly pay from 1979 to 2003.[21]

On March 16, 2005, Jon Honeck, a research analyst at Policy Matters, testified before the Ohio Senate Ways and Means Committee. "The proponents of this bill," Honeck said, "promote it as an economic development package because of the cuts in the income tax rate and the elimination of most of the tangible personal property tax." But, Honeck explained, this was not true: "Our tax code is not a major factor in explaining Ohio s relative economic decline over the last several decades, or the recent precipitous decline in manufacturing employment. In fact, the business share of Ohio s state and local tax burden has declined from nearly 40 percent in 1976 to 30 percent in 2002." And, Honeck argued, neither was it "likely that cuts to income tax rates will affect our employment situation." He pointed out that federal personal and corporate income tax cuts over the last four years had "returned $24.4 billion to Ohio, yet Ohio had lost nearly 200,000 jobs over that time period."[22]

Bluntly put, the challenges facing Ohio's economy were national and global, and they could not be put right by simply giving tax breaks to rich Ohioans. Again, the cumulative effect of cutting income tax rates and raising regressive taxes was a shift in the tax burden from wealthy individuals to the poor and middle class. In addition to sharply reducing the personal income tax, the Republican tax plan called for phasing out the corporate franchise tax, Ohio's corporate income tax.

Conservative arguments to the contrary, as analysts repeatedly pointed out, it is widely acknowledged that cuts to income taxes have little impact on job creation. It is, frankly, just an ideologically driven handout to the wealthy. This probably explains why, as Ohio Republicans drove ahead, the Columbus-based newspaper *Business First* published a poll of central Ohio executives who showed little support for the Republican tax cutting plan.[23] Ordinary business people, unlike political ideologues, seemed to recognize that the need for good schools, good roads, and dependable public services was greater than the need to transfer state revenue to those who least needed it. And small business people certainly realized this was not going help ordinary people buy their products and services.

Policy Matters contradicted the distorted notion that people leave Ohio because of high taxes. A study produced in June 2005 analyzed IRS tax returns for 13 years, ending in 2003. Over that time, Policy Matters found no evidence that people left Ohio because of any changes to the state's tax system. Those who left went to states with a variety of tax systems, some with higher income tax and some with no income tax. Florida was the top destination state, but weather and age would likely be the determining factors there. Florida also was the state that sent the most people to Ohio, perhaps in search of better jobs and pay.

In 2007, nearly two years after the imposition of the series of tax cuts, Policy Matters Ohio reported again on their impact:

> Ohio's total non-farm payroll employment [stood] at 5.43 million, barely higher than in the summer of 2005. The manufacturing sector, which was supposed to be the main beneficiary of tax reduction,

> lost nearly 29,000 jobs since June 2005. House Bill 119 reflects continuation of anemic revenue growth from previous years: Aid to local governments is barely increased after years of being frozen, higher education continues to be squeezed, and it is a struggle to find revenue even to restore parents' coverage under Medicaid to 100 percent of the poverty level.[24]

Policy Matters Ohio went further by asking legislators to halt the income tax cuts and reverse the cuts for the most affluent. It also called on legislators to stop the handouts to the large corporations by not continuing to phase out the corporate income tax. But the Republican-dominated legislature stayed the course.

As the economic tsunami hit in 2008, Policy Matters Ohio, not surprisingly, weighed in once again. "Key economic trends continued to go in the wrong direction after the tax overhaul," Honeck wrote in a new report released January 15, 2009. "The report finds unmistakable evidence that the state's relative economic decline accelerated since H.B. 66 [the tax cut] was passed." The report suggested that hard questions should be asked of those who had argued that this experiment at supply-side economics was going to boost the economy. Now that the recession was upon the state, the think tank called for pushing the tax breaks back, at least to 2007 levels, to avoid the looming budget deficit the tax cuts were creating. "Structural changes in our economy . . . are the primary causes of Ohio's economic problems and for the decline in Ohio's economy. Starving the state of revenue will not address these problems, but it will add to human distress and prohibit Ohio from making the public investments it badly needs."[25]

Once again, and it bears repetition, there is a powerful section in the report where the researchers argue convincingly that there is no evidence that cutting state and local taxes, particularly taxes on the wealthy, boosts economic growth. For many economists this is old news, but it is a fact that has yet to penetrate Republican Party circles where supply-side economics continues to have true believers.[26]

In the 1980s, David Stockman, Ronald Reagan's first director of the Office of Management and Budget was a moderate advocate for supply-side economics. Stockman confessed to reporter William Grieder that the supply-side theory was not a new economic theory. Instead, Grieder writes, Stockman pointed out that it was "only new language and argument to conceal a hoary old Republican doctrine: give the tax cuts to the top brackets, the wealthiest individuals and largest enterprises, and let the good effects 'trickle down' through the economy to reach everyone else." According to Grieder, Stockman conceded that without the new rhetoric that emphasized budget cuts, the theory was just the old Republican orthodoxy of tax cuts for the wealthy. "It's kind of hard to sell 'trickle down,'" he explained to Grieder, without the argument that it is necessary to impose cuts as well.[27]

Newt Gingrich was John Kasich's early chief ideological ally and perhaps the most powerful influence on him. In reading through the news reports of budget cutting efforts after the Republican takeover of Congress in 1994, one is struck by the fact that Gingrich and Kasich were joined at the hip. Gingrich was the figure with stature as a leader of the movement, but Kasich was the enforcer on the House budget committee, working hand-in-glove with Gingrich.

"For months before the House took up the balanced-budget constitutional amendment," Jackie Calmes reported in *The Wall Street Journal* in 1995, "Newt Gingrich had a one-word answer when pressed about the cuts Republicans have in mind: 'Kasich.'" Rep. Kasich himself told Calmes that it was "a chance for us to rewrite and re-route government . . . This is a precious opportunity."[28]

In the story headlined "Point Man: John Kasich Wields the Mighty Budget Axe Granted by Gingrich," Calmes wrote that Kasich's most potent weapon was Gingrich's support. "I don't need Newt to understand all the details of this," Calmes quoted Kasich saying about the partnership, "and he doesn't want to understand all the details of it. But what he has to do—and he has—is just put his confidence in the Budget Committee."[29]

The implications of the Kasich–Gingrich partnership were clear: "This is the New Deal and the Great Society in reverse. Rep. Kasich and his budget allies are considering killing, consolidating or privatizing numerous federal offices, among them the departments of Energy, Education, Transportation, Commerce, Human Services, and Housing," Calmes reported almost breathlessly.

All of this background about Kasich was not prominent in the minds of Ohioans during the 2010 campaign. They had little conception that his goal was to undermine the social supports and institutions that they depended on. He talked about jobs. When Kasich finally came out of the shadows in the days after his electoral victory, Ohioans were in for a terrible surprise.

Instead of examining Kasich's history, Ohioans during the election were focused on the deep shadow that had fallen over the state's economy: the Great Recession of 2008. This broad national recession had taken with it more than 238,000 jobs in Ohio. Despite the many political issues surrounding the 2010 election, it was primarily this economic slump that undermined Strickland's ability to win a second term. Importantly, of course, the recession was a national economic disaster, and there was little that Strickland actually had power to do about it. The Ohio economy began recovering in the last year of the Strickland administration, but the governor got little credit, as the overwhelming impact of the recession was so negative.

Central accomplishments during Strickland's term as governor were in the areas of energy, health care, and education. Strickland made progress on a number of issues where energy was concerned, but Senate Bill 221 stands out for two reasons. First, its Energy, Jobs, and Progress section encouraged energy efficiency by allowing utilities to recover costs for their investment in energy-efficient equipment and practices. It also gave manufacturers the ability to reduce their utility costs and rates by making upgrades to their own systems. One of the primary objectives of Strickland's energy legislation was the creation of a large solar energy project in southeastern Ohio. The project to build a $200 million facility had been making progress until recently and was close to breaking ground on 850 acres of reclaimed coal mining property. The Turning Point Solar project has been expected to produce enough electricity to power 28,000 homes. The solar panels themselves would be built by a Spanish-owned company in Toledo, Ohio, illustrating the multiplier effect of such economic development.[30]

In January 2013, the Kasich administration dealt a blow to the Turning Point project. Since his election, Gov. Kasich has appointed three of the four members of the Public Utilities Commission of Ohio (PUCO). Staunch Republicans in the Kasich camp, they voted 3–1, against the recommendation of PUCO staff, to block American Electric Power (AEP) from using power from Turning Point to meet the state mandate that Ohio utilities generate a portion of their electricity through alternative sources. Democrats pointed out that the decision greatly aids American Electric's competitor, FirstEnergy Corp., whose executives have made significant donations to the GOP. And just to make certain the project is crippled, the Republican majority also ruled that AEP cannot recover its investment in Turning Point by adding the cost to its rate base. "Obviously we're disappointed with the commission's decision," AEP spokesperson Terri Flora told *Business First*, saying it went against an agreement AEP had negotiated with the PUCO staff. "We saw this as an opportunity to leverage Ohio jobs with an environmentally friendly project."

"It's deeply disappointing," Ohio Democratic Party Chair Chris Redfern told *The Columbus Dispatch*, "that Gov. Kasich has given the appearance his administration is more interested in rewarding his campaign donors than supporting a project that would create more than 600 jobs, including many for veterans." As evidence of the ideologically driven objectives—the same blind ideology that drove SB 5—several business groups had argued against the project because they believed it would go against the ideas of free markets.[31]

With regard to health care, using federal funds Gov. Strickland created a high-risk pool that allowed private Ohio insurers to offer coverage to Ohioans with pre-existing conditions. In his budget, Strickland expanded eligibility for the State Children's Health Insurance Program, but the attempt was later blocked by the George W. Bush administration.

But it was in education that Strickland made his most potent advances. In primary and secondary schools, Strickland had planned to direct significantly more funding to education than had been committed during the Taft administration. He had also designed a strategy focused on "evidence-based" funding, which would have required that the state select and fund only educational methods that are supported by research on best practices. This was, in part, an effort to overcome Ohio's long-term problem: its schools are funded on an unconstitutional basis. The Ohio Supreme Court has ruled repeatedly that Ohio's system of funding its schools is unconstitutional because it relies too heavily on the property tax—which means that children in rich school districts (mainly suburban) get advantages denied to students in poor school districts (mainly rural and urban).[32]

The goal of Strickland's evidence-based funding plan was twofold. First, by advocating funding for proven education solutions developed by professional educators, he implicitly opposed the frequent right-wing solutions that are based on the nonprofessional conclusions of lawyers, accountants, and ideologues, who simply oppose public education or fair taxation. Second, it aimed, over the course of ten years, to replace the current system's emphasis on property levies by increasing state funding for public schools.[33]

Candidate Kasich pounced on the evidence-based strategy, saying he would scrap it immediately because, he incorrectly argued, it had only unfunded mandates. Supporters spread the word that this was simply "more spending" by the Democrats. Strickland called Kasich's stance "irresponsible and reckless" and noted that Kasich himself had not outlined any plan for addressing school funding.[34]

Knowing now what would happen after the election, one can see in retrospect where the education issue was heading. Strickland was taking a real-world approach about how Ohio could put public schools on a fair and firm financial footing. The way to do that was clearly to increase state contributions to offset the dependence on the property tax so that all Ohio children would have an opportunity for an equal education. Kasich, on the other hand, during the campaign offered no solution and only criticized the cost of the Strickland plan. Since taking office, Kasich has dramatically cut funding to local schools—some $780 million so far, with plans for more cuts. Far from addressing the unconstitutional overreliance on local property taxes, Kasich is making the problem much worse and moving in the opposite direction than Strickland had envisioned.

Kasich and Strickland also locked horns over an ambitious plan for a light-rail system. Strickland and other Democrats developed a plan to connect Cincinnati, Columbus, and Cleveland with a high-speed rail line. Strickland argued that it would be a great economic development lever, and that even its construction would create thousands of new jobs. The Obama administration had, early on, targeted the plan for a large portion of federal funds, about $400 million, as part of the stimulus plan. Kasich and the Republicans attacked the plan relentlessly: it was a worthless boondoggle, not a fast train but a slow train, no one would ride it, and on and on. Far from benefitting Ohio, Republicans argued, the state would be left holding the bag for huge amounts of maintenance. While any of those points could be debated, the central problem Kasich seemed to have with the plan was that the federal government would be funding it.[35]

In the end, after Kasich was elected, he, like Gov. Walker in Wisconsin, refused for ideological reasons to accept the $400 million, despite Ohio's high unemployment rate and crippled economy. The money was later sent to other states, including nearby rival Michigan, whose political leaders took a more reasonable view of passenger rail. Work is currently progressing on track improvements between Detroit and Chicago to allow 100-mile-per-hour passenger trains.[36]

Another significant rift between Strickland and Kasich developed over the issue of privatization. Kasich clearly embraced the cult of privatization that has been so popular among conservatives. Working from the premise that the private sector and the market can always do things better than the government, Kasich talked about privatization in several areas: economic development, the Ohio Turnpike, prisons, and schools. Reflecting his heavy funding from the corporate school sector, Kasich was very supportive of the idea of increasing the scale of the charter school movement in Ohio—another way he clashed with Strickland on education. While Kasich would be reducing state funding for public education, he also hoped to off-load more of that responsibility onto the private sector. During the campaign he also proposed to sell the state's prisons and the turnpike in northern Ohio. In both cases, he argued that these plans would bring an influx of cash and divest the state of expenses.[37]

While the failure of charter schools to perform as well as public schools is clear, studies of whether privatized prisons are less expensive and more effective have reached mixed conclusions. Those studies performed by the prison industry have tended to paint a rosy picture. Those performed by organizations representing the workers who actually know the prisons show the national prison privatization effort as a failure, except with regard to funneling public money into private corporations. In Arizona, which is well down the road of privatization, a study by a Quaker group found that Arizona's private prisons are not cost-effective for taxpayers and are more difficult to monitor than state prisons. The study also found that much violence and even riots that had occurred in private prisons had not been reported. And an earlier study of the controversial prison industry by *Arizona Republic* staff raised real questions about whether the state could hold the corporate managers of private prisons accountable. Further, it had become obvious that the private prisons, driven by the profit motive, were more expensive than the state-owned and -managed prisons.[38] In contrast to Kasich's devotion to privatization, Gov. Strickland's plans for prison reform did not include privatization but focused on reducing costs through sentencing reform with the aim of reducing the numbers of nonviolent offenders imprisoned.

Finally, Kasich's most radical plan, spoken of only sketchily in the campaign, has been to turn over Ohio's economic development efforts to a private organization made up primarily of CEOs and other leaders in the business community. In the early twentieth century, of course, such an idea would have been seen as obvious graft and corruption but not among the new breed of conservatives who won power in the 2010 election in Ohio. When the concept was first introduced in the campaign during August 2010, Kasich promised to do away with the state Department of Development, replacing it with a new private board called JobsOhio that would, as Kasich has been fond of saying, "move at the speed of business." This plan immediately created opposition, some of it from those who believed it was unconstitutional to turn over that much government funding to a group of private individuals. To provide funding for JobsOhio, now dubbed "RobsOhio" by its critics, the state would lease, and thus privatize, the state's lucrative wholesale liquor profits. Further controversy ensued over the shadowy operation of JobsOhio in early 2013. State Auditor David Yost had insisted on his right to audit JobsOhio because it is funded with taxpayer money. Gov. Kasich and JobsOhio officials had resisted the audit, fighting to preserve the secrecy of their operation, before finally agreeing to pay back to the state at least $7.5 million in grants the organization had received from Kasich administration officials. This revelation of the largely unknown taxpayer funding stream to the privatized agency raised doubts about the ability of JobsOhio to adequately administer public funds. Of course, the timing of this decision to pay back the funds was linked with JobsOhio finally gaining access to Ohio retail liquor tax revenues totaling about $100 million a year. The *Cleveland Plain Dealer* editorial board criticized the secrecy surrounding JobsOhio in March 2013: "The rule in Ohio should be that public funds are the people's funds, and that the officials in whose custody that money happens to be are merely trustees for the people."[39] Shockingly, in June 2013, the Republican legislature passed and Gov. Kasich signed legislation that specifically prevents JobsOhio from being audited, thereby protecting what many see as the obvious misuse of taxpayer money.

Kasich's plan would seriously undermine "oversight and transparency for job creation efforts in Ohio," then–Atty. Gen. Richard Cordray predicted in 2011, perhaps foreseeing the problems JobsOhio would generate. Cordray went on to call the plan "murky" and "unclear" and expressed doubts about its constitutionality. Criticism of the plan was not limited to Democratic politicians. Columbus-based *Business First* carried a detailed article about the failure of such plans elsewhere. In Michigan in 1999, the paper reported, then-Gov. John Engler, also a Republican, tried a similar approach. In the years since, Michigan's economy has slipped so precipitously that there have been calls to abolish the organization and arguments that a more effective use of its funding would be to simply pay down the state deficit.[40]

In Indiana, Republican Gov. Mitch Daniels has worked diligently to portray his privatized Indiana Economic Development Corp. as a success. But when the news media began to look beneath the claims, they have found more costly failure. In March 2010, an investigative story by Indianapolis television station WTHR found that in reality Indiana's job creation numbers "just don't add up" because of numerous fabrications. "In fact," the station found, "as many as 40% of statewide jobs listed as so-called economic successes have not happened—and most of them never will."[41]

Nevertheless, on November 2, John Kasich won election by a tiny margin: 1,889,180 to 1,812,047, a mere 77,000 votes—49 percent to 47 percent. Kasich's strongest support came from the suburban Cincinnati counties of Butler, Clermont, and Warren, while Strickland ran strongest in northeast Ohio in the Cleveland region and Cuyahoga County. Kasich could not know it at the time, but in November 2011 more Ohioans would vote against his signature piece of legislation, Senate Bill 5, than had voted for him in 2010.

Gov. Kasich immediately began to behave as though his narrow win was a mandate. Flush with victory, he announced that Ohio's public school teachers should take out a full-page ad in the state's newspapers to apologize for what they had said about him during the campaign. And a few days after the election, he gathered important stakeholders in the statehouse in Columbus to hear his governing strategy: "Please leave the cynicism and the political maneuvering at the door. Because we need you on the bus, and if you're not on the bus, we will run over you with the bus. And I'm not kidding . . . If you think you're going to stop us, you're crazy. You will not stop us. We will beat you."[42]

Remembering that it was a very narrow victory, there are a few explanations for the election results. First, as the collapse of the national economy hit Ohio, throwing hundreds of thousands of people out of work, the typical voter was shell-shocked and looking for answers. Largely because of Barack Obama's popularity, the Democrats in 2008 had won several state offices and the Ohio House. The downside of this was that as the economy collapsed, desperate voters looked to throw out the party then in power—the Democrats.

Second, the GOP at the time, and even since then, has been able to turn attention away from Republican Party responsibility for policies that led to the Great Recession by focusing instead on the budget deficit, both nationally and in Ohio. The constant refrain from both state and national GOP figures about the perceived need to cut the deficit (despite the fact that it has largely been generated by Republican state and federal tax cuts) has inaccurately supported their claims that "excessive spending" is the culprit. And their answer to the problem is to make drastic cuts in public services.

Third, Gov. Ted Strickland clearly understood the threat Ohio faced from a Kasich administration. But he was largely unsuccessful in connecting Kasich with the investment bankers who brought on the Great Recession and the destructive ideology that connection represented. Certainly, Strickland's response to many of Kasich's sketchy plans was understandable indignation, and he frequently pointed out the inherent irresponsibility of Kasich's proposals. But once again, Ohioans needed to hear more often and more clearly exactly how Kasich's policies would damage the lives of ordinary citizens.

Finally, after a number of defeats over the years, the Ohio labor movement was not energized. Leaders of the labor movement warned their members about a Kasich administration. For example, Joe Rugola, president of the Ohio AFL-CIO in 2010, told a Youngstown audience at the time: "The forces that are arrayed against us today, their voices of intolerance that we hear on the airwaves and their moneyed allies on Wall Street, have one motivation and one plan in mind only. And that is to destroy and wreck the American middle class."[43] Still, caught up on that old canard that there was little difference between the parties, too many union members, especially police officers and firefighters, voted Republican. Further, it is no secret that divisions run in various directions through the labor movement, and unity in recent decades had not been a strong point.

Only a direct attack on the labor movement and the middle class through extremist legislation would create unity. As it happened, Kasich and his right-wing allies targeted the unions with just such an attack with the introduction of Senate Bill 5.

Chapter 2

Disaster Republicanism

In *The Shock Doctrine: The Rise of Disaster Capitalism*, Naomi Klein describes how corporate interests exploited the crisis created by the Hurricane Katrina disaster in order to make radical changes that people in normal circumstances would never make. She cites other instances in Chile under Augusto Pinochet and in Russia under Boris Yeltsin as further examples of crises either precipitated or used as opportunities to take radical actions.[1]

Referring to the rush of charter schools into New Orleans to undermine the public schools after Katrina, Klein observed: "I call these orchestrated raids on the public sphere in the wake of catastrophic events, combined with the treatment of disasters as exciting market opportunities, 'disaster capitalism.'"[2]

Similarly, as explained earlier, the budget "crisis" in Ohio in 2011 was a manufactured one—generated by years of sharp tax reductions that rewarded the wealthiest Ohioans—that presented a similar "market opportunity" to conservative ideologues. Once that crisis was created, Republican stalwarts like John Kasich and Shannon Jones would bluntly state, "There is no money left," wrongly implying that "extraordinary demands" by unionized public employees had drained the treasury. McClatchy Newspapers, alone among the major media groups, were quick to pick up on this. "The tax cuts were supposed to stimulate Ohio's economy and create jobs," McClatchy reporters observed, "But that didn't happen once the economy tanked. Instead, the changes ended up costing Ohio more than $2 billion a year in lost tax revenue, money that would have gone a long way toward closing the state's $8 billion budget gap for fiscal year 2012."[3]

But the particular brand of conservatism that played out in Ohio in 2011 has deeper ideological origins beyond the facts of the political, social, and economic situation in the state. It has its roots in a battle that today is largely forgotten but nonetheless remains at the center of conflict between those who see their government as a tool for balancing interests and regulating the worst abuses of the free-enterprise system and those who see government as an obstacle to the unrestricted environment in which they believe these forces should operate.

While it is possible to draw this conflict back to Woodrow Wilson and issues raised in his second inaugural address in 1916, in modern America, this conflict first burst into the open when Franklin D. Roosevelt took office in 1933. There have been small and ineffective attempts by some conservative commentators to introduce novel theories about the economic collapse of the 1920s and to suggest that the Great Depression was not caused by unregulated capitalism and that the New Deal did not "work." Chief among the works advocating these theories is the deeply flawed *The Forgotten Man*, written by right-wing pundit Amity Shlaes. Published in 2009, the book provides a mix of anecdotal stories and a largely ideologically driven and inaccurate history of the New Deal. A more recent antigovernment screed, similarly long on ideology and short on facts, is *The Battle*, by the current president of the right-wing American Enterprise Institute, Arthur C. Brooks. As his central premise and reason for writing the book, Brooks suggests that 70 percent of Americans support free-market principles and 30 percent do not. Brooks argues that the 30 percent is foisting onto the majority a collection of policies that they do not want. But as another conservative commentator, Bryan Caplan—an economist at George Mason University who reviewed Brooks's book—points out, polling does not, in fact, support Brooks's central premise. Polls, instead, consistently show that Americans, when asked about specific policies, *want* government intervention in the economy. "Once you take a more realistic view of American public opinion," Caplan writes, "there's not much of a split between the policies voters want and the policies voters get."[4]

Unfortunately, now that there are few people living who actually experienced and remember the New Deal of the 1930s, a Republican mythology has grown about its ineffectiveness. This is not to say that every single program sponsored by the New Deal worked. FDR was a pragmatic thinker and not the zealot his enemies have often portrayed. His efforts were directed toward putting political power back in the hands of ordinary people and finding strategies that actually boosted the economy and aided the unemployed. Certainly, most of the time he embraced Keynesian economics, which posited that the government could and should intervene to correct the inadequacies of the market. But even FDR could not imagine the huge scale of government spending it would take to really transform the economy. When FDR backed off on government spending in 1937, the economy worsened once again. It was only World War II that created the political will necessary for politicians to commit to the level of massive government spending, unhindered by ideology, that ended up working—and, in fact, created an economic expansion that lasted into the 1970s.

Yet economic stimulus was only part of the New Deal, and certainly the scale of the stimulus in the 1930s was not enough to begin to drive the economy forward. The New Deal was much more than simple fiscal stimulation efforts. Through the Works Project Administration (WPA), the Civilian Conservation Corps (CCC), and other publicly funded projects, the New Deal changed people's lives for the better. My father, in Depression-ridden western Montana, was the beneficiary of work and pay provided by the WPA. Every time we had the opportunity over the years to drive over Flint Creek Pass in the rugged mountains of southwestern Montana, we benefited from the New Deal project on which he had worked in the summer of 1938.

Besides throwing a lifeline to people in need, the New Deal also created the Securities and Exchange Commission and the Federal Deposit Insurance Corporation, which have combined to make banking and investing much safer—which never would have been accomplished by conservatives of the 1920s or today. Social Security has transformed retirement for older Americans. But by far the most successful actions of the New Deal involved protections for workers and for unions, because it was through these reforms that the great American middle class was created. Given the corporate desire to maximize profits, corporations would never have created a middle class on their own.[5]

Since the Industrial Revolution began in America, corporations and business leaders could confidently call on government police or military forces to crush strikes and enforce their will on workers. The New Deal leveled the playing field. With the Wagner Act, Americans gained the right to organize. Beating and bullying workers to intimidate them against voting to unionize was made illegal. Through the power of unions, ordinary workers were able to wrest decent salaries and benefits from powerful corporate interests.[6]

The wealthy barons of industry opposed all of FDR's New Deal programs, from the AAA to the SEC to the TVA—programs that created modern America. To business magnates, FDR's chief offenses were taking the United States off the gold standard and openly encouraging labor unions. Naturally, those with the most to gain by keeping workers' wages low and their own profits high were strongly opposed to these developments.

But these wealthiest Americans needed someone to craft for them the beginning of a new ideology that could provide an explanation for the economic world in which they felt most comfortable. They needed a theory that would conceal their personal and corporate greed and undermine the ability of the government to defend ordinary people. With this in mind, the likely touchstone of the modern conservative economic movement began with the publication of *The Road to Serfdom* in 1944 by Frederick August Von Hayek, an Austrian economist who was then teaching at the London School of Economics. The book contains a number of contradictions, but one of the clearest points that Hayek makes is that a planned economy would lead to the downfall of democracy. This reflects a body of economic theory that was developed by a group of European economists, including Hayek and Ludwig von Mises (Hayek's mentor), known as the Austrian School. There was nothing particularly new about much of what Hayek was saying—his book was first and foremost a defense of nineteenth-century Robber Baron-style free enterprise—and thus it is difficult to understand how the book, a short but rather dense text, became such a wildly popular bestseller.[7] The key to understanding its popularity, however, is the cover it provided for greed by clothing it in the rhetoric of "freedom," a strategy that today has become common in Republican circles. GOP presidential candidate Mitt Romney, short on details about any economic plan, continually repeated instead the Hayek-inspired mantra: "America's economy runs on freedom."[8]

The embrace of Hayek has much to do with the fact that many of the assumptions about the capitalistic system lay in tatters in the wake of the Great Depression. The assumption of the competence of the wealthy barons of industry had been destroyed by their own actions and inability to manage the economy. The New Deal and the massive government intervention in the economy during World War II represented a rejection of the way the world had worked before FDR. Thus, for the wealthy elite, Hayek's work was a vindication of all they had done to bring on the economic calamity.

To be sure, Hayek's book had its critics from the beginning. George Orwell, for example, warned in the British context that a "return to free market competition means for the great mass of people a tyranny worse, because more irresponsible, than that of the state." John Maynard Keynes himself said, although he got on well with Hayek personally, "what rubbish his theory is." He said that Hayek had started "with a mistake" and proceeded to "bedlam." Keynes described one Hayek article as "the wildest farrago of nonsense." The British journalist, Nicholas Wapshot, has written a revealing study of the conflict between Keynes and Hayek. The two economists engaged in a lengthy correspondence in the 1930s over their respective economic theories. At one point, in a journal publication, Keynes confessed that in his relationship with Hayek a "thick . . . bank of fog still separates his mind from mine."[9]

Over the years, Hayek's work has garnered many critics, including noted economist Jeffrey Sachs. In an article subtitled "Frederick von Hayek Was Wrong," Sachs notes that countries that have much higher taxation rates than the United States and better-funded public services, and that spend more generously for research and development as well as for public education—Canada and the Nordic countries, for example—rank higher in most measures of economic performance. "The U.S. spends the least of all rich countries on social services for the poor and disabled," wrote Sachs in 2006, and it gets what it pays for: "the highest poverty rate among the rich countries and an exploding prison population."[10]

This collection of disparate concepts held by the Austrian School gradually moved over the years from fringe to mainstream in the Republican Party. In contemporary times, the view holds that "social good" will be "maximized by maximizing the reach and frequency of market transactions, and it seeks to bring all human action into the domain of the market," as David Harvey writes in his important study, *A Brief History of Neoliberalism*. The curious "neoliberal" tag can be attached to this economic theory because it has its roots in classical European liberal economics. Harvey writes that the "battle of ideas" was central to Hayek's argument. But Harvey and other critics have pointed to the weakness inherent in Hayek's theory. "The scientific rigor of its neoclassical economics," Harvey notes, "does not sit easily with its political commitment to ideals of individual freedom, nor does its supposed distrust of all state power fit with the need for a strong and, if necessary, coercive state that will defend" the principles of the theory.[11]

To read Hayek's *Road to Serfdom* today is to be struck by the truism that it is difficult to understand a crisis when you are in it. Written during the rise of the Nazis and World War II, Hayek's argument that Nazism is rooted in economic policy is inaccurate and has been overwhelmed by decades of historical writing about the roots of fascism and its particular German variant. It is, however, the kind of deeply flawed argument that an economist might make when trying to write a history book on a topic about which he knows very little. Hayek's little book, after all, is not an economic study but is an effort at contemporary history and politics. There is no evidence of an understanding of the driving forces of nationalism that forged the German nation in 1871. Racism or anti-semitism, so central to Nazi ideology go unmentioned. Perhaps this is because an Austrian of Hayek's generation likely shared these prejudices and so they go unquestioned. There is no appreciation of Hitler's *Mein Kampf*, the text so central to Hitler's ideology. All that exists in the book is the argument that any government intervention in the economy leads to dictatorship—a fact that has been completely discredited by the decades of historical evidence since Hayek wrote his book. The great social democracies of Europe are not dictatorships. Hayek quotes FDR without citing him but FDR and the New Deal ushered in a great deal of social legislation and government regulation. And yet the United States has become more democratic, not less, in the intervening decades. In the midst of all this government intervention in the economy, there has been enormous economic expansion. One can see why John Maynard Keynes must have been so frustrated by Hayek's largely imagined history.

Hayek won the Nobel Prize in economics in 1974—but not for his political ideology. Instead, the award honored his genuine theoretical advances in understanding business cycles. The timing of the Nobel Prize, however, drew important attention to his flawed political concepts, which, just as they had done in the 1930s, wealthy conservatives picked up to defend their "Greed is good" ideology that blossomed in the 1980s. "Is Greed Good?" Britain's conservative *Economist* magazine asked in 2002. "Only if it is properly governed," the magazine concluded.[12]

Nevertheless, despite its flaws, in the wake of the New Deal, many of the wealthiest moguls in the United States came to back an organization that was Hayek's brainchild, the Mont Pelerin Society, named after a mountain resort in Switzerland near where the group first met in 1947. That first meeting was mainly made up of intellectuals—including a young Milton Friedman—who, absorbing and elaborating on the Austrian school over the years, created at the University of Chicago an intellectual hub for what was originally Hayek's Austrian economic ideology.[13]

By the mid-1950s, many of the most powerful American financial figures supported the Society, including Sun Oil's J. Howard Pew, and salt magnate Sterling Morton. The Mont Pelerin Society's first American meeting in 1958 was the society's largest meeting up to that time, but it was nevertheless not the success organizers desired.

Except for its attraction for wealthy business leaders, the Mont Pelerin Society was out of step with 1950s America which had largely embraced the New Deal and its policies. In fact, it played largely a background role in future years as other right-wing think tanks took over its role. Meanwhile, in university departments, as historian Kim Phillips-Fein writes, economists were developing sophisticated mathematical theories about business and trade. In contrast, never focused on mathematical analysis, Hayek and von Mises wrote "political tracts not equations." Believing that the central theme of the economy was "freedom," their views gained much support among businessmen who would rather understand their success through the fuzzy concept of the "growth of freedom" rather than the exploitation of workers. "The work of these two thinkers," Phillips-Fein writes, "became . . . a bible for those who wanted to turn back the New Deal"—and, certainly, for modern corporate raiders and Wall Street traders as well, who would prefer to portray their business activities in the language of "freedom" and "liberty."[14]

Funded by wealthy corporate leaders, many new organizations sprung up in the 1950s, devoted to the supposed defense of free enterprise. This coincided with the period historians have called "The Great Fear," a time when Americans imagined Communists under their beds and in control of their government. "The free-market conservatives," Phillips-Fein writes, "took the nightmarish fears inspired by anticommunism and turned them against the entire liberal state, making it seem as though the minimum wage and labor unions were about to usher in a new era of political enslavement."[15]

This played out in an important way in Ohio and involved a famous Ohioan, Robert Taft. In some ways Taft, nicknamed "Mr. Republican," would not fit well with today's even more radical right, which has left a traditional sense of social responsibility behind. Moreover, Taft was opposed to war, rather than enthusiastic about it as per the neoconservatives, and he was more a protectionist than a free trader. But Taft, coming from the famous and wealthy Cincinnati family, was very pro-business and was strictly opposed to Franklin Roosevelt's promotion of government's role in the economy, no matter how much it benefited individual Americans. Harshly criticizing New Deal policies, Taft called FDR a socialist and argued that his program was taking the United States down the road to a totalitarian dictatorship.[16]

Taft was elected to the Senate three times, in 1938, 1944, and 1950. The 1944 election is essential to understanding his conflict with labor unions. His opponent, William G. Pickrel, a Dayton attorney and former Democratic lieutenant governor, ran a strong campaign, but the key to the close election was a new political dynamic. Labor unions and the workers they represented had been made powerful by the New Deal and, by 1944, were working to make their power felt. The Congress of Industrial Organizations, known as the CIO, had formed a political action committee and targeted Sen. Taft for defeat.

The CIO PAC was involved in a series of campaigns across the country, but the Taft–Pickrel race was one of the most heated and most important. Taking a page out of FDR's critique of conservatives, historian David Farber writes, the CIO accused Taft of waging "a systematic campaign to force America back into the Robber Baron days when a few big business kings ran both the government and the country from a few offices in Wall Street."[17]

Pickrel himself picked up the argument to hammer Taft: "Taft comes from one of Ohio's wealthiest families . . . He represents wealth and large corporations." Internationalists, meanwhile, laid into "Mr. Republican" for being an isolationist. Taft, who had been opposed to war until Pearl Harbor, was attacked for being soft on fascism in Japan and Germany. The result of this furious criticism was an extremely close election in which Taft won by 50.3 percent of the vote to Pickrel's 49.7 percent.[18]

Not surprisingly, upon being elected, Taft began to target the growing power of organized labor, which he saw as the enemy of his allies: the business community and other pro-business politicians. When Republicans won back control of Congress in the 1946 elections, they began to push through pieces of legislation that would limit labor's power, at the behest of their traditional allies—the National Association of Manufacturers, the Chamber of Commerce, and other business groups. Taft's agenda was clear, according to Farber: "He intended to increase the power of employers and reduce the strength of organized labor."[19]

Interestingly, although Taft's animosity toward workers was shared by the bulk of legislative supporters of Senate Bill 5, in contrast to them, Taft announced, in 1947, that he supported workers' rights to organize and to engage in collective bargaining. This is in contrast to the Republican stance in 2011 because the truth of Senate Bill 5 is that it *did* eliminate any real collective bargaining power for public employees. SB 5 allowed for the continued existence of public unions, but it outlawed strikes and binding arbitration. Thus, if the two sides could not reach agreement, SB 5 permitted the management to simply impose its last offer. As was pointed out repeatedly, this would be not collective bargaining but collective begging.

The Taft-Hartley Act of 1947 placed a series of restrictions on what labor unions could do to pressure employers to negotiate fairly with them. Probably most importantly, the law gave employers the ability to work with state legislatures to pass "right-to-work" laws that would cripple union power. Right-to-work was a particularly ruthless portion of the Senate Bill 5 attack on public unions. In Ohio, it is illegal to force employees to join unions. But at a workplace where the majority of employees have democratically chosen to unionize, employees who choose not to join are still responsible for paying Fair Share fees. These are fees that help pay for the fair share of expenses incurred in negotiating and defending the contract that supports all the employees, union members or not. Many proposents of so-called right-to-work bills inaccurately call them "Workplace Freedom" bills but they in fact undermine freedom at the work place because they undermine the democratic processes that the union has established through a majority vote to unionize. It is obviously unfair for a worker to benefit from the union's work on their behalf and to "freeload" on their fellow workers who share the cost of maintaining the union and defending the contract.[20]

Through the 1950s, the Republicans enjoyed ascendancy. Comfortably in control of the White House with the popular World War II hero Dwight D. Eisenhower, Republicans did little to impose the growing radical ideological strand that was developing within the party. Eisenhower himself was a moderate who purposely chose not to attack the New Deal's legacy, primarily because he was not opposed to it. That is not to say that during the campaign he did not criticize Democrats and the New Deal, but he saw the programs of the New Deal as accomplished fact and, as he wrote to his brother, "Should any political party attempt to abolish Social Security and eliminate labor laws and farm programs, you would not hear of that party again in our political history." When faced with the wrath of conservatives for not attacking New Deal programs, he countered they had "now become accepted in our civilization."[21]

Among the hallmarks of the Eisenhower administration were calculation, caution, and compromise. As he wrote, "Some of the intellectuals (and particularly some of the pseudo-intellectuals) . . . are prone to forget that leadership in a democracy consists of making progress by compromise." In this spirit of compromise, Eisenhower took a number of actions that would make him unelectable to today's Republican Party. For example, he extended both the Housing Act and the Social Security Act. But chief among Eisenhower's virtues was his lack of hostility toward the labor movement: "Only a handful of unreconstructed reactionaries harbor the ugly thought of breaking unions," he wrote. "Only a fool would try to deprive working men and women of joining the union of their choice."[22]

But behind the scenes in the 1950s, the insidious ideology of the Mont Pelerin group and the Austrian economists had taken root in corporate boardrooms. Historian Kim Phillips-Fein has written about the "determined few" who, beginning in the 1950s, worked for more than 40 years to undermine the system of labor unions. One of the key figures in this effort was Lemuel Ricketts Boulware, the man who managed General Electric's labor relations and community affairs program. And there is another connection to the attack that would one day be brought against the labor movement: when Ronald Reagan's movie career began to fade, he became a corporate spokesman for GE, introducing the corporation's television drama programs and touring plants to give pep talks to workers. During this time, Boulware was able to transform the former Screen Actors Guild president into an ardent union-busting political figure.[23]

Boulware's antiunion strategy was so widespread that it grew to be known in the industry as "Boulwarism." Basically, it consisted of management meeting with the union for negotiations, pretending to listen, and then releasing to the public what it said was its "last, best, and final offer." Boulware's response to having this unfair labor practice tagged with his name is telling: "The term was coined by some bad people," Boulware wrote, "who have been desperately trying the emotional diversion of putting what they have hoped would be the worst possible name on the very fine thing which our GE relations program—of striving all year long to do right voluntarily and be known to do so." But Boulwarism was not only about blowing up contract negotiations; Boulware launched a complex and detailed indoctrination program of GE employees.[24]

"Starting in 1947," Phillips-Fein writes, "all of GE's supervisors—whom Boulware referred to as job salesmen—were given manuals containing suggested answers to workers' tough questions. They were supposed to respond by reciting 'the catechism of the marketplace.'" Always the intent was to direct the employee along an approved political track of indoctrination. For example, if an employee complained about not getting a Christmas bonus, managers were to respond, "We feel that every time the state, an employee, or anyone else, takes over one of our individual responsibilities completely, we are one step further along the road to socialism and a halt to progress." Boulware believed that all supervisors and managers were "thought-leaders," and he put them in charge of the indoctrination of thousands of GE employees over a long period of time.[25]

Certainly not every huge American corporation fought unions with the same tenacity and belligerency as did GE. But, as Phillips-Fein points out, Boulware's labor relations techniques began to spread through the business community. In the late 1950s, inspired by GE, the National Association of Manufacturers began to hold management training sessions to teach managers how to derail unionization drives using Boulware's tactics. And under Eisenhower, the National Labor Relations Board moved rightward, issuing several decisions that aided employers against workers.[26] Finally, for the purpose of our study, we should not underestimate GE's significant presence in Ohio—particularly in Cincinnati, historically a hotbed of Republicanism and home to a large GE Aviation plant since the 1950s.

What the Mont Pelerin Society, the virulent anti–New Dealers, and Boulwarism and other corporate clones represented in the 1950s was a fringe radical element within the Republican Party. This fringe element thus already had a significant history before Barry Goldwater's devastating defeat at the hands of Lyndon Johnson in 1964. But several issues had caused conservative extremist views to bridge the gap between the corporate and political worlds. Chief among these was the civil rights movement.

Of course, today the Republican Party dominates the American South, the states of the Old Confederacy. But this wasn't always the case. From the Civil War until the 1960s, the South had been solidly Democratic—a tradition stemming from the Civil War, when the Democratic Party was the party of secession. But today, that's no longer the case: if the South were not solidly Republican, the Republican Party would no longer be a national party.[27]

The 1964 election allowed the bridging of the divide between corporate ideology and mainstream Republican Party politics. Throughout the 1950s, there had been a struggle within the party between moderates, represented by Nelson Rockefeller, and conservative extremists, represented by Barry Goldwater. In 1957, Goldwater, the Senate campaign committee chair, and Meade Alcorn, the Republican Party chair, spearheaded an effort that became known as "Operation Dixie." Leadership in the Republican Party could see that the only way to win elections nationally was to break the Democratic Party's control of the South.

Initially, directed by Eisenhower's moderate supporters, Operation Dixie targeted the growing cities in the south, trying to convince professionals and white-collar workers that there was a new future possible for the South and it lay in breaking free from the old Democratic Party and the racial divisions connected with that history. Most of those connected with the campaign believed that they were making progress, and there was evidence that this class of urban voters might well be moving toward the Republican Party. But then Eisenhower ordered the intervention of federal troops in the desegregation crisis at Little Rock's Central High School.

Heading Operation Dixie was I. Lee Potter, former state party chairman of Virginia and a Republican National Committee staff member. Potter had been given a budget of nearly $21,000 in the second half of 1957 and set himself the goal of creating a feeling of "respectability in being a Republican candidate." Even small victories would build the idea that it was possible to have a two-party system in the South. But the "Little Rock situation," Potter reported, "threw us into quite a tailspin," adding that he had traveled to each Southern state in the wake of the crisis and "there has been severe damage done." To appease the civil rights opposition in the South, Potter urged the Eisenhower administration to pull the troops out, turning the responsibility "back over to the states." Potter said it was the only way of "getting candidates and raising money in 1958. We've lost the enthusiasm and appear to have lost the votes."[28]

While even Alcorn thought that perhaps it was better to simply give up at this point, Eisenhower insisted on persevering. In fact, Operation Dixie extended beyond Eisenhower's administration and into new conservative leadership. Even after the defeat of Richard Nixon in the 1960 election, the GOP continued the fight to move into the South. Now, however, with moderates under heavy fire, conservatives moved within the party to make use of Operation Dixie's machinery to take the drive in a new radical direction.

William E. Miller replaced the more moderate Alcorn and began to pour even greater resources into Operation Dixie. By 1964, the operation was taking up nearly a third of the RNC's expenditures. And its character had changed as well. Under Miller, Operation Dixie operatives and candidates no longer shied away from racial issues. They very often made distinctly racial and segregationist appeals.[29]

Alcorn regretted the strategy's transformation under Miller and later Goldwater; he would later remark, "[Operation Dixie's] whole purpose was perverted." He held that although his effort had been to set up a structure to promote a progressive Republican Party in the South, "the machinery was taken over to create a lily-white Republican organization." The appeals to the segregationists, Alcorn maintained, were sharply against the goals set during the Eisenhower administration to create a party in the South that would "obliterate any division or segregation between white Republicans and negro Republicans."[30] Instead, Operation Dixie was used for opposite purposes: to plant the seeds of a new and radical Republican Party. Unrecognized at the time, this development would provide an avenue for the fringe economic ideas rooted in the Austrian ideology to find a route toward electoral power because, in its resistance to civil rights, the South moved to support the Republican Party and so provided a political base to the Hayek-inspired ideologues.[31]

This puzzling collage of ideas came together in the person of Barry Goldwater. The Arizona senator's most famous expression about his philosophy was, ironically, not written by Goldwater at all. His ghostwriter for *Conscience of a Conservative* was Brent Bozell, the brother-in-law of William Buckley. Bozell had already done some speechwriting for Goldwater and must have had a good sense of the ideas that Goldwater would feel comfortable having published under his name. Although anyone reading *Conscience of a Conservative* might suspect from its fine writing that Goldwater had not actually been the author, the book nevertheless became a massive bestseller.[32]

In *Conscience*, one can see the blending of the two conceptions that had once not been Republican—or, in the case of the Austrian economics, not even American. The book used harsh language in writing off all social legislation as simply dependency-creating nonsense that would destroy the individual discipline and strength on which America was posited to have been built. But then, echoing the Austrian economists, Goldwater argues that this is not about helping poor people but is all about "liberty." "The effect of Welfarism will be felt later on—after its beneficiaries have become its victims, after dependence on government has turned into bondage, and it is too late to unlock the jail."[33]

It should come as no surprise that Goldwater also attacked unions in *Conscience*; today's Republicans who attack unions are definitely taking a page from Goldwater. He advocates all the traditional arguments in favor of union busting, including right-to-work legislation, and counters labor's arguments with all the inaccurate clichés so common among those who railroaded Senate Bill 5 through the Ohio legislature. For example, Goldwater complains that unions donate to political candidates without consulting with the members who pay dues. Of course, every union has democratic processes in place to elect a leadership that is responsive to the membership; however imperfect those processes, they are certainly in sharp contrast to corporate political donations, where there is no democracy for employees and no limits to what those fortunate few in the boardroom may decide to do with the corporation's vast resources that are, after all, generated by the employees. But Goldwater and the contemporary conservatives who are regularly attacking the involvement of unions in politics fail to recognize this hypocrisy.

As conservatives took over the Republican Party, they combined the racial and cultural attitudes of the South with the Mont Pelerin Society's hostility to labor. Neither of these strains would prove electorally successful in the short run. In the Republican Party in the early 1960s, Nelson Rockefeller reflected the moderate mainstream inside the party rather well, but he carried with him some unfortunate baggage. A divorce and a new wife nearly 20 years his junior did not endear him to many GOP voters. Further, his wealth and East Coast connections breathed "establishment" to those who wanted their party to take a fresh approach. Rockefeller did two things to greatly boost his chances. He hired the political team of Stuart Spencer and William Roberts, who, as Spencer-Roberts Consultants, introduced much that was modern into the old campaign model. They eventually went on to future triumphs as Ronald Reagan's gubernatorial and presidential campaign advisors. Rockefeller also leaned on his family's history of support for historically black colleges in the South to reach out to blacks and even Hispanics.[34]

During the campaign, as George Kabaservice writes in his aptly titled *Rule and Ruin: The Downfall of Moderation and the Destruction of the Republican Party*, Rockefeller hammered at Goldwater's philosophy, "depicting him not as a conservative but as a radical reactionary, backed by extremists, who would abolish Social Security, renounce civil rights, and the United Nations." While these descriptions are mainstream in some parts of the Republican Party today, Goldwater further damaged his image by appearing to be a dangerous madman by suggesting that it would be appropriate to use nuclear weapons in Vietnam. Rockefeller emphasized, rightly, that his opponent was outside the mainstream of American public opinion.[35]

One of the ironies of this takeover of the Republican Party by the extremists is that, in a sense, the party deserves some credit for one of the greatest political accomplishments of the twentieth century—the Civil Rights Act of 1964. For years, more Republicans than Democrats had pushed for federal action against the obviously racist policies of the Old South. The Democrats had been hindered from taking action by having so many conservative senators from Southern states. It took a political magician of the stature of Lyndon Johnson to create a large enough coalition of Southern Democrats as well as the political will to push the bill through. A majority of Republicans as well as Democrats voted to pass the bill when the opportunity finally came.

But not Goldwater. He felt that the federal government had no business legislating the civil rights of those African Americans living under Jim Crow. In *Conscience*, he maintained that he was "unimpressed by the claim that the Supreme Court's decision on school integration is the law of the land." These sentiments were, of course, exactly what the white supremacists in the South wanted to hear. So Goldwater voted against the Civil Rights Act and, as Kabaservice observes, "put his stamp—and, by association, that of the Republican Party—on the side of Southern resistance to what was now the law of the land."[36]

Opinion pieces in the wake of Goldwater's vote compared the Arizonan unfavorably to Ohio's Robert Taft. The contrast was clear, as Kabaservice writes: "The Taft tradition was supportive of civil rights in a way that ideological conservatism was not." Longtime Republican political operative William Rusher was editor of the *National Review* magazine at the time of this change. He was unapologetic: "The Republican Party, like it or not, has a rendezvous with a brand new idea," he wrote. All the party needed to do in the South was offer anti–civil rights candidates. He suggested that the party should be appealing to the moderates, but the message was clear: the GOP should not be an ally to national civil rights legislation.[37]

This was, of course, music to the ears of supporters of Sheriff Bull Connor and Gov. George Wallace. Historian Dan T. Carter has made a careful study of the political transformation of the South during this era, and his book *From George Wallace to Newt Gingrich: Race in the Conservative Counterrevolution, 1963–1994* is particularly impressive in outlining the roots of contemporary Republican power and its connection to the likes of Gov. Wallace. Carter acknowledges that today's Republicans are naturally reluctant to admit that Wallace and the strain of American politics that he represents are largely responsible for the rise to power of the new conservative movement. But, Carter maintains that

> the fundamental differences between the public rhetoric of the Alabama governor and the new conservatism sometimes seem more a matter of style than substance. In Barry Goldwater's vote against the Civil Rights Bill of 1964, in Richard Nixon's subtle manipulation of the busing issue, in Ronald Reagan's genial demolition of affirmative action, in George Bush's use of the Willie Horton ads, and in Newt Gingrich's demonization of welfare mothers, the Wallace music played on.[38]

At the 1964 Republican Convention in San Francisco, Nelson Rockefeller took the stage to address the extremists who were seizing control of the party: "These extremists feed on fear, hate, and terror. They encourage disunity. These are people who have nothing in common with Americanism. The Republican Party must repudiate these people," Rockefeller shouted above the booing and jeers that eventually drove him from the stage. Later, in a statement much more widely quoted, Goldwater asserted, "Extremism in defense of liberty is no vice." The power in the Republican Party had passed to the extremists.

So out of step with America were those who had taken over the Republican Party that in the election of 1964, Lyndon Johnson had no problem painting Goldwater as someone who held views too dangerous to be allowed into the White House. Republicans faced a complete repudiation of their radical policies in their landslide defeat in 1964.

But from the depths of that defeat, with the extremists largely in control, the Republicans began to rebuild the party from the ground up, without the baggage of moderation. Some of this had to consist of developing a more sophisticated way of expressing their new and somewhat foreign political philosophy. In other words, this new Republican ideology had to be crafted in such a way to sound to ordinary people as though it was about more than defending the wealthy—even if a great deal of deception was necessary. The result of this goal was the development of a series of think tanks in which significant amounts of money were invested by the wealthiest and most powerful people and corporations in America.

The American Enterprise Institute, founded in 1943 at roughly the same time as the Mont Pelerin Society, initially worked at creating professional critiques of government policy from a conservative perspective. From the beginning, it tried to create an intellectual façade, granting its staff seemingly academic titles and chairs. However, it began to come into its own in the wake of the Goldwater disaster. William Baroody, Sr., president from 1962 to 1978, began to hire more professional and ideologically oriented staff and to seek out a great deal of corporate and private funding. A former U.S. Chamber of Commerce official, Baroody was the right man for the job, having been a principal adviser to the Goldwater campaign.

John Micklethwait and Adrian Wooldridge, British journalists with the magazine *The Economist*, have written a perceptive study of the conservative movement in America. Most importantly, they follow the money. They argue that the constellation of right-wing think tanks that have generated this ideological offensive—especially the Heritage Foundation, the American Enterprise Institute, and the Cato Institute—have been funded by sources they call the "Big Five."

"The first of these Medici of the conservative Renaissance was Joseph Coors," Micklethwait and Wooldridge note. The wealthy brewery magnate provided $250,000 in seed money for Heritage and also contributed to other right-wing organizations, including the Committee for the Survival of a Free Congress, the Independence Institute, and Accuracy in Media. The next major source of funding for right-wing thinkers was Richard Mellon Scaife, heir to the Mellon fortune and thus possessing historic connections to his family's resistance to the New Deal. One of the early financial advisers to Goldwater, the candidates's complete defeat "convinced [Scaife] that conservatism needed to match the enemy's intellectual firepower." By 1973, he began to turn the spigot on. His first contribution to Heritage was $900,000. In 1976, he donated another $420,000, which was then 42 percent of Heritage's income. Micklethwait and Wooldridge write, "The Washington Post has calculated that in four decades after 1960 Scaife and his family's trust gave at least $340 million to conservative causes—or about $620 million in current [2004] dollars."[39]

The third major benefactors are no strangers to Ohio. Friends of John Kasich, Wisconsin's Gov. Scott Walker, and their Republican allies, David and Charles Koch have been "prolific givers to libertarian causes." Their father, Fred Koch, had made his money in the oil business, built fifteen oil refineries in Stalin's Russia, and became a founding member of the John Birch Society. Charles was a cofounder of the Cato Institute in 1977. The Koch brothers developed a large network of fellowships, grants, and scholarship to nurture libertarians.[40] The Kochs have been especially generous benefactors to the American Legislative Exchange Council, the right-wing group that is particularly responsible for Senate Bill 5 and other undemocratic legislation in Ohio and elsewhere.[41]

The fourth largest funder of right-wing think tanks has been the Lynde and Harry Bradley Foundation. With a fortune made in a Milwaukee-based electronics company, Allen-Bradley, Harry Bradley was a committed John Birch Society member. The founder of the Birch Society, Robert Welch, was a frequent speaker at Allen-Bradley sales meetings in the late 1950s. Harry Bradley also supported the conservative journal the *National Review*, contributing both money and articles. Although Bradley died in 1965, his foundation has continued to give money to right-wing causes and, in fact, received a huge cash injection when Rockwell International bought Allen-Bradley, pushing the foundation's assets above $260 million.[42]

The John M. Olin Foundation makes up the last of the "Big Five" conservative financial benefactors. John Merrill Olin "was another right-wing businessman obsessed with the threat to liberty," write Micklethwait and Wooldridge. Olin focused on trying to plant seeds of his ideology in academia. He supported the law and economics program at the University of Chicago and tried to encourage imitators elsewhere. Olin was particularly generous to a "handful of favored scholars" such as Robert Bork, who was chair of legal studies at the American Enterprise Institute for several years, and Irving Kristol, a journalist and writer who has been dubbed the "godfather of neo-conservatism."[43]

Other foundations also contributed huge sums to right-wing think tanks, including the Smith Richardson Foundation and the Howard Pew Freedom Trust. Perhaps even more importantly, the political activities of business organizations expanded during this time. The Chamber of Commerce had long been working against unions and workers, especially through suppression of the minimum wage, and in Ohio has played a particularly damaging role. But in 1972, the five hundred largest corporations created the Business Roundtable specifically to lobby for their interests: union-busting, deregulation, and tax cuts. The contrast between labor union political action committees and corporate ones is also illustrative of the transformation that had taken place by the early 1970s. Labor PACs outnumbered corporate PACs in 1974 by 201 to 89. But just two years later, corporate America had turned that around, with 433 corporate PACs and 224 labor ones. By 1984, corporate PACs had a 4-to-1 advantage.[44]

The Heritage Foundation, one of the chief benefactors of all this money, is more extremist than even AEI and "wrote the book on how to market and popularize political ideas," according to Jacob Weisberg, writing in *Salon*, the online magazine. Why have the Heritage Foundation and its allies been so successful at promulgating ideas that are bad for most of the population and the nation at large?[45]

Money, Weisberg says. Corporations and the wealthy are eager to pour money into Heritage and other right-wing think tanks that will push ideas that will directly benefit them by passing the tax burden on to those less able to pay and by freeing business from government oversight as much as possible. While some would point to the Brookings Foundation as a liberal counterpart, Weisberg points out that this is not true. Brookings could only dream of the wealth lavished on the Heritage Foundation, not to mention the other right-wing think tanks pumping out justifications for bad policy. Further, Brookings sees itself much more as a scholarly organization not driven completely by base political motivations. By contrast, the former president of Heritage, Ed Feulner, has said, "We conduct warfare in the battle of ideas." Whereas some of the other right-wing think tanks maintain some standards of scholarship, Heritage is unconcerned by such niceties, Weisberg notes.[46]

Evidence of the impact of the funding of "research" and reports that conclude that various right-wing policies are effective and helpful with problems facing the nation—however wrong-headed such reports may be—are easy to find. Jude Wanniski, a one-time *Wall Street Journal* editorial page writer, for example, used an AEI grant to write his book *The Way the World Works*, wildly popular in right-wing circles for promulgating the theory of supply-side economics.

Wanniski, a native of Pennsylvania like Kasich, began his career as a newspaper reporter in Alaska, then moved on to Las Vegas, and finally, in 1965, started working for *The National Observer*, a Dow Jones publication. He served as associate editor of *The Wall Street Journal* from 1971 to 1978. Wanniski left that position when he was spotted handing out brochures for a New Jersey Republican candidate, a violation of journalistic ethics. "Wanniski was a genius, the smartest man I ever met," conservative columnist Robert Novak wrote after his colleague's death. "While he made his living as an economic consultant, his real profession was changing the way the world worked."[47]

The conservative journal *National Review* listed Wanniski's book as one of the one hundred most influential books of the twentieth century. *The Way the World Works* had a great impact on the "Republican Revolution" of 1994 and was inspirational not only for Newt Gingrich but for John Kasich. Wanniski became the cheerleader for economic ideas that he discovered quite by chance at a dinner with Professor Arthur Laffer of the University of Chicago. Different versions of this event have appeared, but I will provide here Laffer's own recollection, as offered to the Heritage Foundation in 2004:

> The story of how the Laffer Curve got its name begins with a 1978 article by Jude Wanniski in *The Public Interest* entitled, "Taxes, Revenues, and the 'Laffer Curve.'" As recounted by Wanniski (associate editor of *The Wall Street Journal* at the time), in December 1974, he had dinner with me (then professor at the University of Chicago), Donald Rumsfeld (Chief of Staff to President Gerald Ford), and Dick Cheney (Rumsfeld's deputy and my former classmate at Yale) at the

> Two Continents Restaurant at the Washington Hotel in Washington, D.C. While discussing President Ford's "WIN" (Whip Inflation Now) proposal for tax increases, I supposedly grabbed my napkin and a pen and sketched a curve on the napkin illustrating the trade-off between tax rates and tax revenues. Wanniski named the trade-off "The Laffer Curve."[48]

Interestingly, Laffer, who said he has no exact memory of this, went on to say that the roots of the supply-side concept that would be so thoroughly embraced by the Republican Party came from the seventeenth-century Islamic historian Ibn Khaldun in his famous work *The Muqaddimah* and had also been expressed with "incredible clarity" by the liberal economist John Maynard Keynes.[49]

The bearing that this has on John Kasich is that Wanniski was a great fan as Kasich rose to prominence in Congress as the chief dismantler of the New Deal legacy. Wanniski often sent "memos" to people he wanted to influence, and on the Polyconomics Institute website still devoted to Wanniski, there are several memos to and about Congressman Kasich. Polyconomics was established in 1978 as an economic forecasting firm consulting with banks and corporations.

"If there is one big reason to be optimistic," Wanniski wrote in 1995, "it is the leadership, enthusiasm and vision of House Budget Director John Kasich. Of all the players, Kasich is the one who clearly has no ax to grind other than the national interest. He is passionate in making the case to the other boys that they put their narrow interests aside."[50] In memos to Kasich, Wanniski often offered advice on ways that Kasich could sharpen his argument, or take different approaches, or change his mind—for instance, regarding most favored nation status for China. Often, Wanniski offered his enthusiastic support: "Your Sunday appearance on NBC's 'Meet The Press,'" Wanniski wrote in 1998, "was as good as I've ever seen you . . . I must say you were almost, shall I say, presidential in handling [the tough questions]."[51]

It is important that we recognize this relationship between Wanniski and Kasich because it demonstrates that Kasich was a leading proponent at the very beginning of the flawed "supply-side" economic theory that has nearly bankrupted the nation and crippled governments in Ohio and elsewhere. So tied was Kasich to Wanniski that he attended the Polyconomics Institute annual meeting in 1997, along with a number of other important and controversial figures. But the star, according to Wanniski, was Nation of Islam leader Louis Farrakhan. Wanniski had a habit of embracing controversial figures, including Moammar Khadafy and Saddam Hussein.

And Wanniski gushed with enthusiasm over Farrakhan. "Of all the speakers," Wanniski reported, "Min. Farrakhan clearly enjoyed John Kasich the most, three times standing to applaud Kasich's impassioned statements on the interference of government in our lives. [Farrakhan] noted that with people like Kasich, and [Jack] Kemp, in the Republican Party, there may be a brighter future for the GOP in the black community."[52]

Although there is no question that Wanniski's *The Way the World Works* has become a formative book for current conservative philosophy, many experts believe that the book is full of silly platitudes based more on fantasy than reality. I am going to quote generously from the review written by noted economist Benjamin J. Cohen:

> The book would be much less distressing if we were permitted to read it as satire rather than as scholarship. Then we might merely smile and wink when Wanniski assures us that the [*Wall Street*] *Journal* is "without commitment to economic dogma." We might grin when he argues that of all of the world's economic problems in the postwar era, the most serious has been the personal income tax rate. We might guffaw when he asserts that high taxes are "the primary cause by a long shot of the poverty of the world . . . But, the book, [Wanniski] insists, is to be taken seriously . . . For all of his erudition, he does not appear to appreciate the dangers of the colorful historical generalization, the univariate theory of history. For all of his sophistication, he still insists on trying to reduce complex reality to trite oversimplification . . . Readers of Das Kapital will be amused to learn that "The Marxian idea does not concern itself with economic growth, but with economic contraction"; readers of Keynes' General Theory will be amused to learn that his book was written "to systemize [socialism] into an economic model."[53]

Concluding his authoritative review of what is a very poor book, Cohen summarizes the problem: "Nothing like a convenient twisting of the facts to fit one's own theory. Serious scholars can expect to learn little from this type of approach to historical problems." Even David Stockman, Reagan's budget director, has criticized Wanniski's extremist support for supply-side economics calling him, "the real prince of darkness, a fanatic," among the cadre of supply-siders inside the administration.[54]

The year of publication of Wanniski's book, 1978, is important since the administration of Ronald Reagan warmly embraced many of the book's nonsensical principles to drive new policy decisions. Even more importantly, the Heritage Foundation also produced *Mandate for Leadership*, a detailed program for the incoming Reagan administration, a catalog of various ideologically driven policies that shared much with the flawed tracts of both Hayek and Wanniski.[55]

While Reagan often cast himself in the image of FDR, his administration began to systematically undo the social progress that had been made since the New Deal. For our purposes, one of the most brutal attacks came in the context of his crushing of the Professional Air Traffic Controllers Organization, the air traffic controllers' union. "This signaled," Harvey notes in his study of neoliberalism, "an all-out assault on the powers of organized labor." Harvey argues that PATCO was more than just an ordinary union because it was a white-collar union that had the "character of a skilled professional association." And PATCO was an icon of middle-class unionism, the middle class that, in fact, unionism had built since World War II.[56]

"The effect on the condition of labor across the board was dramatic," Harvey writes, "perhaps best captured by the fact that the Federal minimum wage, which stood on a par with the poverty level in 1980, had fallen to 30 percent below that level by 1990." What ensued after this brutal and ideologically driven action was a long and steady decline in real wage levels across the country. As Harvey points out, the whole complex of neoliberal policies championed by the Republican Party since that time has driven down wages, deindustrialized the nation, chopped away at the middle class and the American standard of living, and dramatically expanded the gap between the very wealthy and everyone else. Generous tax breaks to the wealthy and to corporations, Harvey notes, have only made it easier for them to extract money from the United States and invest it overseas.[57]

So, has there been a huge revolt by taxpayers at seeing both state and national treasuries emptied for the purpose of rewarding the wealthy primarily for being wealthy? Has the attack on workers caused a huge blowback? As universities are steadily being privatized and our public schools slowly turned over to corporations, has there been enormous outrage? For the most part, the answer to these questions is no, and the reason is the hugely effective propaganda campaign that has convinced the public that these changes are reasonable and pragmatic. Nothing, of course, could be further from the truth.

And in the face of this assault on the American way of life, we have actually seen this process being accelerated by Republican Party figures who seem to be acting out of desperation to transform the country into something it has never been. The wave of Republican victories in 2010 brought a series of radical governors into office and won back the U.S. House. The governors of Ohio, Florida, Michigan, and Wisconsin have been particularly aggressive in pushing radical right-wing policies. Union busting, of course, leads the way, but voter suppression laws and the privatization of government services are obviously also extremely important to their strategies.

But why the desperation, and why now, when it appears the GOP is actually in a powerful position? Jonathan Chait, former senior editor at *The New Republic*, got a hint from the preamble to conservative star Sen. Paul Ryan's budget proposal: "America is approaching a 'tipping point' beyond which the Nation will be unable to change course." This is a sentiment that both Rick Santorum and Gingrich also echoed on the campaign trail in 2012.[58]

What are these people talking about? Chait believes that the Republicans have become acutely aware of demographics. The modern GOP, Chait argues, is "staring down its own demographic extinction." The Republican Party, as Chait outlines, has become increasingly narrow in the people it represents, mainly rural whites and whites without a college education. The Democratic Party, by contrast, does better with college-educated whites and is dominant among racial minorities. With the American population growing more educated and dramatically less white, Chait argues, the Democratic Party is en route to a natural Democratic majority.[59]

Chait tempers his argument by noting that no coalition is permanent, but the changes that are taking place cannot be underestimated. As I've noted, the Republican Party has built its coalition by embracing the racial attitudes of the states of the Old Confederacy and used the resulting political base to promote the economic policies of the Austrian School. Barack Obama's election and re-election demonstrate that the Republican strategy does not have the power that it once did. When a party or nation is in an inevitable decline, one might think that the wise strategy would be one of careful management. Instead, the Republicans have opted for outright confrontation. But, as Chait points out, it was this kind of thinking that led the South to start a war with the North, the Japanese to start a war with the United States, wars hopeless from the start. "At varying levels of conscious and subconscious thought," Chait argues, "this is also the reasoning that has driven Republicans in the Obama era. Surveying the landscape, they have concluded that they must strike quickly and decisively at the opposition before all hope is lost."

Chait, of course, did not have the benefit of having seen the 2012 presidential campaign when he wrote the material quoted here. In the wake of President Obama's impressive victory, there was clear evidence of the durability of a coalition based on a more diverse electorate than the white men the Republicans have been trying to target. *Washington*

Post commentator E. J. Dionne cited exit polls that demonstrated that the electorate may be becoming aware of the stacked economic deck that conservative policies champion. In the exit polls, only 10 percent of those polled said that Obama's policies aided the rich, while 54 percent said that Romney's policies favored the rich. More importantly, as Dionne points out, "voters rejected a core Republican proposition: that the economy works on behalf of everyone." Polls showed instead that 54 percent of the voters believed that the economy works for the rich, while only 39 percent said it was fair to most Americans. Attacks on what conservatives called "class warfare," Dionne wrote, were ineffective because "a majority thinks there is a class war and the wealthy are winning it."[60]

Even right-wing South Carolina Republican Sen. Jim DeMint's recent book, aptly titled *Now or Never: Saving America from Economic Collapse*, claims that 2012 may be the last chance for the Republican Party.[61] And in Ohio, the desperation has been clear, and not only as reflected in Senate Bill 5. Republican majorities in both houses have passed voter suppression laws, and there has been a grotesque Republican attempt at drawing new legislative and congressional districts showing genuine desperation on their part. In a state split roughly 50–50 between Democrats and Republicans, but trending Democratic, the GOP has already gerrymandered a situation in which they have 13 out of 18 congressional seats. And the newly-gerrymandered map ushered in more power for the Republicans in 2012 with a 12–4 majority in congressional seats. "Even though most Ohio voters backed Democrats in this year's presidential and U.S. Senate elections," *The Cleveland Plain Dealer* reported after the November elections, "new congressional maps designed to protect GOP incumbents kept three quarters of the state's U.S. House of Representatives seats in Republican hands." And this is in the context of Republicans winning only 52 percent of the votes cast in Ohio congressional races. "This is a tossup state, the battleground of battlegrounds, except when you stack the deck," Steve Fought, a Democrat who worked on the Democratic congressional campaigns, told the *Plain Dealer*. "That is the only way they were able to hold their power in Ohio and the only way they were able to hold their power in the House of Representatives. But you have to give them credit. They knew what they were doing and it worked."[62]

Many Americans, even some Republicans, have recognized the destructive nature of the conservative policies that have been imposed on the nation. George H. W. Bush was right when he pronounced this ideology "voodoo" economics. And Judge Richard

Posner of the Seventh U.S. Circuit Court of Appeals in Chicago, in an interview after the Supreme Court ruled that the Affordable Care Act was constitutional, said that he has become less conservative as the Republican Party has become more "goofy." Perhaps it is best to quote Posner in some detail, to understand just what a moderate and sophisticated Republican thinks about the drastic turn his party has taken. Speaking about right-wing criticism of Chief Justice John Roberts, Posner said:

> Because if you put [yourself] in his position . . . what's he supposed to think? That he finds his allies to be a bunch of crackpots? Does that help the conservative movement? I mean, what would you do if you were Roberts? All of a sudden you find out that the people you thought were your friends have turned against you, they despise you, they mistreat you, they leak to the press. What do you do? Do you become more conservative? Or do you say, "What am I doing with this crowd of lunatics?" Right? Maybe you have to re-examine your position.[63]

Similarly, longtime GOP economic guru Bruce Bartlett has come to a new understanding of his right-wing colleagues. "Frankly, I think I'm at ground zero in the saga of Republicans closing their eyes to any facts or evidence that conflict with their dogma," Bartlett wrote recently in an essay titled "Revenge of the Reality-Based Community." Rather than listening to him, Bartlett wrote, "they threw me under a bus." Bartlett's study of the 1930s convinced him that, contrary to what he had previously thought, Keynes had been correct in the policies he advocated. Uncomfortable though it was, "facts were facts." Further, Bartlett now believed that more Keynesian intervention was necessary in the wake of the 2008 collapse. Uncomfortably, he found himself "joined at the hip with Paul Krugman," an economist he had formerly considered his intellectual enemy. "For the record," Bartlett wrote, "no one has been more correct in his analysis and prescriptions for the economy's problems than Paul Krugman. The blind hatred for him on the right simply pushed me further away from my old allies and comrades."[64] Bartlett further wrote,

> The economy continues to conform to textbook Keynesianism. We still need more aggregate demand, and the Republican idea that tax cuts for the rich will save us becomes more ridiculous by the day. People will long remember Mitt Romney's politically tone-deaf attack on half the nation's population for being losers, leeches, and moochers because he accurately articulated the right-wing worldview.[65]

This chapter has been an attempt to understand where the radicalism of the proponents of Senate Bill 5 came from so that politics in Ohio and beyond can move in a direction that addresses real issues and real problems. Hopefully, the behavior of the Republican Party in Ohio and across the nation in recent years will cause many Americans to re-examine the GOP and its ideology. Ohio provided a case study of the problem in 2011, when a series of policies driven by this extreme, conservative ideology, with roots in a foreign economic philosophy, created a battleground in the Buckeye State.[66]

Chapter 3

The Battle Begins

After state Sen. Shannon Jones dropped Senate Bill 5 on the legislature on February 1, we at the AAUP immediately began to formulate a strategy to preserve the things that were most important to us—defending academic freedom and shared governance at the University of Cincinnati and other colleges and universities.

Keys to the success of our struggle were two people who, by chance, were in place in Ohio to help. Debby Herman was executive director of the UC chapter of the AAUP. I had been on the search committee that hired her back in 2004, and I'd advocated strongly for the hire. Herman came from a union family and had real labor union experience with the UE.[1] Coming to us with a doctorate from the University of Iowa, Dr. Herman was a natural organizer whose skills were essential to us as we met this crisis. The AAUP Ohio Conference had also made the important step in January 2011 of hiring a new executive director. Sara Kilpatrick's first day of work was February 1, the day SB 5 was introduced. She hit the ground running. With a master's in public administration from Ohio State University, Kilpatrick had worked as staff for the Ohio Senate Democratic Caucus as well as the Ohio State Medical Association. Kilpatrick knew her way around the political world of Columbus on a level that no one else in the AAUP did because of our traditional nonpolitical stance, and this made her invaluable. The decision by Dr. John Cuppoletti, professor of physiology at UC and then-president of the Ohio Conference, and the Conference board of trustees to hire Kilpatrick proved essential to our cause.[2]

We took some cold comfort in the fact that Senate Bill 5 never garnered another cosponsor, a very unusual situation and testimony to the fact that it was such bad legislation. In the first day or two, we reached out to others across the state and tried to absorb the broad dimensions of this attack on working people. Until we had a better understanding of this attack on us, we decided to stay low, "beneath the radar," as Herman described it, joking that "beneath the radar means hiding and lying on the ground, where you often get rolled over by tanks anyway. So, whatever . . ." Dark humor served us well in the months to come.

Our national office and state conference soon sprang into action. The state conference and national AAUP president Cary Nelson worked to coordinate a strategy to defend the faculty. All across Ohio, AAUP chapters began planning how to defend their universities. The state conference created a communications committee—consisting of Marty Kich of Wright State and Dave Witt and Steve Aby of the University of Akron—and their work over the coming months was invaluable. Another of our great assets was Gary Rhoades, executive secretary in the national office. As a scholar at the University of Arizona in the history and practice of higher education, Rhoades was also an activist on national issues regarding higher education. His knowledge, enthusiasm, and positive attitude helped a great deal. As word about Senate Bill 5 spread across the country, Rhoades immediately contacted us, offering assistance and the resources of the national office of the AAUP.

Dr. Herman and I reached out to some of our contacts with the Ohio Federation of Teachers (OFT) and had a conference call with OFT president Sue Taylor and her staff. We were looking, in particular, for ways to tap into the political and union network in Ohio with which we had so little experience. This led to an invitation a few weeks later, through Taylor, from Tim Burga, Ohio AFL-CIO executive director, for us to attend a major meeting of labor organizations on January 28 at the Ohio State campus in Columbus. It was an important step for us because we made contacts there that have lasted to the present. Key political figures were in attendance including Sen. Sherrod Brown and a large number of state legislators. Especially impressive was former governor Ted Strickland, who gave an impassioned speech and said that he had just turned down an opportunity to serve at the International Labor Organization in Geneva because he wanted to stay and fight against these radical attacks on Ohio's middle class. We also met with the head of the Cincinnati AFL-CIO, Doug Sizemore, and his staff. Sizemore, who would become a great ally in the coming months, agreed to allow us to have a representative sit in on their labor council meetings as a nonvoting member, since the AAUP is not an AFL-CIO affiliate. We also made contacts with Progress Ohio, Innovation Ohio, and Policy Matters Ohio, important organizations producing research and reports that could be used to combat the flawed right-wing narrative.

There were more than a hundred representatives from different labor organizations and progressive groups at the meeting, and we knew almost no one. At the beginning, representatives from the many organizations took turns standing and being introduced, going around the big room. Much to our surprise, Herman and I were also introduced. As we stood, the crowd gave us a good long round of applause, perhaps surprised that the professors, too, were in the house. It was a bond that would be solidified in the coming months.

It is time to be specific about what aspects of Senate Bill 5, which was more than five hundred pages long, were most disturbing to us. The bill had changed in some ways since its introduction and through its transfer to the House and its final passage. But it clearly was not moderated by the changes. In fact, especially in the case of university faculty, it became more radical as it moved through the Republican-dominated legislature. First and foremost, contrary to continuing statements from Gov. Kasich, Sen. Shannon Jones, Senate President Tom Niehaus, House Majority Leader William Batchelder, and other Republicans, Senate Bill 5 did not leave collective bargaining intact. Although it did allow unions to technically still exist, it eliminated their ability to genuinely engage in collective bargaining. It was immensely frustrating to me, as a former newspaper reporter, to see newspapers all over the state allowing the proponents of SB 5 to be dishonest on this central issue.

Republicans tried to use these minor tweaks in the bill to suggest that they were listening and being reasonable. Not true. The bill outlawed strikes for all public workers, thus eliminating the only real pressure union members can bring to bear on their employers—the right to withhold their work. Although the bill technically allowed for negotiations on wages, hours, and terms and conditions of employment, more than a dozen other issues, including health care, were off the table. Obviously, if you can't negotiate for health care, any increase in pay could be taken back by an increase in health care premiums—clearly a union-busting strategy used by extremists.[3]

Republicans never budged an inch on their central goal of eliminating the reality of collective bargaining. This is clear in the impasse resolution process. In the past, when an impasse was reached in negotiations, a professionally trained arbitrator would come into the process, analyze the situation, and impose a "fair" settlement. In the public safety sector (i.e., police and firefighters), arbitration had worked historically as a strike-prevention option. A study of arbitrators' decisions over the years would show that arbitration was rarely used and that the decisions went against the union just about as often as against management. But the Republicans wrongly insisted that arbitration somehow gave enormous advantages to the unions, which was not true.

Having eliminated strikes and binding arbitration, Republican legislators created a process wherein, if the two sides reached impasse, the decision would go to the nearest responsible elected body—the school board, the county commission, or the university board of trustees. These bodies were, of course, the management and thus management could then just impose its last offer. So, at any university, for example, both sides could talk as long as the administration wanted. Once impasse had been reached, the university board of trustees—the management—could simply impose its last offer. Clearly, this process was not collective bargaining; at best it would be mere conversation.

Under Senate Bill 5, current contracts would be in effect until their terms ended. But even those could be eliminated if the state auditor declared a state of fiscal emergency. We expected that Gov. Kasich would do exactly that, to complete this political power play. For public school teachers, each new contract would have to be negotiated from scratch. No old language could be carried forward as teachers would have to engage in these new phony nonnegotiations. Pay could only be based on merit. In schools and universities, the ability to defend tenure would disappear. In one of the more bizarre requirements, an early version of SB 5 included provisions to make it illegal (an unfair labor practice) for any union leader to speak to persons such as school board or university board members during the course of contract negotiations about any matter that was "or may become" a subject of bargaining. Among the most common untruths repeated by proponents of SB 5 had to do with health insurance and pension plans. Sen. Jones led the way in suggesting that state employees paid for neither of these benefits. That has never been true. In the universities, for example, most unionized faculty pay between 10–15 percent of the cost of health care premiums, although it varies by contract. For retirement in the State Teachers Retirement System, faculty contribute 10 percent of their salary and do not qualify for Social Security.

Part of SB 5 also contained elements of typical right-to-work laws and made it illegal for employers to collect dues for its union employees through payroll deduction. Additionally, there could be no "fair share" fees collected from those who benefited from the union contract but chose not to join the union. All of this, of course, was the central reason for the attack on the unions. In the wake of *Citizens United*, the court decision that allows unlimited corporate political donations, the Republicans wanted to also eliminate the only force that balanced out those political contributions—political donations from labor unions. Crippling a major funding source for the Democratic Party was, without question, what Senate Bill 5 was all about.

Senate Bill 5 was, thus, a cold and calculated power grab. The Republicans were determined to take full advantage of the 2010 election that had put them in control of Ohio state government to impose a right-wing ideology on the state. "Flexibility" became the code word for union busting. Meanwhile, the AAUP, which had been determinedly not political for decades was caught in the middle and targeted for elimination.

While digesting all this, we communicated a great deal with our colleagues at other universities. In Ohio, the AAUP's collective bargaining chapters include, UC, the University of Akron, Wright State University, Kent State University, the University of Toledo, Cincinnati State, Central State University, Cleveland State, Wilberforce University, North Central State, and Cuyahoga Community College. Bowling Green State University faculty had won a certification vote during 2010, but its administration stalled negotiations during the SB 5 battle. A first contract was finally completed in April 2013. Advocacy chapters, many of which were very active during the SB 5 fight, are located at Ohio University, Case Western Reserve University, Ohio State University, John Carroll College, Lake Erie College, Sinclair Community College, the University of Dayton, Ohio Dominican University, Wilmington College, Defiance College, and Xavier University. By standing up for principles of academic freedom, shared governance, fair treatment of faculty, and devotion of resources to the instructional and research mission, the AAUP has helped set standards for public and private, union and nonunion, institutions alike. This is why the nonunion chapters were just as adamantly opposed to SB 5 as were the collective bargaining chapters.

This collection of colleges and universities gave us a statewide network of faculty interested in defending their institutions from the damage promised by SB 5. It also presented us a challenge. The AAUP is not a top-down organization, and each chapter has its own culture and traditions. Thus, we had to work in the early weeks to find a way of balancing statewide coordination with the fact of independent chapters. In the end, through the work of a great many people, we reached a mode of operation that represented a lot of sharing of information and ideas but based on local actions. One of our greatest moments was coming together on several occasions in large numbers at the statehouse in Columbus, with other unions and fair-minded groups, to try to make our voices heard by the legislature.

This collaboration led to a communication to our statewide members from Kilpatrick and Dave Witt, chair of the communications committee, on February 8. "Our goal is to provide you with informative, data-driven, objective arguments," they wrote, "that we hope you will build upon and take action. In the coming days and months, the Ohio Conference will provide our members with details of the legislation as these unfold, talking points for communicating directly with state legislators in your respective districts, sample letters to the editor, and research materials that will help effectively address this issue."

They continued: "We also encourage each AAUP member to work closely with your local chapter leadership in the months to come. We will keep you informed so that your individual or chapter response can be most effective. Watch for our Action Alert in the next few days."

There was no time to waste, after all, because the first hearing on the bill was set for Wednesday, February 9, just a little over a week after it was introduced. This clearly indicated Kasich and his right-wing allies were determined to railroad the bill through the legislature as quickly as possible. The first hearing was in the Senate's Insurance, Commerce, and Labor committee.

Herman and I and several other faculty members carpooled to Columbus for the hearing, not knowing at all what to expect. What we encountered on that cold day in Columbus was inspiring. Inside the huge hall of the capitol building were at least a thousand people, many with signs and buttons identifying themselves as members of various unions from all over Ohio. The crowds continued to build all day as hundreds and hundreds more continued to arrive at the statehouse. No longer able to get into the statehouse, union members with signs crowded the grounds. The sound of automobile horns could constantly be heard as people driving past honked in support. As I sat in the hall, I looked up to see a plaque on a pillar. It said that Abraham Lincoln had spoken once from those very steps. I could not help but think what Lincoln, the Great Emancipator and the first Republican president, would think about today's Republicans and the threat to our civil rights represented by Senate Bill 5. I reflected on the fact that each generation has to fight its own battles to preserve their liberty, as we were now doing.

Union members packed the rotunda of the capital and roared their opposition to the bill. I talked with firemen and schoolteachers, students and policemen, janitors and professors. This diverse crowd was united against this ruthless attack against all of us. In the large hall, some of the testimony was piped in so we could hear it. Former governor Ted Strickland made his way through the crowd, to loud cheers. Some Democratic lawmakers set up a microphone from which they spoke defiantly, helpless as they were to stop the process.

Particularly appalling was Sen. Jones's testimony. Jones did not use the state budget crisis as a major reason for the legislation. She said there might be "some savings" that year. In fact, Jones did not have a single projection of any cost savings for the short or long term, but said that she "thought" there would be savings in the future. A few of Jones's own Republican colleagues asked very damning questions and seemed not to be very supportive of the bill's intent. Although they were fewer in number, we became aware that there would be some Republicans on our side. Even though Jones explicitly said this bill wasn't "political payback," it became clear that diminishing union power was her intent. She could barely answer any questions about her own bill, which told many observers that her main goal was to punish unions and not get caught up in the details.

Some of the testimony is revealing:

Sen. Bill Beagle (R-Tipp City) Q: How will this bill ensure that public employee salaries aren't totally gutted?

Jones A: There may be salary adjustments, up or down. The main point is that it gives employers flexibility.

Sen. Joe Schiavoni (D-Youngstown, Ranking Member) Q: Do you realize that state employees took $250 million in concessions last year? It seems to me that public employees are willingly trying to adjust to meet the challenges of the new budget and economy.

Jones A: But employers are still limited. We have to look at all contracts. This bill addresses structure.

Sen. Schiavoni Q: Do you think state employees are getting paid too much?

Jones A: I don't know, but it needs to be disclosed.

Sen. Kris Jordan (R-Delaware) Q: What are the cost savings that will result from this bill, and how do you arrive at them?

Jones A: I can't specify any specific dollar amount in the short term. But what this does is give Cabinet members ability to adjust as they need to.

Sen. Tim Schaeffer (R-Lancaster) Q: What replaces binding arbitration?

Jones A: If there is no agreement reached after an alternative dispute resolution process, the current agreement would continue for one year until a new agreement can be reached.

Sen. Bill Seitz (R-Cincinnati) Q: As a follow-up to Sen. Schaeffer's question, what happens if the current contract that provides for salary increases ends in 2010 and doesn't prescribe an increase for the following year? What happens then?

Jones A: Then salaries are frozen.

Seitz Follow-Up: That certainly seems like that overwhelmingly favors the employer.

Sen. Seitz Q: Why are we prohibiting this totally, not even giving people the option to enter into a CBA? It may be the best choice in some situations.

Jones A: [When Jones failed to answer the question, the questioning continued.]

Sen. Hughes (R-Columbus) Q: How do we keep experienced and knowledgeable people under this new system?

Jones A: The system would be based on merit, so it would allow employers to keep high-quality people. Longevity shouldn't drive salary.

Sen. Schiavoni Q: Do you know how many cuts and freezes that state employees have taken over the past six years?

Jones A: The public doesn't know, which is why we need transparency so the public can understand.

Sen. Schiavoni Q: Am I correct in stating that you have not identified any cost savings that would result from this bill?

Jones A: This doesn't have to do with the short-term budget situation, but I do believe it will yield some savings.

Sen. Faber (R-Celina) Q: Am I correct in that this bill would prescribe employees to pay 20 percent of their own health-care costs?

Jones A: Yes, public employees need to take more responsibility for their health care costs, have "skin in it." This will help save the state money.

Sen. Faber Q: Why 20 percent?

Jones A: It is somewhat of an arbitrary number.

Sen. Tom Sawyer (D-Akron) Q: Do you know how much personnel and wages have risen since 1983, when the CB law first went into effect?

Jones A: No, I don't.

Sawyer Follow-Up: They haven't. State government levels are now the same as they were in 1983.

Sen. Sawyer Q: Can you give any examples of how employers don't have enough flexibility?

Jones A: There will be people coming in to testify about that.

Sen. Sawyer Q: Do you know the number of CBAs that have been enacted in the last 27 years?

Jones A: No.

Sawyer Follow-Up: I think that's a number you should know. It would be helpful to know how many CBAs resulted in strikes. My point is that the 1983 law has worked. The threat of binding arbitration keeps people bargaining amicably.

Sen. Eric Kearney (D-Cincinnati) Q: Do you know how this bill would impact current retirees?

Jones A: This bill in no way addresses the public pension systems.

Sen. Kearney Q: Do you think this bill will attract better teachers?

Jones A: Interesting question. I do think this bill lays the groundwork for innovation. The outcomes of children should be the driving factor determining salary, not longevity.

Kearney Follow-Up: I think we're in danger of having good teachers leave if this bill would pass.

Sen. Kearney Q: Binding arbitration is rarely used . . .

Jones A: Then why are we so upset about it? It's used as a stick and parties agree out of fear. That's not how it should be.

Sen. Edna Brown (D-Toledo) Q: Will state employees be able to be represented by a union under this bill?

Jones A: I don't know. I'm not a union member, and I'm not sure how exactly they would be affected.[4]

As *The Columbus Dispatch* noted the next day, the response to the bill from unions had been "quick and furious." The *Dispatch* quoted Eddie Parks, president of the Ohio Civil Service Employee Association (OCSEA), who noted that state workers had taken five pay cuts in nine years and saved the state $250 million in its current contract alone. "No economic problem was ever solved by cutting the middle class," he said.[5]

John Lyall, president of AFSCME Ohio Council 8, told *The Cleveland Plain Dealer* that Jones' proposal was part of a national GOP effort to defund unions that have historically backed Democrats, including former governor Ted Strickland. "She's nothing if not consistent in her hypocrisies," Lyall said. "She would rather shove her right-wing politics down the throats of Ohioans than fix the economy."[6]

Stephen Loomis, president of the Cleveland Police Patrolmen's Association, and Jay McDonald, president of the Fraternal Order of Police of Ohio, both told *The Plain Dealer* that they didn't like the proposed plan but would work to improve it for their members. "We're going to be involved in this to the end," Loomis said. "It's going to be a long struggle." We were particularly pleased when later in February, the firefighters and the police, when offered the opportunity to get out of SB 5 and negotiate something separately, both chose to stick with all of the unions. "Never in their wildest dreams," Mark Sanders, president of the Ohio Association of Professional Firefighters, told *The Plain Dealer*, "did they think a governor who talked about examining collective bargaining would end up with something gutting their livelihood. I haven't seen this response ever, really, after almost 30 years in fire service."[7]

Our national staff was keeping up on events. Nseabasi Ufot, a member from the national office, communicated to us and shared some photos of the huge crowds at the statehouse. "Rooms FILLED with union members and supporters," she wrote. "Very powerful." Meanwhile, our chapter had its monthly meeting on the UC campus the next day. I had billed it to our membership as an opportunity to make plans to defend higher education in Ohio and begin coalition building. Executive Director Sara Kilpatrick and John Cuppoletti, president of the state conference, would be our special guests.

"Of course as higher education faculty," I wrote to my colleagues, "we have particular concerns about this legislation which specifically targets us. But it was good today to be seated in an overflow room side-by-side with hundreds of uniformed police, firefighters, and nurses showing our shared opposition to this bill. [As] stalwarts of the AAUP . . . you know this struggle is not just about dollars and cents. It is about shared governance and academic freedom as well—about our ability to continue our work to enhance the university for our students and our communities."

Our chapter meetings are usually modest affairs, with light turnout unless there is some burning issue. Nothing could be more "burning" than politicians trying to eliminate the AAUP, so there was a big crowd and some unanticipated guests: a crew from a local television station. I allowed the crew to film the meeting briefly and then stepped out in the hallway to talk with them, my first television interview. I can't remember exactly what I said on the spur of the moment, but I did criticize the legislature's actions as harshly as I could, and I remember that I pointed out that the impact of union busting would be lower wages, lower standards of living, lower educational attainment, and an undermining of the university system. Proponents of this legislation, I concluded, "were trying to re-create Mississippi with ice here in Ohio."

One thing that became perfectly clear to us was that the ideologically driven Republicans in control of the legislature intended to move like lightning to adopt this destructive legislation before the state's unions could move to counter the attack on the middle class. In the background, leadership of the major unions were coming together to consider a strategy, especially the big public unions—AFSCME, SEIU, AFT, NEA—where both the membership numbers and the money were. Early on, we became determined to work as closely as we could with them as only they had the resources to defend us. Alone, we faculty would easily be crushed by an administration whose leader had once referred to us contemptuously as "eggheads."[8] As the legislation worsened over the course of the political process, professors were targeted in a way that shocked even our union partners. "Why do they hate you?" they asked us, as puzzled as we were. Thus, we consulted with them as Senate Bill 5 rapidly moved forward. Keeping the AAUP in contact with our larger partners was part of Sara Kilpatrick's job.

Looking back on the communications through February and March of 2011, the sense of doom was palpable. An avalanche of completely unexpected animosity was being directed at professors, and we seemed powerless to stop it. Yet still there was plucky determination.

"No matter what happens," wrote Debby Herman in a communication to the state leadership, "we will live to fight another day. I promise."

"I don't know if we can pull this off," wrote Rudy Fichtenbaum, professor of economics at Wright State (who would be elected national AAUP president in 2012), "but I'm willing to go down fighting . . . I don't want to concede that all the gains we have are gone. Of course, I have been known to tilt at windmills."

"We are very proud of what you are doing in Ohio," wrote Howard Bunsis, chair of the AAUP's Collective Bargaining Congress and a professor of accounting at Eastern Michigan University, "and I promise you that we will stand with you no matter what. Each day is a new fight, and I know we will continue to stand up for what is right."

The crisis made it clear that if we were to mobilize our resources, we had to get better at communication. The state board and its communications committee did a great job as a catalyst in this effort. Our staff, Kilpatrick in Columbus and Herman and Stephanie Spanja and Eric Palmer at Cincinnati, as well as faculty and staff across the state, worked hard to put together a "tool kit" with information about SB 5. This included names and addresses of legislators to contact and talking points to coordinate our message. We could not know at the time that the legislature was so determined to crush us that talking to them would be a pointless exercise. We had faith in the political process, that we could make it respond to the injustice represented by Senate Bill 5.

As we and our colleagues across the state wrestled with developing a strategy, we became aware that one option was a statewide ballot referendum to repeal the bill if it was passed. The state's major unions were discussing this, but one issue was paramount. Unlike the corporate community, union financial resources are limited and comparatively small. If unions, the AAUP included, were going to fund a statewide ballot referendum, it was going to be necessary to conserve financial resources for that fight and not squander money during the ideologically driven political process that was taking place in Columbus. Therefore, by the end of February, it became clear that there was going to be no big and expensive media campaign or funds expended on organizing while the bill was in process.

Of course, we recognized that staging and winning a statewide referendum was a long shot. "You're absolutely right that a veto referendum or constitutional amendment will be extremely difficult to pull off," Kilpatrick advised us. "It is a measure of last resort, and as many of our union allies see it, it may very well be our only option to defeat this thing."

We were going to have to do this the old-fashioned way, through contacting our legislators and reasoning with them. We knew that the Democrats were opposed to this legislation, but they were outnumbered in both the House and the Senate. We also knew that there were a handful of Republicans who were either persuadable or were already opposed to the legislation. We hoped that it might be possible to convince a couple more Republicans to be more reasonable so that we could put a stop to this. In retrospect, we underestimated the determination of the conservative ideologues in the legislature and their ability, jointly with Gov. Kasich, to intimidate their colleagues to vote in lockstep. In the end, only a very few very strong individuals on the Republican side were able to stand up for what was right.

A column written by then-AAUP president Cary Nelson at this point caught the character of what was going on the Buckeye State. "Ohio Is at War," was the title of his piece. Although he had spent most of his academic career at the University of Illinois, he had spent time in Ohio. "[M]y decades of AAUP activism," he wrote, "have added a new and more telling element to my fondness for the state: respect for Ohio's brand of faculty activism and union solidarity . . . Like so many other principled struggles, the battle in Ohio and Wisconsin to retain faculty rights is really a struggle on behalf of faculty members and public sector employees everywhere. It is also a struggle over the soul of our democracy."

Nelson was correct, of course, and what we were watching in Ohio were some of the worst abuses of the democratic process. And then there was Wisconsin. The battle in the Badger State hung over all of our work in Ohio. We were inspired by our friends and colleagues in Wisconsin as they fought against their own right-wing political extremists, headed by another Republican governor bent on destroying the political fabric of the state. We watched as their Senate, over massive public protests, passed legislation to end collective bargaining. Then we watched the Democratic members of the Wisconsin House flee the state to avoid being party to such infamous legislation. We began to see clearly what Debby Herman told us bluntly:

> Ohio's SB5 (and the simultaneous moves in Wisconsin, Michigan and Indiana) is not about what's good for the state or the country. *It's an exercise in raw political power.* These guys want to gut public employee unions before we get to 2012 . . . so that unions cannot effectively get out the base to vote for Democrats and to ensure that unions are financially weakened and cannot support Democrats in those races. (It's no coincidence . . . Wisconsin and Ohio are swing states in presidential election years.)

Still, Gov. Kasich and his allies forged ahead. Given the huge public outcry over SB 5, the Senate planned a couple of more hearings and made time for more testimony. But because of the imposed need to rush, the testimony would go late into the wee hours of the morning. On February 17, Phil Hayes, the grandson of legendary Ohio State coach Woody Hayes, spoke to the committee. Hayes is a high school social studies teacher in Columbus. He spoke about the many teachers who had been important in his life:

> Think about your favorite teacher. The one who motivated you to do more than the assignment or the class asked for; the one that inspired you to be where you are now.
>
> These are the people who have helped you win; these are the people that, if they are still living, you should thank on National Teachers' Day in person.
>
> I wonder; if you were to tell them where you are, where you have been, what you have been through to get where you are and what you have done, what would they say about what you're doing now in regards to Senate Bill 5?[9]

Saying that his grandfather had told him that the things you send into other people's lives come back to you, Hayes made a special appeal directly to Sen. Kevin Bacon, who chaired the committee and was one of those Republicans primarily responsible for forcing the bill through so quickly. He pointed out that their fathers were lawyers, and they both have children with autism who have especially benefited from public school teachers. Hayes noted that his own daughter has been able to receive special therapy because of the health insurance negotiated by his union. "Senator Bacon, members of the committee," Hayes testified, "this legislation will not just affect me, but my children. They are my family. This legislation punishes teachers, firefighters, police officers, state workers and their families. I urge you to pigeonhole this bill; to not send it to the floor for a vote."

On February 18, a column I wrote for *The Cincinnati Enquirer* appeared side-by-side with a piece by Senate Bill 5 sponsor Shannon Jones, whose district encompasses part of the Cincinnati metro. It appears that after receiving my piece, Ray Cooklis, editorial page editor at the time, sought out a piece from Jones since I had sent mine unsolicited. My piece was intended as an op-ed, so it was suitably long at about six hundred words, roughly three times the length of a letter to the editor. I had had a couple of op-eds published by the now-defunct *Cincinnati Post* a few years earlier of roughly that length, so I knew it was appropriate. The *Enquirer* cut it to 341 words. Meanwhile, Shannon Jones was able to extol the virtues of Senate Bill 5 for 460 words.

The nearby Hamilton *Journal-News* ran my piece, with tiny changes, at its full length on February 18. More importantly, the *Journal-News* did not take out the heart of my argument and critique of Senate Bill 5 as the *Enquirer* had. "It's hard to see how it is not political payback against unions who supported Ted Strickland in the last election," I wrote to readers of the *Journal-News*. "Is this really how we want politics in the United States to operate: Those who vote the 'wrong' way are punished by the next administration? Not surprisingly, new Republican Gov. John Kasich says he is happy with the bill and is only concerned that it will not go far enough."[10]

The *Journal-News* gave me room to explain some of the most important aspects of this attack on the university: "The AAUP champions shared governance in which faculty and administrators share in the decision-making process to ensure quality education and good financial stewardship. It is our experience that decisions made solely by business managers or accountants end in failure." I also emphasized the importance of academic freedom: "Being able to teach students and engage in research that benefits the public without fear from political reprisal is what makes the university a great place for students and faculty alike. This is a faculty-driven organization at UC with dozens of faculty directly involved in work that makes this university a great place to be."

While all this activity was moving forward, we began to reach out to other contacts. In Columbus, we cultivated some former Cincinnatians who lived in the city and had more regular contact with the state government and legislature. During our participation in the protests, we often met with our contacts to try to get a deeper understanding of the forces arrayed against the universities and the unions.

An important part of this process of reaching out to allies was building relationships with students who cared about the fate of their university. Even in my op-ed, I had closed with an appeal to UC alumni to stand by the faculty in this attack on the university: "We ask for Bearcats everywhere and the public at large to join with us to defend UC and higher education statewide." Since nearly all the employees at UC are unionized workers, from the food service to the janitors to the security, we saw this correctly as an attack on the university community, not just the faculty. Students, by and large, agreed with us because they cared about the university.

A small coalition of student activists organized what would be the first of many protests on February 21 on McMicken Commons at the main campus. In a press release, the students wrote, "The rally intends to express the students' solidarity with public workers across the state. Anyone who values democracy, education, and the work of UC's professors and other public workers should be there. The future of Ohio depends on it." Years ago when I was an undergraduate, I was not politically active. Through the SB 5 fight, I came to have great admiration for the many students at UC and across the state that I met through the campaign, who cared deeply about their state and their country and were willing to stand up against these destructive actions. Dan Traicoff at the University of Cincinnati and Will Klatt at Ohio State were particularly helpful.

It was, however, a regular disappointment that we could not generate really big crowds of students. There are a variety of reasons for this, but they mostly revolve around the fact that between work, school, and family, students have very little flexible time. That was all the more reason to genuinely appreciate those students who came to rallies, wrote letters, and talked to their families about Senate Bill 5 and other damaging legislation.

The day of the rally was cold and rainy, but dozens of students turned out. Several students spoke, giving voice to the defiance they had for what was being done in Columbus. I had a chance to speak briefly: "We will stand in rain, we'll stand in the wind, we'll stand in the snow, we'll even stand in the dark, but we won't stand for this attack on our right to collectively bargain," I told them. The students responded with a roar of enthusiasm. We were going to be partners in this fight, I could see. The students soon created a Facebook site appropriately titled "Defend UC."

In Columbus, the push to rapidly pass Senate Bill 5 continued unabated. Powerful testimony was given to the Senate committee by Sean Grayson, general counsel for AFSCME in Ohio. Piece by piece, Grayson explained why Senate Bill 5 was not needed for the "flexibility" that Jones said was so necessary. He questioned why universities would be specifically barred from negotiating with their employees. "Why?" he asked, noting that Jones had offered no reason for this prohibition. He added that AFSCME represented about five thousand union employees at state colleges and universities. Grayson talked about all the concessions, including furlough days, that his members have already agreed to at state and local levels. "SB 5 seeks to control local government in its collective bargaining relationships rather than letting local government make its own decisions," Grayson said. "If you are concerned about preserving local government control, these proposals should concern you. Those who loathe government mandates should oppose SB 5."[11]

In discussions among AAUP leadership, we had chosen Dr. Rudy Fichtenbaum, a leader in the Wright State University chapter, to testify for the AAUP before the Senate committee, and Kilpatrick was able to get him on the list. Fichtenbaum was a labor economist, so we felt he could speak from his position of expertise about the financially illegitimate aspects of Senate Bill 5. Fichtenbaum's hard-hitting testimony on February 17 ultimately proved futile, but that just underlines what an ideologically blinded collection of politicians we were up against.

Fichtenbaum noted that Jones had said that punishing unions and seeking political retribution was not why she had submitted Senate Bill 5. If that was true, then the only possible reason for the bill must be the belief that collective bargaining had created the budget crisis, or that eliminating unions would solve the crisis. "Perhaps this is based on the myth that public employees are overpaid relative to employees in the private sector," Fichtenbaum testified, "a myth stemming from simple comparisons of earnings between public and private sector employees. Such comparisons fail to take into account differences in education between public and private sector employees."[12]

Fichtenbaum went on to cite several recent research studies that, in fact, demonstrate that the opposite about state employee compensation is true. For example, Fichtenbaum testified that, in an authoritative study that controlled for education and several other variables, it is clear that full-time state and local public employees earn about 5.9% less than their private sector counterparts. When hours worked are factored in, they earn 3.3% less. The same study also analyzed total compensation (wages plus benefits) and found state and local public employees receive annual compensation of about 6% less, and hourly compensation of about 3.5% less.[13]

Research also points out other facts that run counter to the pro-Senate Bill 5 argument, Fichtenbaum emphasized. For example, states without collective bargaining are actually in worse financial condition, with bigger deficits, than states that do have collective bargaining. Further, Fichtenbaum argued that the statistics point to the real problem undermining Ohio's economy. For years, Ohio has underfunded its university system. Ohio is thirty-seventh in the nation in the percentage of its citizens who have a college degree. Fichtenbaum agreed with Sen. Jones on one point: that the world has changed. That new world's economy is knowledge-based and needs a well-educated workforce "In short," Fichtenbaum testified, "to create the high-paying middle-class jobs of the future, we need a world-class system of higher education, and this means attracting the best and brightest from around the world to come teach and undertake research at state universities in Ohio."

But there is a growing gap in compensation between Ohio's public universities and the private colleges and universities. Eliminating collective bargaining would further expand that wage gap and further undermine public education in Ohio. It would "make it more difficult for us to attract the faculty we need to build a world-class system of public colleges and universities." And, Fichtenbaum observed, a great system of higher education needs a well-funded public school system to prepare students for colleges and universities, and so the attack on public school teachers would be counterproductive. There is even a correlation, he said, between higher teacher salaries and greater numbers of college graduates in a state.

In a line that drew a rousing roar from the crowd even at that late hour, Fichtenbaum testified, "We need police and firefighters. These people put their lives on the line every day. There are no statues of Wall Street bankers who have died keeping us safe or carrying children from burning buildings."

Fichtenbaum concluded his testimony:

> So the bottom line is that public employees in Ohio are not overpaid, and they are not responsible for the current budget crisis. Ohio's public employees are not the problem. They are part of the solution! It is unfortunate that the issue of collective bargaining rights for public employees has even come up at this time when Ohio faces a budget

> crisis. The Bill's sponsor, Senator Jones, acknowledged in her testimony that eliminating collective bargaining rights for public employees would have little if any effect on Ohio's immediate budget problems. I submit that curtailing collective bargaining rights for public employees will be outright harmful to Ohio in the longer term—by weakening our state's competitive position in having a well-educated citizenry, a safe environment in which to raise families, and workplace conditions that engender satisfied employees who will stay with their public employer rather than leaving at the first opportunity.

February 22 was one of our biggest turnouts during the whole protest process. Although we were never able to match the throngs that turned out in Madison, Wisconsin, to protest similar legislation, we had at least ten thousand at the statehouse that day. Even Gary Rhoades, the executive secretary at the national AAUP office, had flown in to stand with us. It is hard to say how many UC faculty were there, certainly more than 40. Others, of course, had class and other university responsibilities. We carpooled again to Columbus, and after a stop by the AAUP office only a block from the capitol, we bundled up for the walk over to the rally taking place.

It was then that we encountered a most shocking situation. The Capitol police, apparently under the direction of the Republican leadership, were to allow only 1,200 people into the building, leaving thousands more stranded on the steps and sidewalk. This was another example of the Republican disdain for the people whose unions they were trying to undermine. On the positive side, anyone who, like me that day, saw this unreasonable act by the people in power in Columbus had to be convinced, as I was, that this was not an ordinary political action going on in the American tradition but something alien and ugly. As it began to snow, thousands of people sang "God Bless America" to the accompaniment of the bagpipers from the various firemen's unions. "This is our house. Let us in," the people chanted repeatedly. Under threat of legal action from the Democratic Party leadership, the police relented and allowed more people into the building. But along with most of the crowd, I was never able to get into the Capitol that day.[14]

In the opposing testimony in the Senate committee, the only one that was really unpredictable and surprising was that of Bruce Johnson, president of the Inter-University Council. Sad to say, Ohio's faculty discovered that the Inter-University Council, the organization of university presidents, was actually a Trojan horse working against its own faculty.

The group had previously been relatively inactive except as a place for presidents of the universities to discuss common issues among themselves. Johnson was a lawyer with a law degree from Capital University in Columbus but no experience in higher education. His appealing qualifications for being a Kasich appointee were that he was a Republican and had served in the Senate and also in several capacities in the Gov. Bob Taft administration, including as lieutenant governor. Thus he was clearly someone who could push the governor's agenda for higher education, which, in this case, included union busting.

In his testimony in support of Senate Bill 5, Johnson said the collective bargaining system "results in higher labor costs, unnecessary duplication of personnel, and inefficient operations because of limits on what workers can and cannot do." Johnson said Senate Bill 5 would help Ohio's public colleges and universities build an environment that fosters efficiency, creativity, and productivity.[15] Anyone who knows firsthand about the academic world knows that what Johnson said was highly inaccurate and inflammatory. This distortion of the facts by Senate Bill 5's proponents, however, became par for the course as the political process unfolded and later as the campaign against it took place.

First and foremost, it is well known that a primary driver of higher labor costs, unnecessary duplication of personnel, and inefficient operations can be attributed to poor management decisions by university administrations across the state. The Goldwater Institute, no left-leaning think tank, determined in 2010 that between 1993 and 2007 administrative costs had grown by 61.2 percent, while instructional expenses trailed at only 39.3 percent. Similarly, the number of full-time administrators per hundred students increased more than 39 percent, but the number of faculty devoted to teaching, research, and service increased by only 17.6 percent.[16]

Anyone familiar with Ohio's universities can testify to the burgeoning corps of administrators, vice provosts, deans, assistant deans, and deanlets across the system. By comparison, there is constant pressure to replace retiring full-time faculty with part-time instructors so that benefits and decent pay do not have to be provided. That a spokesman for Ohio's university presidents would distort the facts so completely was a harbinger of worse things yet to come.

CHAPTER 4

GOP FORCES SENATE BILL 5 ON OHIO

The absolute determination of Republicans to force Senate Bill 5 on the people of Ohio became crystal clear in the struggle that occurred in the Senate committee where the bill was sourced.

Sen. Bill Seitz is a Republican stalwart from Cincinnati. He is an attorney of the venerable law firm Taft, Stennius & Hollister, the firm that was home to "Mr. Republican" Robert Taft. As noted on its website, "The firm's labor department led by J. Mack Swigert was instrumental in helping Senator Taft draft and pass 1947's groundbreaking Taft-Hartley Act despite President Harry S. Truman's veto."[1]

In the Senate Bill 5 fight, however, Seitz was an early critic. He was an acknowledged expert on labor law, and certainly any bill that was going to make historic changes to Ohio labor law should have included him in its formation. Neither he nor other experts on labor law in the Senate were consulted. Seitz believed, as he said more than once, that some changes ought to be made to Ohio's labor law. But he was opposed to Senate Bill 5 because it failed the basic test of fairness. And he did not mince words. He emphasized that, contrary to pronouncements by Sen. Jones, Sen. Bacon, and others, Senate Bill 5 unilaterally eliminated the reality of collective bargaining in Ohio.

The problem for the Republicans was that Seitz was chair of the Senate Insurance, Labor, and Commerce Committee that held Senate Bill 5, and with Seitz in charge, it was unlikely that the bill would get out of committee. So Senate President Tom Niehaus, a close ally of Gov. Kasich and an ardent supporter of the union-busting legislation, made Sen. Kevin Bacon chair instead and then kicked Seitz off the committee just 30 minutes before the committee was to meet to decide on the bill. Niehaus then replaced Seitz with Cliff Hite, a reliable pro-SB 5 senator. "It was not lost on our hundreds of thousands of police and firefighters and others that if that's what can be done to a senator, what will happen to other workers?" Seitz told *The Wall Street Journal.*[2]

With Seitz off the committee and the threat of a tie vote gone, the committee quickly voted 7–5 to approve Senate Bill 5 and send it on to the full Senate. Ironically, Seitz and Niehaus shared the same residence in Columbus. No matter how often Niehaus emphasized that such a politically ruthless action was normal, no union member who witnessed that pure political power play aimed at their own livelihood would ever forget it. Senate Democratic Leader Capri Cafaro of Mahoning County correctly called the last-minute committee changes "an abuse of power." A couple of weeks later, Seitz had also been bounced from his lodging with Niehaus and was looking for a new place to live in Columbus.[3]

After all the fireworks on March 2, the committee vote led to even more rapid action. Only a few hours after passing the committee, the full Senate picked up the bill in the afternoon. Many Senators spoke with anger and eloquence and emotion. It was, in many ways, a great debate in Ohio history. Like the one that would play out in the House, it asked basic questions about fairness, about honesty, about the role of government, about responsibility—and about the kind of state Ohioans wanted and about the values that we held.

I don't doubt that most of the advocates of Senate Bill 5 really believed the things that they said. But I have become ever more convinced that such an ideology is rooted in economic ideas that are divorced from reality and from American traditions. There was no practical need to so vilify public workers and unions. What members of the House and Senate owed to Ohio taxpayers was a more thorough understanding of the problem and a more sophisticated view of the world. Instead, much like the proponents of the Iraq War, they wanted simplistic answers for complex problems and, thus, created an unnecessary and destructive conflict.

Several of the speeches given on the Senate floor were stirring efforts. The scene was tense. Niehaus threatened the spectators on more than one occasion to be quiet or they would be ejected. In the hearing room, firefighters wore their helmets. Union buttons sprouted everywhere. But the crowd outside the Senate chambers, filling the statehouse, was so loud that their cheers and jeers could be heard as the debate was piped through the building. In the Senate chambers, because they had been warned that they would be thrown out if they made vocal their sentiments, the nearly two hundred spectators instead raised their hands over their heads and wiggled their fingers rapidly to indicate applause or agreement with speakers. Much like the whole Senate Bill 5 process itself, the experience was surreal.[4]

Sen. Tom Sawyer (D-Akron) recounted his experience being involved in politics when Senate Bill 133 passed in 1983 and created the existing labor law. As mayor of Akron at that time, he quickly embraced the bill because it provided for a "creative balance." In Akron and elsewhere, he said, the new legislation ended years of labor problems. He reminded people of the labor chaos in those years. There were 183 strikes between 1978 and 1980. Now, he said there have been five strikes in the last three years and none in the last year and a half.

"We just ran through a three-week sprint to destroy collective bargaining for all public workers," said Sen. Joe Schiavoni (D-Canfield). Jobs would not be created, he argued, Instead, Senate Bill 5 would crush job growth. The bill was driving a wedge among Ohioans, he said. It is "not working together" when you tell police they cannot negotiate for bullet-proof vests or when you tell teachers they cannot negotiate for a smaller class size. Senate Bill 5, he said, was "senseless, completely unfair, and will hurt people in so many ways. Thank God we have the ability in Ohio to put a law on the ballot so that the people can override our mistakes."

Sen. Michael Skindell (D-Lakewood) explained the value of public workers by describing a fire in Cleveland, the difficult snowstorm that had recently crippled Ohio, and his own bicycle accident. In each of those cases, he said, public workers saved lives. "There are many myths about this bill. This is not about the budget. The last budget was balanced because collective bargaining units made concessions." "Over $200 million in concessions" by state workers, he pointed out, and that did not include concessions offered by city, county, and school employees. "Ohio is the seventh largest state in the nation, yet we have the least number of public employees of any state in the nation. Our public employees make a huge investment for us," Skindell said, adding that all studies demonstrate that public employees are paid significantly less than their private sector counterparts when total compensation is considered.

Some African American senators gave particularly effective speeches, perhaps because of their great sensitivity to the violation of civil rights that Senate Bill 5 represented. Sen. Edna Brown (D-Toledo) said the bill would "muzzle public workers" and warned that the elimination of longevity as consideration in layoffs would open the door to age discrimination. Sen. Eric Kearney (D-Cincinnati) continually repeated that "Haste makes waste" as he reviewed the flawed and rushed process. He cited the Ohio Constitution, Article 1, Sec. 3: "The people have the right to assemble together, in a peaceable manner, to consult for their common good; to instruct their representatives; and to petition the general assembly for the redress of grievances." By contrast, Kearney said, the Senate had worked to inhibit the right of the people to petition the General Assembly through the rushed process and even by locking the people out of the statehouse. He went on to mock Gov. Kasich's frequently used line that he was making Ohio "move at the speed of business." Eliminating a 27-year collective bargaining system in three weeks is not the "speed of business," Kearney noted; "it is a bad business decision." You can't create jobs by eliminating jobs, he said.

Sen. Nina Turner (D-Cleveland) gave an impassioned critique of Senate Bill 5 and defended public workers vehemently. As she began, she held up a stack of letters from constituents urging a "No" vote on Senate Bill 5. In American society today, she said, "we have three groups of people: The Have a Lots, the Have Some, and the Have Nots. Senate Bill 5 would destroy this middle group, leaving us with only two groups, the Have a Lots and the Have Nots." Quoting the Rev. Martin Luther King and St. Thomas Aquinas, she said that any law that uplifts human personality is a just law, while any law that degrades human personality is an unjust law. Based on Aquinas, Turner observed, "Senate Bill 5 is an unjust law." It was introduced "under the cloak and guise of fiscal crisis." But, Turner noted, "everybody knows that our public workers did not cause this crisis." It was introduced "under the cloak and guise" of balancing the playing field with the private sector. But she asked, "Who says the private sector has the golden standard on how to treat folks and what it means to serve their community?" Senate Bill 5 was introduced "under the cloak and guise" of taxpayer rights. "Well, my God," Turner said, "the last time I checked, our public service employees were taxpaying citizens."

Apparently, Turner said, the proponents of Senate Bill 5 were following the old advice to "never let the truth get in the way of a good story." She pointed out that there was no correlation between collective bargaining and budget deficits. She went on to cite other states that had banned collective bargaining and have budget deficits, too, some of them worse than Ohio's. "The truth of the matter," she asserted, "is that this bill seeks to vilify our public employees and turn what used to be the virtues of service into a crime . . . The truth of the matter is that Senate Bill 5 destroys the middle class and their families." No matter how the bill was disguised, Turner maintained, "it will criminalize the right of hard-working employees to strike, making them second-class citizens to their private sector counterparts." In a fiery conclusion, Turner told the crowd, "we cannot go back and we will not go back. As Dr. King said, the arc of justice is slow but it bends toward justice. Senate Bill 5 is unjust, Senate Bill 5 is un-American, and Senate Bill is just plain wrong."

As Sen. Turner took her seat, the audience could not help but offer scattered applause as the roars of thousands of people in and around the statehouse filled the Senate chambers. What followed were two very different kinds of testimony from Republican attorneys Bill Seitz of Cincinnati and Tim Grendell of Chester Township.

Seitz opened with a lawyerly description of what he liked in the bill. He noted that he is not known for being a friend of unions and that his law firm, which helped create the Taft-Hartley Act, is typically on the side of the employers. He said he would leave analysis of the process and political implications of passing such a bill to others and focus on the substance. The flaws in the bill were so serious that he would be breaking with his colleagues and voting no on SB 5. Putting his well-honed speaking skills to work, he calmly moved through much of the bill, but when he got to the flaws, his voice rose as he expressed exasperation and outrage. He noted that he had tried to get amendments on many issues but had been rebuffed. For example, he said, the bill would bar school districts from picking up part of the pension costs for their teachers. Seitz noted that school boards choose to use this option because it is often cheaper for taxpayers than providing a pay raise would be, and thus gives the school boards flexibility. "Even public employers," Seitz's own friends and clients, he said, were writing to him and objecting to the ban on pension pickups. He read from a letter he had received from a school administration organization who asked that they not be barred from pension pickup. "Why are we being more pro-employer than the employers?" he asked exasperatedly.

Seitz harshly criticized the restrictions on the ability of safety and emergency forces to bargain for their staffing. "They would be relegated to two men on a fire truck whereas now there are four. That would be dangerous and unsafe," he noted. The bill, he said, nonsensically sharply restricts the number of safety personnel who can join a union. Seitz also focused on what he said was the "critical" issue of layoffs of longtime employees. State employees are not participants in Social Security and thus will not receive Social Security and, by and large, do not have IRAs to depend on for retirement. "Their pension benefits are all they have for retirement," he said, adding that their pension is one of the few advantages the public sector has over private sector workers. "When those older workers are ripped out of the workforce they get a big fat nothing" unless they have reached the "magic number," 25 years for fire departments, 30 years for other state employees. "If they go out with fewer years than that, their pension is much reduced," Seitz said, repeating for effect, "much reduced, ladies and gentlemen." He had proposed an amendment to protect those who have 20 or more years in the system, but it had been rejected. In the private sector, he said, lots of people in their fifties are being "sent out to pasture" by big private corporations. "They are the biggest at-risk group today, and they are great people." They were losing their jobs, he said, not because of bad performance but because those corporations want to "offload those higher-cost employees, get rid of them."

At least those workers have a 401k, a defined contribution plan, and Social Security, Seitz said. "I am concerned that under this bill, our longest-serving employees are at risk of being the most ill-treated, and I do not buy for one minute" that filing a lawsuit or a federal age discrimination case "is an adequate remedy." Seitz was also very critical of the provision to allow the state government to declare a fiscal emergency to abrogate contracts. The problem, he said, was the lack of a definition of what constituted a fiscal emergency. He said there was no reason to grant "carte blanche" to the governor or the state auditor to simply determine this issue unilaterally.

"Finally, and of greatest importance to me," Seitz concluded, "is the woefully, woefully one-sided mechanism that this bill proposes to replace binding arbitration and the right to strike." Once impasse was reached after fact-finding and mediation, the employer would submit the findings, the employer's last best offer, and the union's last best offer to "the legislative body of the public employer." This legislative body, such as the school board or county commission, would hold a hearing for both sides. After the hearing, the legislative body would have to accept either the employer's or the union's last best offer. Obviously, in such an arrangement, there would be no reason for the school board or county commission not to accept what was in reality their own offer rather than the union's. So they would then force the employees into a new three-year contract on the employer's terms. "What a deal," Seitz said sarcastically. "I'm going to negotiate with Senator [Mark] Wagoner. I have the choice of my offer or Senator Wagoner's offer. Uh, I think I'll take my offer." Laughter filled the hearing room. "This 'Heads I win, tails you lose' solution is also, in my opinion, likely unconstitutional,"

Seitz said. "No man can be a judge and advocate in his own cause. That's just Justice 101."

"I support collective bargaining reform," Sen. Timothy Grendell said, "and I want to stress 'reform'"—alluding to Senate Bill 5's virtual elimination of collective bargaining. He said that he supported much in the bill, just as Sen. Seitz did, but that the bill went too far. "I support barring public strikes as long as you have a fair method for resolving the tension between labor and management," Grendell stated. "You cannot take away the strike without providing any fair method for resolving the disputes." The alternative is lawsuits, and Grendell—who, like Seitz, is an attorney—said that any taxpayer who thinks that is a better solution is wrong. "Lawyers," he said, "are more expensive than negotiators."

"My biggest problem with Senate Bill 5," Grendell said, "is that it does not keep the collective bargaining process as is claimed." Under the language of the bill, "as my good friend from Cincinnati explained, there is no collective bargaining process." With much animation, Grendell said loudly, "Senate Bill 5 replaces public worker collective bargaining with public worker collective begging." To have collective bargaining, Grendell said, "both sides have to have something to gain and something to lose; otherwise it is not bargaining, folks." The government side has only two things to lose: one is service, and the other is money. "Senate Bill 5 eliminates both elements, since there are no more strikes and the employer can simply impose its contract," Grendell said. "This is not bargaining. It is simply a conversation." Losing the ability to bargain, he said, leaves police, firefighters, corrections officers, teachers, and everybody else "as beggars." And the employer will not budge because it knows that at the end of the process it can simply impose its will, he said. "It is downright 'Pollyannish' to suggest that the school board, the city council, acting as both advocate and judge, will select the union's last best offer" over their own offer. "Why in heavens would anybody do that?" said Grendell, with disbelief in his voice. "What are they going to say: 'We were stupid last week when we made that offer, but now we've been enlightened'?"

Other Republicans spoke in favor of Senate Bill 5. They were mostly informed by the misconceptions and ideology that has been discussed earlier in this book. They repeatedly implied that the budget deficit was caused by the public employees—"there is no more money left." They wrongly suggested that the bill preserved collective bargaining and only placed commonsense restrictions on unions. They frequently compared average salaries in a community with police and fire salaries, thus comparing fast-food workers and retail clerks with highly skilled professionals who sometimes have to risk their lives. Sen. Keith Faber (R-Celina), one of the ringleaders behind Senate Bill 5, hit on all the clichés during his address: "efficiency," "flexibility," "budgets are under strain," "taxpayers have had enough." He noted that not only was Ohio competing for jobs with neighboring states but also "India and China," apparently suggesting that American wages and work conditions be reduced to those prevalent in the developing world. Particularly glaring in the wake of Seitz and Grendell, Faber wrongly insisted that SB 5 was not about ending collective bargaining and provided the typical unfounded anecdotal evidence. He accused critics of Senate Bill 5 of "hype and hyperbole."

Cliff Hite (R-Findlay), the reliable advocate of SB 5 who had replaced Seitz on the Senate committee, gave one of the most bizarre defenses of the bill. He recounted how he had a 30-year career in teaching and coaching, and had been asked by many teachers how he could now be attacking the profession. At Findlay high school, Hite said, he'd had a chance to play quarterback, and that year the schoolteachers went on strike. Hite didn't know whether he would get a chance to play. But his football coaches crossed the picket line to coach the team, and thus, Hite said, he had a good year and went on to play at the University of Kentucky. "If my coaches had not crossed that picket line, I would not have gotten a full ride to the University of Kentucky and would not have this ring I have on my hand," he said holding his hand aloft, as boos and laughter filled the air from the thousands of union workers in the statehouse. The Republican, who said he was proud of Shannon Jones "for sticking to her guns," insisted he would vote for Senate Bill 5 in honor of his coaches who crossed the picket line. Many in the audience were less than impressed by Hite's heartwarming story about union busting.

Despite the eloquence of the defenders of collective bargaining, the final vote went down nearly along party lines. The bill made it out of the Senate by a 17–16 vote. The Republicans actually had 23 out of the 33 seats in the Ohio Senate. The one-vote margin occurred because courageous Republican Senators Gayle Manning, Bill Seitz, Timothy Grendell, Tom Patton, Jim Hughes, and Scott Oelslager bravely did the right thing and voted against Senate Bill 5.

Cries of "Vote them out" and "Shame on them" shook the statehouse as the huge crowd reacted angrily to the vote. In the hearing room, Senate President Niehaus futilely pounded his gavel as the vocal criticism echoed through the building.

Having taught that day, I was watching the drama between classes from my office via news reports. In hallways and offices across the university, faculty and staff talked about this assault on our institution and the Ohio way of life. As yet unknown to the faculty, the Republicans, claiming they were open to listening, had added much more radical language to the bill that was, without question, an attempt to eliminate the AAUP in Ohio.

Only hours before the Senate voted on the "amended" document, right-wing committee members had stuffed another nearly one hundred pages of amendments into the massive bill. Hours after the passage, as we were trying to untangle the bill, we saw that the amended bill was much worse than the original version, contrary to Republican claims. It represented a new assault on faculty. Our staff at the Cincinnati AAUP that evening cranked out a new edition of our newsletter that spelled out exactly what was being done to us. The changes to Senate Bill 5 would eliminate bargaining rights of any kind for Ohio college and university faculty by declaring them "management-level employees." Herman and I wrote in a message in our newsletter to the University of Cincinnati faculty:

> If SB 5 passes, everything we as faculty have taken for granted will be up for grabs. But what's more, the long-term quality of K–12 and higher education is up for grabs. SB 5 has great potential to undermine our ability to recruit and retain excellent faculty and staff in Ohio's universities. We must stand up for students and their right to a quality public education.[5]

What we uncovered in our examination of the new bill was that it now contained a concept known as "Yeshiva language." This refers to a 1980 U.S. Supreme Court case, *NLRB v. Yeshiva University*, in which the Supreme Court had held by only a narrow 5–4 margin that the faculty at Yeshiva University, a private institution, were considered "managerial employees." As "managerial employees," the Yeshiva faculty would not be covered by the National Labor Relations Act, and thus were denied the right to bargain collectively. Obviously, it was unfair to strip from faculty at private universities the right to collectively bargain, a right that exists in the private sector elsewhere and in the public sector as well. Justice William J. Brennan writing in the dissent maintained that:

> [W]hatever influence the faculty wields in university decision-making is attributable solely to its collective expertise as professional educators, and not to any managerial or supervisory prerogatives. Although the administration may look to the faculty for advice on matters of

> professional and academic concern, the faculty offers its recommendations in order to serve its own independent interest in creating the most effective environment for learning, teaching, and scholarship. And while the administration may attempt to defer to the faculty's competence whenever possible, it must and does apply its own distinct perspective to those recommendations, a perspective that is based on fiscal and other managerial policies which the faculty has no part in developing. The University always retains the ultimate decision-making authority, and the administration gives what weight and import to the faculty's collective judgment as it chooses and deems consistent with its own perception of the institution's needs and objectives.[6]

The language in SB 5 that was specifically designed to eliminate all faculty unions in Ohio read as follows:

> any faculty who, individually or through a faculty senate, or like organization, participate in the governance of the institution, are involved in personnel decisions, selection or review of administrators, planning and use of physical resources, budget preparation, and determination of educational policies related to admissions, curriculum, subject matter, and methods of instruction and research, are management level employees.

The method by which faculty gain appointments, get promoted, gain tenure, and are awarded merit is based on a three-pronged system of responsibilities, a concept developed by the AAUP and broadly accepted nationally. These responsibilities are teaching, research, and service. So the service component is an essential part of the professional contribution of any faculty member. And Senate Bill 5 now said that if you do service—which is good for the university and the students—you can no longer be part of your faculty union.

For example, if a history department is going to hire a historian, it only makes sense that other historians, who are specialists in the field, should be involved in the evaluation of qualified applicants. This makes sense for the department, the university, and the students. People who know the field should contribute to the hiring decision, but the hiring itself is always the responsibility of the administration. It would make no sense to have the administration's accountants, lawyers, or business managers conduct evaluations that rely on the expertise of the faculty. The same is true in promotion and tenure decisions.

And it is hard to imagine university administrators deciding curriculum issues for nonorganic chemistry or the study of medieval literature or conducting a symphony orchestra. Why would you cut the experts out of the decision-making process? And yet that was the logic now being used to destroy Ohio's faculty unions.

If this irrational legislation had gone into effect, university professors all over the state would have had to make the decision to do the service that is so badly needed, or not to do the service so that they could continue to have the union—however badly weakened—to advocate for academic and faculty issues. Some would have chosen service, and some the union. In the wake of the imposition of this legislation, the large numbers of faculty doing service activities would have plummeted. It is also a possible interpretation of the law that if any university rules provided for faculty involvement in these service duties that faculty would then be ruled managers and ineligible for union membership automatically whether they actually participated or not.

I am one of those faculty devoted to the importance of service. In addition to my union activities (all volunteer and unpaid) and service on several college-level committees, I've also served four years on the Faculty Senate, served on a collegiate restructuring task force, and have twice been on provost search committees. That is in addition to several department and college committees, including one focusing on our study-abroad programs and our scholarship and honors committee. I do not know how many faculty would have maintained their enthusiastic engagement in service if the extremists at the state legislature had been successful in crushing the AAUP and depriving us of our voice at the university.

So, where did this radical approach come from, to disband faculty unions? The details of the sordid operation only became clear in the weeks ahead. Much of our knowledge of the roots of the attack can be credited to the work of Sheldon Gelman, a law professor at Cleveland State University. Making a public records request, Gelman received thousands of pages of documents showing the involvement of the Inter-University Council, its executive director Bruce Johnson, and the presidents of Ohio's universities in this attack on their own faculty.

Gelman published his findings in the *Albany Law Review*, and it is a richly detailed story that I cannot recommend highly enough. Gelman used the arguments of Benjamin Ginsberg to frame his analysis. Ginsberg is the author of the widely read *The Fall of the Faculty: The Rise of the All-Administrative University and Why It Matters*. Gelman argues convincingly that the Ohio university presidents tried to transform the universities into what Ginsberg has dubbed "the all-administrative university." "Consistent with that view" in the Senate Bill 5 battle, Gelman argues, "the presidents identified their institutions with themselves, equating presidential authority with institutional freedom and creativity."[7]

In the introduction to his book, Ginsberg explains to those unfamiliar with the way that universities work, why this is such a destructive strategy for the academic mission of the institution. Reflecting the explosion in administrative staffing in the last 20 years, he notes that "universities are filled with armies of functionaries—vice presidents, associate vice presidents, assistant vice presidents, provosts, associate provosts, vice provosts, assistant provosts, dean, deanlets, deanlings, each commanding staffers and assistants—who more and more direct the operations of every school."[8]

This matters, Ginsberg argues, because "controlled by its faculty, the university is capable of not only producing new knowledge but new visions of society." Through their teaching and scholarship, university faculty can show that "new ways of thinking and acting are possible." Controlled by administrators instead, Ginsberg maintains, the university can never be more than a "knowledge factory, offering more or less sophisticated forms of vocational training to meet the needs of other established institutions in the public and private sectors." Vocational training is a good thing, Ginsberg notes, but a university should be more than that. "We cannot all," he writes, "be [University of] Phoenixes."[9]

In Ohio, however, in 2011, the university presidents took actions to eliminate the biggest advocate for shared governance, their faculty unions. "SB 5 singled out university faculty," Gelman points out, "for the most stringent treatment of any group and it did so via a provision—known as the *Yeshiva* amendment—that Ohio's public university presidents drafted and promoted in secret." Pointing to Johnson's committee testimony in favor of Senate Bill 5 and his quoting of the Yeshiva language, Gelman writes that Johnson actually broke from Justice Powell in his view of the faculty role. Powell clearly believed the faculty members were at the core of the university and that shared governance was a very important role for the faculty. Johnson, by comparison, suggests that faculty already have too much power. Gelman goes on to further question Johnson's interpretation of the Yeshiva decision and argues convincingly why, in the Ohio context, it should not apply.[10]

But Gelman's most important contribution was tracing the decision-making process of the IUC that led to the insertion of the language into Senate Bill 5 to destroy the faculty unions. Before Kasich was even elected, at a meeting on October 12, 2010, the presidents had met and had determined to take an aggressive and unified stance with regard to "regulatory relief," code language—as it turned out, for union busting—and the development of "charter" universities. More will be said about the charter concept in a later chapter, but faculty leaders saw this as a move toward privatization, as well as a backdoor method to abrogate union contracts.

In mid-December, after Kasich's victory, Johnson and IUC staff first met with an aide to the governor-elect, Wayne Struble. The minutes of the next meeting, January 11, 2011, reveal that discussions among the presidents, IUC staff, and the Kasich administration representatives had resulted in action: "IUC has submitted our very aggressive recommendations to the Governor's senior staff . . . The details are still unknown but we are making progress." Also, importantly, the IUC had found allies: "Council members can use regulatory reform in discussion, as part of the IUC message. The business community is coming onboard with this approach, [and] we continue to garner business leaders' support." Obviously, the IUC had discussed its proposals with political leaders, business leaders, and administration officials—but not with the faculty.[11]

The presidents wrote Kasich on January 19, 2011. They said, in part, that they wanted "to make sure [he] underst[oo]d how fervently [they] support[ed] the concept of regulatory reform." Among the areas where "reform" should be focused were the Administrative Procedures Act, Public Works Law, Civil Service, Purchasing, Office of Budget and Management regulation, public improvements, and "Public Employee Collective Bargaining." They went on to suggest that charter universities might be a way to move on these reforms.[12]

While it is hard to gauge each president's position on union busting, Carol Cartright, president of Bowling Green State University was clearly most enthusiastic. She wrote a personal follow-up letter to Kasich urging support for the IUC goals. But she went beyond the message of the IUC. She did not just support that the universities be relieved of compliance with the statutes; she asked that state universities be specifically exempted from those statutes. "Applied to collective bargaining," Gelman points out, "that would mean *eliminating* rather than *reforming* it."[13]

Why the extra hostility? The AAUP, using both state and national resources and volunteers, had worked with faculty activists at Bowling Green State to mount a successful unionization drive. In October 2010, with about 85 percent of the eligible faculty voting, BGSU faculty voted 391–293 in favor of unionization. It had been a long battle. Faculty from all over the state pitched in with their BGSU colleagues. I was one of those who volunteered my own time to walk the halls with BGSU faculty to explain the value of collective bargaining in defending shared governance, academic freedom, and keeping the focus of university resources on the central instructional and research mission. I shared the history of how valuable the AAUP was at the University of Cincinnati. The victory of the BGSU faculty was a satisfying one for many Ohio AAUP members. "The faculty at Bowling Green," said the national AAUP's then-president Cary Nelson, "have sent a message to the country—that shared governance and a quality education are best guaranteed by a legally enforceable union contract."[14]

The victory at Bowling Green came against an administration that tried in many ways to thwart the will of the faculty. And now it became clear that if they could not win the vote, the Bowling Green administration would try to undo their own faculty's victory and take the rest of Ohio's faculty unions down as well.

Interestingly, in preparation for his testimony on SB 5, Johnson emailed the presidents saying he would include a mention that a minority of the presidents wanted "reform" and not "elimination" of collective bargaining. This was a bit disingenuous since, as it stood, SB 5 already effectively made collective bargaining a sham for state employees. It is, nevertheless, evidence that some of the university presidents were uneasy with such a blatant attack on their faculty, and that some clearly held more moderate views. Still, as is now clear, that was not enough for a majority of the presidents. Robert J. Pietrykowski, Cleveland State's president, said—revealing a deep misunderstanding of collective bargaining—that the process was "deeply flawed" because sometimes administrators could not achieve complete victory. Writing from Bowling Green, Sean Patrick Fitzgerald, BGSU's general counsel, who probably actually drafted the Yeshiva amendment that found its way into SB 5, also voiced opposition to the bargaining process. To summarize, Fitzgerald's major complaint was that "bargaining required meetings," and he was apparently strictly opposed to having meetings. A ridiculous objection since, as Gelman notes, most administrators spend almost all of their time in meetings—that is the nature of the job.[15]

On February 25, 2011, Johnson wrote to Republican Kevin Bacon, chair of the Senate committee, and proposed the Yeshiva amendment to eliminate faculty unions. David Robinson, a lobbyist for the Bowling Green administration, sent a similar amendment to Johnson and Fitzgerald. The BGSU administration, through either Robinson or Fitzgerald, seems the sure source of the Yeshiva language. "It appears that the BGSU administration," Sara Kilpatrick, executive director of the Ohio AAUP, told *The Toledo Blade* when the news surfaced in September, "scorned by the faculty's success in forming a union, decided that it would get rid of its 'problem' by eliminating collective bargaining rights for all professors across the state of Ohio."[16]

In the uproar that followed, Fitzgerald tried to minimize his role. He said he had made the suggestion of using the Yeshiva case but that if he had not, then others would have. "From there, others ran with it," he said. Johnson, for his part, tried to share the burden of blame for the amendment crafted by Fitzgerald, saying that it was "common sense" to university officials.[17] Not surprisingly, no university president stepped forward publicly to accept responsibility.

When pressed, University of Cincinnati President Gregory Williams would only talk about how the IUC worked to reach "consensus" on issues. Specifically with regard to Senate Bill 5, he would only say that the bill now would be decided by the public in a vote. To paraphrase Williams's public statements at the time, he would say that he had been at universities with unions and at universities without unions, and that working together would continue in either outcome, to strive for excellence at the university. His statements were, in fact, eerily similar to what other presidents were saying. University of Akron CEO Louis Proenza said, for example, that there was nothing to worry about, because things had worked well before the union was formed at the University of Akron in 2002, and things were working well currently and would continue to do so if Senate Bill 5 survived the November referendum. "There are great universities with unions and great universities without them," Proenza said. "and we intend to be a great university." Williams and Proenza must have received the same memo.[18]

One of the most consistent and flawed concepts connected with the university presidents' drive to crush their faculty unions was the idea that doing service—a professional responsibility of every faculty member—made them managers. Managers make decisions. If university faculty actually had decision-making powers, there would certainly be much less administrative bloat. And there would be some better choices made to keep university resources focused on academics.

With Senate Bill 5 now narrowly through the Senate, it would move on to the House. Statewide, there was a historic and broad coalition coming together that would become known as "We Are Ohio." Because of the threat to our existence and to our ability to influence quality education in the state, the AAUP chapters—both individually and at the state conference—embraced with determination outright political action for the first time in our history.

Part of our awakening was the eye-opening realization that while we had been tending to our profession, teaching students, and breaking new ground in research and ideas, the radical right-wing movement had not only been steadily crippling the nation's educational system but was even trying to undermine our democracy. A primary driving force was the innocent-sounding but highly destructive American Legislative Exchange Council.

Chapter 5

Gathering Forces

With Ohio in turmoil over the passage of the union-busting legislation through the Senate, our AAUP team redoubled our efforts to try to turn the bill back in the state House—hoping vainly that now that legislators could see the resistance across the state wiser heads would prevail.

At this point in the struggle, a column appeared in *The New York Times* that began a process of putting into focus this sweeping attack on the labor movement and would provide great clarity to us about the motivations of our opponents.[1]

Dr. William Cronon, professor of history at the University of Wisconsin, wrote the column that appeared as an op-ed on March 21, 2011. Cronon is an important figure in the historical profession, the author of several important historical works, including *Nature's Metropolis: Chicago and the Great West*, about the growth of Chicago. In addition, he was then president-elect of the American Historical Association, the nation's largest organization of historians, a position that commands an enormous amount of respect in the profession.

So when Professor Cronon wrote a piece critical of the Wisconsin union-busting debacle, it was bound to get attention. In his heartfelt essay, one could see that Cronon cared deeply about the tragic way that Gov. Scott Walker and his extremist allies were tearing apart the state of Wisconsin while destroying the state's own traditions. "Republicans in Wisconsin," Cronon wrote, "are seeking to reverse civic traditions that for more than a century have been among the most celebrated achievements not just of their state, but of their own party as well."

Cronon went on to point out that Theodore Roosevelt had called Wisconsin the "laboratory of democracy." It was the first state to introduce worker's compensation (1911), unemployment insurance (1932), and public employee bargaining (1959). Professors at Wisconsin had helped design Social Security and were responsible for founding the union that eventually became the American Federation of State, County, and Municipal Employees (AFSCME). These accomplishments were possible because of collaboration between Democrats and Republicans in Wisconsin.

"The demonizing of government at all levels," Cronon wrote, "that has become such a reflexive impulse for conservatives in the early 21st century would have mystified most elected officials in Wisconsin just a few decades ago." Cronon went on to point out that Walker's policies also broke with the state's tradition because of the lack of transparency. Even open-meetings laws were apparently violated in the rush to crush the unions. The Wisconsin way had been to work jointly for the common good, but these Republicans had adopted an "ends justify the means" attitude, an exercise of "power in abusively nontransparent ways that represent such a radical break from the state's tradition of open government."

The Republicans were creating harsh divisions in the state that had not existed since the Vietnam War, and Cronon said that he found himself asking the question of Wisconsin political leaders that was once posed to another Badger Stater, Sen. Joseph McCarthy: "Have you no sense of decency, sir, at long last? Have you left no sense of decency?"

Cronon concluded:

> The turmoil in Wisconsin is not only about bargaining rights or the pension payments of public employees. It is about transparency and openness. It is about neighborliness, decency and mutual respect. Joe McCarthy forgot these lessons of good government, and so, I fear, has Mr. Walker. Wisconsin's citizens have not.

Cronon's column created an instant sensation and, perhaps more importantly, drew me and many others to his blog. It was really by reading his blog that eyes began to be opened about the sweeping nature of the attack on the middle class. The blog, Scholar as Citizen, contained a detailed entry entitled, "Who's Really Behind Recent Republican Legislation in Wisconsin and Elsewhere? (Hint: It Didn't Start Here)."[2]

In what he aptly described as a "study guide," Cronon explained that it had occurred to him that the huge amount of radical legislation sweeping the country could not be just the product of a couple of wealthy conservative activists, like the Koch brothers. Pointing out that many such organizations had gotten their start in the wake of Barry Goldwater's defeat, he said that some of them were very obvious, like the Heritage Foundation, but others were largely invisible. "That's why events like the ones we've just experienced in Wisconsin," Cronon wrote, "can seem to come out of nowhere. Few outside the conservative movement have been paying much attention, and that is ill-advised."

Cronon provided readers with a couple of good sources to investigate the secret right-wing organizations on their own (www.sourcewatch.com, www.rightwingwatch.org), but he added that, as far as he could tell, the most important organization was the American Legislative Exchange Council (ALEC). In a section titled, "Telling Your State Legislators What To Do," Cronon focused closely on ALEC. He explained that because the organization's information is open only to members, it is not easy to see exactly what ALEC is doing or proposing. And despite Wisconsin having one of the strictest open-meetings laws in the country, the legislature carved out a special exception so that they could meet in secret with ALEC.

There has been substantial reporting on ALEC, and Cronon cites a good deal of that on his blog. Essentially, as Cronon points out, ALEC partners with corporations and the wealthy to craft legislation that will bend state laws in their favor. The "model" bills are then brought back to their home states by ALEC legislators and introduced, sometimes with little or no change, in their state legislatures.

Before we move on to ALEC's involvement in Ohio, it is necessary to discuss what befell Cronon because of his willingness to speak the truth about this right-wing organization. In an intimidation tactic, the Wisconsin Republican Party immediately issued an Open Records Law request to see all of Professor Cronon's email. Such a hostile act was an obvious attempt to silence an important critic. Wasting no time, on March 28, 2011, the AAUP national office sent a strongly worded statement to Biddy Martin, chancellor of the University of Wisconsin, urging her not to comply with the Republican demand. Terming it "an outrageous request," the AAUP agreed with Cronon's own initial response that this was "an assault on academic freedom." Eventually, the university, exercising its discretion, released only those emails that did not compromise the personal privacy of students or other respondents. It found no incidents of Cronon using his email for partisan political activity.[3]

In an eloquent defense of the faculty, Dr. Martin wrote to the members of the UW community: "To our faculty, I say: Continue to ask difficult questions, explore unpopular lines of thought and exercise your academic freedom, regardless of your point of view. As always, we will take our cue from the bronze plaque on the walls of Bascom Hall. It calls for the 'continual and fearless sifting and winnowing' of ideas. It is our tradition, our defining value, and the way to a better society."[4]

Cronon's experience at the hands of the Wisconsin Republicans and his lifting the corner of the tent on the sordid attacks that were being launched against faculty and other union members was an important moment. We saw clearly that we were not simply facing some old-school Republicans fighting old battles; rather, this was a new and destructive political movement, something that threatened not only university values of academic freedom and shared governance but ultimately, as we shall see, the democratic process itself.[5]

Discovering ALEC as the creative force behind Senate Bill 5 also solved another puzzling issue for us. Shannon Jones, the only sponsor of the bill, was continually and completely unable to answer any questions about the legislation. Time and again, when asked about some complex issue regarding the destructive impact of the bill, she would respond with her two or three talking points. These one-liners concluded so often with the catch words "flexibility" or "skin in the game" that we joked we should have a drinking game during her testimony: take a drink every time she said "skin in the game." Even a hardy drinker would be under the table in no time.

Since Jones knew so little about the issues herself (except having a disdain for unions), where had the bill originated? ALEC gave us the answer. Although the Ohio legislation was more radical than what appeared in Wisconsin, it was quite similar, and we had begun to believe they had some shared source. That source, as it turned out, was ALEC. But cutting through the secrecy was a challenge.

It took a while for the full realization to unfold, and by the time it did, we were deeply engaged in the fight to repeal Senate Bill 5 as well as battling other extremist legislation generated by ALEC and strongly supported by Republican legislators. Just as we were beginning to understand the assault that was underway, we discovered that ALEC was planning a national conference in downtown Cincinnati in the historic Hilton Netherland Plaza Hotel. To us, in the wake of Senate Bill 5 and as we began to understand the organization's responsibility for the bill, it looked like they intended to do a victory dance. Student activists and others who cared about Ohio took the lead in making ALEC understand that they might be meeting in Cincinnati but they were not welcome.

An important part of the coalition was a joining together of students from Miami University at Oxford, some 20 miles north of the city, and students from the University of Cincinnati. Other community groups were important, too, but this synergy between students at UC and Miami—both state universities—as well as Ohio State and other colleges and universities, would play an important role in coming months.

The organizers planned a protest that would garner assistance from students nationwide. Today, when ALEC meets, they can expect protestors. But it all started in Cincinnati. The students had only weeks to create this important action, and they did a superb job. I often thought, as I saw them at work, how surprised the right-wing politicians and corporate titans who considered them irrelevant would be at their creativity, their ingenuity, and their courage. It was a good thing that they were on our side.

The staging area for the protest was the downtown landmark Fountain Square, across the street from the Netherlands Hotel. A special feature of the protest was some creative street theater featuring a 15-foot-tall puppet that represented ALEC, ravaging the lives and livelihoods of ordinary people. The crowd cheered as the protestors fought back against their exploitation based on the history of the organization since its founding in the 1970s. Eventually, after speakers outlined the threat to Ohio that ALEC represented, the group marched around the hotel, beating drums and calling for more transparency. It was a powerful sight as the line of people stretched from corner to corner around the block. Large numbers of spectators, including a lot of office workers, gathered to watch the spectacle. During the day, some of the protestors ventured into the hotel to try to engage the ALEC participants in debate. They were somewhat successful in their quest and had civil contacts with participants, who seemed surprised that anyone knew about their meeting. Hotel security, however, siding with ALEC since they were paying the bills, were careful about ejecting anyone who was not a conference attendee.

Later in the day, activists held a well-attended teach-in at a former school in the Over-the-Rhine neighborhood, about ALEC and its activities as well as other corporate attempts to undermine democratic processes in Ohio and across the country. They also sent a letter to

Ron Scheberle, the executive director of ALEC and former lead lobbyist for Verizon, with a list of requests. The powerful letter, signed by the "ALEC Protest Team, Cincinnati, OH," cited Abraham Lincoln's Gettysburg Address, pointing out that the dead on that Civil War battlefield had not died in vain but to make certain that "government of the people, by the people, and for the people shall not perish from the earth."

ALEC, the Protest Team argued, threatens that promise: "We write to you today because we believe that your organization's actions dishonor those dead and place in peril the system of government they died to defend. The least that you owe them is the decency to acknowledge your actions so that a democratic discussion may be had on the policies that you have pushed." The Protest Team then made a series of requests. First, they wanted disclosure of the list of ALEC donors. Second, they wanted the names of elected officials who were members of ALEC. Third, ALEC should give them the full texts of their model bills. Fourth, when legislators submit bills based on ALEC models, they should honestly say so. The letter concluded that the team did not expect to be able to agree on issues with ALEC but did hope "that we can bring you to accept a code of conduct for your organization that accords with our democratic system of government." Not surprisingly, ALEC's Scheberle did not respond to the Protest Team.[6]

The next episode in the pursuit of ALEC, and the organization's responsibility for Senate Bill 5 and other antidemocratic pieces of legislation, was told in detail in the Cincinnati alternative newsweekly *City Beat*, in August. Aliya Rahman, a doctoral student at Miami and a labor activist, had, like many of us, been alerted to ALEC by Cronon's work and had done some research herself. She was one of the lead organizers of the Cincinnati protest. A couple of hours after the protest and teach-ins, Rahman was at her apartment in Over-the-Rhine, exhausted and evaluating the effort, when she got a phone call. "I have information on ALEC," the caller told her. As *City Beat* reported:

> "What kind of information do you have?" Rahman asked the caller, expecting little after weeks of phone calls from activists whose enthusiasm sometimes veered into conspiracy theory.
>
> This one left her trembling.
>
> A whistleblower with full access to ALEC's documents wanted to deliver 800 model bills to the protest's organizers. So Rahman . . . agreed to act as conduit.
>
> She passed the documents along to the Center for Media and Democracy, a nonprofit investigative newsgroup, which organized

them onto a website that it activated July 13. Overtly critical, alecexposed.org allows anyone to cross-check wording from the leaked bills against laws in their own states to see where ALEC's invisible hand might appear."[7]

In May 2011, the Center for Media and Democracy (CMD) had produced a riveting report entitled "Quid pro Status Quo: ALEC and State-Sanctioned Corruption in Ohio." The report detailed the close relationships between the Ohio legislature, under Republican control, and ALEC, particularly through the State Rep. John Adams (R-Sidney). Adams was ALEC's Ohio public sector chair. He worked particularly closely with the private sector chair, Time Warner Cable's Ed Kozelek, regional vice president for government relations. They had both worked diligently in 2011 to prepare for ALEC's spring conference in Cincinnati. By the end of February 2011, CMD reported, they had received pledges for more than $107,000 from more than 50 corporations and lobby firms for ALEC's Ohio operations. These monies were held in the Ohio ALEC "scholarship fund."[8]

A series of emails that CMD obtained through public records requests show that Faith Williams, a lobbyist with the law firm Bricker and Eckler, LLP, had a discussion with Adams on the morning of March 23, 2011, about "an economic development study" created by some of her clients in the life insurance industry. CMD reports that they discussed a proposed amendment of the state's 2011 budget and possible support for ALEC's scholarship fund. The amendment would be "a 12-page portion of the more than 80-page piece of 'model legislation' known as the 'Insurer Receivership Model Act.'" In short, this would allow insurance companies to lump their assets, losses, and obligations into one tradable commodity. Not only did House Speaker William Batchelder agree to slip this into the budget bill (thus allowing it to avoid further scrutiny), but later emails demonstrate that contacts for Cincinnati insurance companies were provided by Williams to Adams's office at Adams's request. American Financial Group, along with Western & Southern, were added to the roster of potential donor corporations.[9]

The story of a baseball game can provide evidence to the insidious influence of ALEC in the Ohio legislature. No trip to Cincinnati would be complete without a Reds game, so Time Warner stepped up to sponsor the event. At least 40 tickets were given to at least 22 lawmakers and others, ranging from legislative aides to lobbyists. A large ALEC contingent saw the Reds lose to the Florida Marlins, 7–6, with food and drinks provided.[10]

The complication that the CMD uncovered was that Ohio law prohibits lawmakers from accepting gifts valued at more than $75 from a lobbyist. CMD pressed the Joint Legislative Ethics Committee (JLEC) and the Office of the Ohio Legislative Inspector General (OLIG) to investigate this apparent violation. Tony Bledsoe, OLIG executive director, eventually responded by splitting legal hairs: Time Warner's Kozelek may well have been a lobbyist, but ALEC was a group to which the Ohio legislature pays membership fees. Thus, in a convoluted interpretation, Bledsoe concluded that the legislators who received the boodle had no need to report it. The interpretation, as CMD suggests, may just boil down to who controls OLIG, which is, of course the 12-member Joint Legislative Ethics Committee. Eight members are required to vote to remove the legislative inspector general. Not surprisingly, five of the 12 were ALEC members—including JLEC Chair Sen. Tom Niehaus and Vice Chair Speaker William Batchelder—and three of them (Sen. Niehaus, Sen. Keith Farber, and Rep. Matt Huffman) received tickets to the game.[11]

On July 12, 2011, *The Nation* newsmagazine, in collaboration with CMD, led with a series of powerful articles about the impact of ALEC on public schools, health care, prison labor, and rigged elections. An essay by veteran reporter John Nichols introduced the package, citing the importance of Rahman's coup. Other stories, written by the journal's excellent reporters, outlined the involvement of billionaire brothers David and Charles Koch and the overwhelming emphasis on gaining partisan political advantages for corporations.

Joel Rogers and Laura Dresser wrote in *The Nation* about ALEC's ruthless attack on unions. ALEC's view of government is that, outside of providing security in which corporations can operate, it should be "demonized, starved, or privatized. Any force in civil society, especially labor, that contests the right of business to grab all social surplus for itself, and to treat people like road kill and the earth like a sewer, should be crushed." Not knowing what lay in the future, Rogers and Dresser speculated that perhaps a mass movement to defend the rights of workers and the middle class might develop to successfully oppose ALEC and its supporters. But "we can be sure that ALEC will fight them fiercely in the states, while pressing forward with its own project: the complete business domination of American public life." Certainly harsh language but our experience in Ohio in 2011 provided evidence for such a view.[12]

Perhaps the most definitive report on ALEC's involvement in Ohio was not published until February 6, 2012. "ALEC in Ohio: The Corporate Special Interests That Help Write Ohio's Laws" was coauthored by a coalition of progressive groups, including CMD, Common Cause, People for the American Way, and Progress Ohio. The ALEC in Ohio (AIO) report spelled out the cold reality of ALEC's capture of the Ohio legislature in 2011. I am going to quote liberally from the report, which is available at the websites of the above organizations and on other sites concerned with defending democratic processes.[13]

"ALEC's internal talking points," AIO reports, "praise Gov. John Kasich as someone who 'helped mold ALEC in its formative years.'" Kasich served as legislative aide to ALEC's longest-serving national chairman, former Ohio State Sen. Donald "Buz" Lukens. Kasich, AIO notes, has tried to distance himself from the organization in recent years, and his office reports that he is not an "active" member, since he is not a legislator. But the reality is that Kasich has "put forward major proposals that share titles, messaging strategies, and policy elements with ALEC model legislation."

And, of course, Rep. John Adams (named 2010 ALEC State Legislator of the Year) is famous for working closely with ALEC. Adams credits the group with influencing his legislative proposals, such as a $12 billion plan to eliminate Ohio's income tax. In fact, between January and October of 2011, "33 bills were introduced in the Ohio legislature that are identical or contain elements from 64 different ALEC 'model' proposals." Nationally, about a thousand bills based to some extent on ALEC models are introduced each year. And each year about 17 percent become law.

The AIO study reported that in the past ten years, employees of the 22 corporations on ALEC's Private Enterprise Board have spent more than $9.3 million on political campaigns in Ohio. This does not include the many other ALEC member corporations that underwrite ALEC's operations but do not have a seat on the corporate board. The report specifically points to Time Warner's Ed Kozelek as a power broker in the Ohio state organization, creating links between ALEC and state legislators.

Legislators pay $50 a year to join ALEC—a tiny proportion of the vast sums that ALEC expends. About 98 percent of the group's revenues come from nonmembership sources. Wealthy business magnates and huge corporations provide the rest of the funding as a way to produce legislative results. The Koch brothers, for example, have contributed more than $1.4 million to ALEC since 1998. Wealthy foundations have also contributed loads of cash, including the Scaife family's Allegheny Foundation and the Coors family's Castle Rock Foundation.

ALEC's "scholarship" fund is a way to funnel corporate money to legislators. The scholarships are used to fund travel and expenses to ALEC events. Through a Freedom of Information Act request, the coalition of progressive groups received a ledger sheet about ALEC's financial transactions. On the credit side for corporation donations, several of the names were not surprising. They included Procter and Gamble, Duke Energy, the National Rifle Association, Ohio Farmers Insurance, AT&T, Diageo North America (a major liquor distributor), Abbot Laboratories, Key Bank, Purdue Pharma, Cable Telecommunications Association, and the American Petroleum Institute.

On the debit side of the ledger were 20 Ohio legislators, including Speaker Batchelder, Rep. Louis Blessing, and Rep. John Adams. The legislators received an average of $1,900 from the "scholarships." Though this is a small number for the giant corporations involved, the AIO report notes that this money "goes a long way in providing ALEC legislators with the perk of trips to luxury resorts to be wined and dined alongside corporate lobbyists and prospective donors." ALEC provides funds in other ways, too, such as child care so that legislators can bring their whole family. In fact, in 2009, ALEC spent $250,000 on child care expenses. As of January 2012, 57 members, or roughly 43 percent, of the Ohio legislature were members of ALEC, and all but one were Republicans. Several Ohio legislators serve on ALEC task forces.

The bulk of the AIO study, however, details the parallel language that links ALEC "model" bills with bills that were introduced into the Ohio legislature. It clearly demonstrates that many bills introduced during 2011, including Senate Bill 5, were clones of ALEC bills. Going back to an earlier point, this explains why Sen. Jones was unable to answer questions about her union-busting bill. ALEC in fact, has a sweeping collection of antiunion laws readily available, according to the AIO analysis. They include the Right to Work Act, which eliminates employee obligation to pay the costs of collective bargaining; the Public Employee Freedom Act, which bars almost any action to create a union; the Public Employer Payroll Deduction Act, which bars automatic dues collection; and the Voluntary Contribution Act, which bars the use of dues for political activity.[14]

In the face of this legislative assault and evidence that ALEC had stacked the deck against working people and the middle class, the labor movement in Ohio began to do what it does best: organize. As already mentioned, meetings had begun early in earnest, such as the one my executive director and I attended in Columbus, in order to mount resistance to these radical destructive forces that were moving against professional and working people in Ohio.

As early as the end of February, it had become clear that compromise with the Republicans pushing Senate Bill 5 was unlikely. In the face of unprecedented protests, Senate President Niehaus insisted, "There will be a bill." Ohio Democratic Party Chairman Chris Redfern countered that if Kasich and the Republicans insisted on pushing the bill through the legislature, there would be a ballot challenge. "The people of the state will gather together and we'll put this on the ballot. We will repeal it and that will happen," Redfern predicted.[15]

Throughout March 2011, as the Republicans were pushing Senate Bill 5 through the legislature, union members and community leaders were talking about creating a coalition to fight Senate Bill 5 by putting the legislation up to a vote of the people. The public announcement of the new organization came the day after Kasich had—quickly and with great fanfare—signed Senate Bill 5 into law. The news came at a rally in Columbus at the IBEW hall.[16]

"We will deal a setback to the wealthy elitists who've taken over our state," Ohio AFL-CIO President Tim Burga told the crowd, according to the Columbus *Free Press*. "We've been given a tremendous opportunity to educate the public on the fact that unions created the middle class, public education and the eight-hour day, child labor laws and a decent living standard for working people. It will be a tough, difficult fight." But Burga insisted, "It's a fight that, with our friends and allies, we *will* win!"[17]

We Are Ohio was thus born, a historic coalition between labor, community, religious, and political groups that would fight this important battle for the middle class. Initially, labor leaders were meeting as part of the "Unity Table" or "Labor Table," which is an affiliate of the National Unity Table in Washington DC, as Sara Kilpatrick, AAUP State Conference executive director, remembered. "Once it became clear that SB 5 was a serious threat, labor unions outside of the Unity Table were welcomed to participate," Kilpatrick said. She added that once it became clear that SB 5 was going to pass, the Unity Table decided that it would not offer any amendments but would instead pursue the referendum route. "At that point," Kilpatrick recalls, "we knew we were heading into a full-fledged campaign. We quickly hired A. J. Stokes as campaign director, and the Executive Committee decided upon the name We Are Ohio, mostly because the Wisconsin effort was called We Are Wisconsin."[18]

The initial structure of We Are Ohio was based on the ability of the various labor organizations to commit resources, manpower, and money. The top decision-making tier, called the Executive Committee, included the Ohio Education Association (OEA), Service Employees

International Union (SEIU), Ohio Federation of Teachers (OFT), United Food and Commercial Workers (UFCW), Communication Workers of America (CWA), American Federation of State, County, and Municipal Employees (AFSCME), and American Federation of Labor and Congress of Industrial Organizations (AFL-CIO).

On the next level was the Steering Committee. This consisted of all of the groups on the Executive Committee, plus the Ohio Conference of the American Association of University Professors (OCAAUP), the Fraternal Order of Police (FOP), the International Association of Fire Fighters (IAFF), the Ohio Nurses Association (ONA), the United Auto Workers (UAW), and the United Steelworkers (USW).

This somewhat clinical explanation of how the organization was structured does not do justice to the many other community and religious groups that worked side by side with the labor movement to turn back Senate Bill 5. Among the nonunion organizations that contributed to our efforts were African American ministers' groups, the Catholic Church's Amos Project, the Cincinnati Interfaith Labor Council, the Farmer's Union, the Blue-Green Alliance of the Sierra Club, and many student organizations.

So, by early April, the battle was joined. A ruthless union-busting bill had been railroaded through the legislature by a group of ideologically driven extremists. In response, an historic coalition of progressive organizations would try to defend rights that one would have thought had been settled long ago—after the Triangle Fire, at Ludlow, or along Anaconda Road.[19]

Chapter 6

Extremism's High Tide

Early on the morning of March 18, I was reading *The Cincinnati Enquirer* online and saw a brief notice that Gov. Kasich was going to be at the University of Cincinnati late that afternoon to meet with President Gregory Williams and the media about the success of a research program. Naturally, we saw this as an opportunity to question the governor about the attack that he and his supporters had launched against faculty across Ohio.

One of the characteristics of Gov. Kasich's style is his insistence on never being in a situation where he might face questions from Ohioans—whether hostile or otherwise. My personal experience in Montana had been quite different. When I was a journalist in the Big Sky State, the then-governor of Montana, Ted Schwinden, a Democrat, had his home phone number listed in the Helena phone book. If you needed to talk to him, you just called him. One night, working on deadline and needing a quote from Schwinden, I called him. The governor answered the phone: "Hello." Since I knew Schwinden from my years of reporting, I identified myself, apologized for calling him at home, and said I needed to ask him a question. "No problem, John. What can I do for you?"

I did not anticipate that the situation would work exactly the same in Ohio, but I believed then—and I believe now—that politicians should be prepared to answer questions and face the public. They are public servants and should not view the public as their enemy. It is part of the job to endure questioning—to face people opposed to political decisions that have been made. As Harry Truman famously said, "If you can't take the heat, get out of the kitchen." If a politician cannot face his critics when pushing harsh and unreasonable policies, then he should either find another profession or adopt more rational and collaborative policies. Gov. Kasich, from the beginning, was only interested in forcing through his own ideologically driven union-busting policy with Senate Bill 5, and those who refused to get on the bus would get "run over by the bus." His unwillingness ever to face his critics became crystal clear during his visit to UC. It is no surprise that this visit was scheduled on the first day of spring break so that there would be minimal opportunity for the governor to encounter any students or faculty.

Word spread quickly through the union and beyond that the governor would be visiting a laboratory on campus, in Rhodes Hall. On campus that morning, a group of students and faculty assembled outside Baldwin Hall, which is connected to Rhodes. Many were wearing anti-SB 5 buttons and carrying signs protesting Senate Bill 5 and other extreme legislative proposals. It was already clear that this was going to be an odd situation. Two large black SUVs with darkened windows were parked on the sidewalk in front of Baldwin Hall, a historic quad in the center of campus. Two state patrol cars were also parked nearby. Clearly, rather than walking across the campus, our visitors had ridden in their vehicles across campus sidewalks to get there. Given the heavy security presence, the governor and his party were apparently seeking protection from someone. But from whom?

In total, there were probably about 20 to 25 of us, split roughly equally between students and faculty. Very soon after entering Rhodes Hall, we were confronted by plainclothes and uniformed and armed UC security, who blocked the hallway. We told them that we were there to talk to the governor since he had come to our university. They told us that, given our signs and buttons, we were protesting, and "protestors" had to use the small "free speech zone" on the lawn behind McMicken Hall, quite a distance from where we were. In an effort to be cooperative, we took off our buttons and put our signs into garbage cans. Thus, we were only citizens wanting to speak with our governor.

But our request to see the governor was of no avail. The anger that faculty began to express about these restrictions came largely because we considered UC to be our university, where freedom of inquiry and expression were encouraged, not suppressed. These were hallways that faculty walked every day. Our last effort was to try to get a glimpse of the governor when he exited the building to get into the black SUV with the darkened windows. We were reduced to the hope that we might be able to at least shout to him. But then things got worse. As we waited outside Baldwin Hall, UC security backed by state police told us that we could not be in the quad, a very large space ringed by three historic buildings, with the governor. We had to go to the "free speech zone."

The university's notorious "free speech zone" deserves some comment. Although the exact history of the zone is not clear, it seems to have been created initially in the late 1960s or early 1970s because of regular Vietnam War protests that disrupted the campus. But over time it had become institutionalized as a small patch of lawn behind McMicken Hall.

So, security forced both faculty and students (we really could not abandon the students at this point) back away from Baldwin Hall about a hundred yards—about the length of a football field—to corral everyone into the free speech zone. By the time faculty and students were cornered in the free speech zone, leaders of other city unions had also arrived, including Doug Sizemore, executive secretary of the Cincinnati AFL-CIO, and stood by us. By this time, it was 5 p.m., and some staff getting off work at administrative offices joined us to show their support. One of them said to me, "We saw what they were doing to you. This is completely wrong." One campus police officer, sitting in his patrol car "guarding us," watching the spectacle, remarked, "They should just come out and talk with you. It would solve the whole problem."

Then it began to rain. In the distance now, we could see people, including President Williams and Gov. Kasich, coming out of the building and getting into the SUVs. We stood our ground because they were going to have to drive on the sidewalk past us to get out. It was the closest we would get to the governor. They took their time as they approached us, but then the drivers stepped on the gas, and the SUVs sped past us. Students chanted, "This is what democracy looks like" as the governor and the president left us standing in the rain.

In retrospect, it is not just the complete lack of respect for Ohioans that the governor demonstrated—though that was bad enough—that concerns me. The events of that day remind me that, as faculty, we must continually press our administrations to understand what the true values of the university are and to defend those values. Not surprisingly, Gov. Kasich never came back to UC during the SB 5 struggle.[1]

In spite of the Senate's vote in favor of Senate Bill 5, we remained hopeful that, with the enormous resistance that had been demonstrated against this attack on working people and union workers, we might be able to turn the tide in the House. We had, after all, won over some reasonable Republicans in the Senate, and we aimed, win or lose, to do the same in the House.

The gallery was packed as the House convened late on the morning of March 30. The Democrats, expecting to be run over by the Republican majority, tried delaying tactics. Rep. Connie Pillich (D-Cincinnati) asked that the five-hundred-page bill be read in its entirety. That was quickly defeated on a party-line vote. Later in the debate, Rep. Ted Celeste (D-Columbus) tried to table the bill, which was defeated by another vote, also split along party lines.[2]

Rep. Joe Uecker (R-Miami Township) opened the Republican attack, saying he was "happy" to be returning to local governments the power to manage their budgets. Uecker seemed to express exasperation at what he perceived as the long and tedious process to which the representatives had been subjected. In reality, it had been a rapid process. He wrongly suggested that substantive changes had been made in the bill, and he criticized the Democrats for making no attempts to amend the bill. As they had in the Senate, Democrats in the House took the position that the whole bill needed to be rejected, not tinkered with. Rep. Uecker portrayed as generous such changes as no longer requiring strikers to be jailed, or that it would no longer be an unfair labor practice to talk to elected officials during contract negotiations, or allowing emergency and medical staff to negotiate for personal safety equipment. In fact, such changes were either common sense or were made to address some of the unconstitutional aspects of Senate Bill 5.

Republican Rep. Louis Blessing of Cincinnati, a longtime opponent of unions, noted that he had voted against the collective bargaining bill back in 1983, and he would vote to eliminate it again through his support of Senate Bill 5. He presented a badly distorted view of the rarely used arbitration process and, quoting Thomas Jefferson in misguided Tea Party parlance, suggested there was "no consent of the governed" in the process that had obviously been established by the people through their elected representatives by legislative action. He particularly criticized the use of union funds to back political candidates but, like other Republicans, did not recognize the parallel situation of corporate political use of revenue generated by employees who, unlike the unions, have no democratic process.

"I rise in opposition to Senate Bill 5," Rep. Kenny Yuko (D-Toledo) announced. "We call this the People's House for a reason," he continued. "It's because this is where our constituents get their voices heard and get their rights protected. It greatly concerns me that the direction that Senate Bill 5 takes us in tramples on the rights of lots of Ohio workers, it tramples on the very heart and soul of what makes this the great state that it is. That's our working families." Yuko, in his fourth term in the Ohio House, said, to warm applause from the gallery as Speaker Batchelder pounded his gavel for order, that he was "very proud to be a union member." Yuko, a 37-year member of Laborers' Union Local 310 where he had also served as a union organizer for 25 years, said that he was proud that for more than a hundred years his union had "worked to improve the working rights of every man and woman" and had won for their workers decent pay, a retirement plan, and safe job conditions. "They've done a tremendous job . . . They are here today, in force, and I thank them for that and for their friendship and support over the years," he said.

The 1983 collective bargaining act, Senate Bill 133, had stood the test of time, Yuko said. He noted the state had endured hundreds of strikes before it was adopted but that now strikes were rare. "We keep hearing that if unions don't get their way, they call a strike. Let's look at 2010. No strikes. Zero." In fact, he said, Ohio had had only five strikes in the last three years. "It is not broken. Collective bargaining is working, and it is working well," he said.

"This is certainly not the first day that middle-class Ohioans have been under attack," said Matt Szollosi, a Democrat from Oregon, a Toledo suburb—adding that, based on Gov. Kasich's budget, it would not be the last. Szollosi, the assistant minority leader, said that the governor had tipped his hand during the campaign when he said "we need to break the back of organized labor in the schools" and that workers having a collective voice "threatens our American values." It was no surprise, then, Szollosi said, that after the election Kasich announced that all the teachers' unions should take out full-page ads apologizing for the things they had said about him.

The attack on workers in Senate Bill 5 was veiled beneath the argument that "we need to give our managers the tools they need to control their costs," Szollosi said. "If this were truly about the budget, here is a radical idea: Ask for concessions. Communicate. Not one phone call was made to the state unions offering to reopen negotiations, because Kasich would not have taken yes for an answer."

The truth, Szollosi said, was that the "underlying purpose of Senate Bill 5 is to weaken the traditional political adversaries of Gov. Kasich and the Republican Party." Coupled with voter suppression legislation, also being adopted by the legislature despite Democratic resistance, Szollosi argued that "a very clear message" was being sent to working-class Ohioans: "You weren't on the bus, so you are getting run over."[3]

Szollosi specifically corrected Rep. Uecker about the changes that had been made since the bill's initial introduction in the Senate. The changes had made Senate Bill 5 worse and even more vindictive against the unions and public workers. Szollosi noted that unions are required by federal law to provide fair representation to all members, so for Senate Bill 5 to bar the unions from collecting "fair share" fees for services provided to bargaining unit members who have chosen not be members was not only unfair but was solely designed to cripple the unions politically. Meanwhile, the unions would still be required to represent all members, but those who chose to opt out of membership would get the services for free. Such an attack on the unions, Szollosi said, would do nothing to provide the "tools" and "flexibility" that backers of the bill said they wanted to give to local governments. "What will this do to create jobs? Nothing! What will this do to lower costs? Nothing," Szollosi thundered. He said that a colleague in the Commerce and Labor Committee, where the provision had been inserted, had told him in explanation, "I like freedom." Szollosi said, "I think what he should have said was, 'I like freeloaders.'" Again the gallery burst into applause as Batchelder pounded his gavel.

Szollosi expressed doubt that the Republicans had met with any union correctional officers. He said the supporters of Senate Bill 5 see public employees only as costs. He recounted the dangers faced and injuries suffered by the correctional officers. Szollosi said that during this process he had heard that belonging to a union was a sin, and union members, like those in the gallery, were referred to as "union thugs." Szollosi introduced Beth Earl in the gallery, president of Franklin County Federation of Children Services Employees, noting to general laughter that she was one of the alleged "union thugs."

In a particularly aggressive speech, Rep. Lynn Wachtmann (R-Napoleon) said he had "never before heard such outrageous comments from the other side." An ALEC member who has been "honored" as an ALEC Legislator of the Year, Wachtmann said he came to Columbus to represent all workers, not just union workers. "Anyone who has worked in the private sector—or, as I call it, 'the real world'—needs to understand that we need to have a productive workforce." He said of Rep. Szollosi, "I won't call you a liar, but you are wrong." He said that many Republicans had met with union members from all over the state, "so you're dead wrong, representative from Toledo," jabbing his finger toward Szollosi. "For those of you who claim that we don't listen to all the parties, you're dead wrong," he said, glaring around the chamber. He complained about high taxes and poor government services. The current collective bargaining law, he asserted, had been "rammed through the legislature on a 100 percent partisan basis back in 1983" and makes the workforce "unflexible and unproductive compared to the private sector." Wachtmann idealized the private sector, apparently overlooking the private sector financial collapse of 2008 and Ohio's own governor's links to the failed Lehman Brothers. He said that workers and management could get along much better if not for unions getting in the way. Discounting union efforts to create safe working conditions, he essentially blamed the unions for on-the-job injuries.

As Wachtmann went on with his wide-ranging attack on public employees and their unions, a roar of protest from the crowds gathered around the capitol building could be heard. Wachtmann was breathing hard and stopped to catch his breath while boos and jeers filled the room from the protestors in other parts of the capitol. For the most part, the audience in the gallery had remained quiet during Wachtmann's tirade, but when he said Ohio had "crumbled" under former Gov. Strickland, the gallery erupted in laughter. As he went on and had to speak louder to be heard he said, "I hope there are no school groups taking a tour, because the rudeness and the loudness of people . . ." he paused again as laughter again filled the room and Speaker Batchelder pounded his gavel. "I'm dead serious. You think it's funny. Hundreds of school kids come in the building every week to learn about Ohio history," he continued as more laughter rippled through the room. If there were any children in the building, they were getting a lesson from Rep. Wachtmann in what ruthless, ideologically driven politics was all about.[4]

Democrat Dennis Murray of Sandusky said that such an important piece of legislation, which would so dramatically change the lives of hundreds of thousands of people, deserved a careful dialogue with the unions and with management. Instead, there was only a "monologue." Because of the billions of dollars in budget cuts being imposed on school districts and local governments by the Republican-controlled legislature, "Senate Bill 5 is a union-busting bill masquerading as cost-control." Far from offering "flexibility," Murray maintained, Senate Bill 5 would be the precursor of "vastly more top-down control of local governments." He scoffed at Republicans who wanted to get credit for not having language in the bill requiring jail time for strikers. Because the bill makes strikes illegal and gives administrations the right to ask for court injunctions, "it is obvious that the only way to enforce an injunction is either a fine or jail time."

"These are moral issues" that the legislature was dealing with, Murray asserted, "involving principles of justice and participation," not just dollars and cents. While Americans were living through the greatest disparity of wealth in American history, he said, the corporate greed that had really caused the great recession was fueling a national scheme to scapegoat unions. "Unions are the thin blue line for the middle class," Murray said. And, make no mistake, he said, antiunion forces would next take on private unions through so-called right-to-work legislation as soon as Senate Bill 5 was accomplished.

Rep. Ron Young (R-Leroy Township) said he supported Senate Bill 5, not because he was part of some huge corporate conspiracy to destroy unions, but because it was a matter of "pure mathematics." Echoing the discredited claims of Sen. Jones, Young said, "we simply don't have the money any longer." And although he accurately recounted the heavy job losses that Ohio had faced in the last ten years, he inaccurately said that the number of public employees had stayed the same—and, most importantly, he did not point out that public unions had made large concessions over the last several years or that Republican tax policies were largely responsible for manufacturing the revenue shortage.

Several other Republican representatives echoed the same inaccurate depictions of Senate Bill 5's provisions, tweaking them a bit for their own personal interests, to express support of the bill. They included Rep. Kristina Roegner of Hudson (near Akron), Rep. Mike Dovilla of Berea (suburban Cleveland), and Rep. Michael Henne of Clayton (suburban Dayton).

Rep. Dan Ramos (D-Lorain) said he had many problems with the bill, given its "gaping holes, glaring omissions, and rampant contradictions." He noted, for example, that new provisions in the bill would bar university professors from union membership simply for doing their jobs, like designing courses. "Every professor who testified before us, and others who have contacted us separately, have maintained that this just doesn't make sense," he noted, adding that "professors do not run our public colleges" and should not be wrongly defined as management.

Rep. John Adams (R-Sidney) provided a lengthy statement in favor of Senate Bill 5. Although the Ohio legislature is packed with ALEC members, Adams is the most prominent. Ohio's ALEC cochair, not only was Adams a 2010 recipient of ALEC's Legislator of the Year award but he has been a longtime member of the organization's Tax and Fiscal Policy Task Force. Having such a stalwart as majority whip of the Ohio House really put ALEC in the driver's seat for getting legislation hostile to the middle class enacted as long as Adams and his Republican colleagues had control of the legislature. Even Adams's legislative aide Kara Joseph won the 2011 ALEC Volunteer of the Year Award.

In a classic political strategy, Adams worked to keep the issue focused locally by attacking his own school district. Interestingly, in the Republican primary in 2012, self-employed engineer Dave Easton ran against Adams and was particularly opposed to Adams's support for private school vouchers because they would undermine the local school district. Further, Easton said he would have opposed Senate Bill 5. Adams handily defeated Easton in the primary.[5]

In clinical terms, Adams said that if costs are never realigned with tax revenues, then greater levies will become a constant. "Over and over again," he said, "my school district has failed to control costs." Adams complained about steady and significant increases in per-pupil spending that greatly outpaced inflation. He was, however, quoting numbers and comments from an essay by Mary McCleary from the right-wing Buckeye Institute about the Sidney school district.[6] As any public employee knows, the Buckeye Institute's numbers about public employee compensation are often inaccurate because of over-estimating compensation. For example, they provide inflated pension estimates for members of the State Teachers Retirement System (STRS) but then do not check to see whether the person in question is actually a member of STRS. To further obscure the reality, the Buckeye Institute shows Social Security totals for Ohio public employees despite the fact that they are ineligible for Social Security.[7]

Rep. Bob Hagan (D-Youngstown), known for his fiery speeches, said he had made some notes for his address that underlined the advice "Don't get angry." "But," he said, "as I listen to my Republican colleagues, in more cases than not, they sound like concession speeches at the next election." Once again Batchelder pounded his gavel to silence the laughter and applause. "We have to be mindful of what is transpiring here today," Hagan continued. "Think about what we're doing." He noted that March 25 marked the hundredth anniversary of the Triangle Shirtwaist Factory fire in New York City, in which 146 union workers were killed, most of them immigrant women. They were "killed because the greed of that owner made him decide it was more important to lock the doors because someone might take a break on the fire escape." Because of that tragedy, the nation started to adopt labor laws, fire codes, and child labor laws. "I know you are thinking 'these are private sector people,'" Hagan said. But, he said, he himself was marking his fortieth year as a locomotive engineer for the CSX Railway. "For 24 years, I've sat in this chamber and listened to people denigrate working people as if they were a scourge on America, as if they were responsible for the budget," he said. He reminded the Republicans that they had voted to cut more than $4 billion from the budget in 2004 under the Taft Administration, a giveaway largely to big corporations and the wealthy.

"Now you are saying the cookie jar is empty. But you are responsible for the largest corporate tax break in the history of Ohio," Hagan said, because "you wanted to make sure that your friends were taken care of." Continuing to hammer away at the Republican position, he said, "Some of you have said you 'listened' to the testimony. Apparently, you didn't 'hear.'" Hagan noted that his father, as a legislator, had voted in favor of the collective bargaining bill back in 1983 and that now he, too, would be voting to protect working people. "This is an attack on the middle class," he roared. "Don't try to dance around it."

Rep. Nickie Antonio (D-Lakewood) said she had heard much in the debate about how SB 5 protected "traditional management rights." She then talked about her mother, who had worked in a bank. It was a private sector job, and there was no union. Because of discrimination against women in the workplace, her mother had had to train a young man to be her supervisor. "He was going to make twice as much, and if my mother didn't like it," Antonio said, "she was told, 'There's the door. Go, because there are ten other people who want your job.'" Antonio said that during the testimony they heard stories of families being hurt by breaking the unions. "What in the world are we doing?" she asked. "What have we come to that we are trying so hard to lower the bar?"

Antonio also objected to apparent Republican displeasure that 85 percent of the budgets at public schools are directed toward teacher salaries. "What else would we be paying for?" she asked in disbelief. "Chalk?" Antonio said she was ashamed that many of the public employees in their testimony felt the need to apologize for their modest salaries. "I think it is appalling that their right to make a decent middle-class living has been demonized," she said.

Perhaps the most puzzling statement came from Rep. James Butler, a Republican from Oakwood, a suburb of Dayton. "I'm disappointed," he said, "about what I'm seeing from the other side of the aisle. I see anger, I see separation. We are all in this together." The gallery laughed out loud at this comment. "Yeah," he said, "people are angry, people are pointing, you can see it in their eyes. That's the system, 'Us versus Them,'" he continued. "The underlying disease," Butler said, finally getting to his point, "is public sector collective bargaining—collective bargaining, in general, for that matter." Contrary to Butler's comments, the disease, in the eyes of many, was the extremism that had seized the legislature.

"We are undergoing a profound change," said Rep. James Barnes (D-Cleveland), "and I know that on Election Day in November, the people of Ohio did not vote for radical change." Ohioans, he said, had voted for an "opportunity for access to the American dream: Life, Liberty, and the Pursuit of Happiness." Calling the debate a "historic day," Barnes predicted that what the House was about to do would be mocked across the nation. "We are sending a message that the welcome mat is not out in the state of Ohio for workers. We are sending a very definite message . . . 'Don't come to Ohio if you want a fair shake in the workplace,'" he said, adding that supporters of Senate Bill 5 had been "demonizing" workers. "That's wrong, and we shouldn't be doing this in this day and time." Barnes noted that he has been very involved in the labor movement through his work with AFSCME. An African American, he said that in the history of that union, perhaps the most significant single event was on April 4, 1968, when the Rev. Martin Luther King Jr. was assassinated while helping over thirteen hundred sanitation workers, members of AFSCME, in Memphis. "Dr. King went down to Memphis," Barnes said, "and he tried to help people in a peaceful way to recognize the importance of the dignity of man and to understand the collective bargaining process and the inherent rights guaranteed by our Constitution."

Barnes noted that the sponsor and supporters of Senate Bill 5 continually claimed it was needed to give tools to the government to cut costs. Barnes picked up a copy of an AFSCME contract, noting that many contracts have similar provisions, including a management-rights section. He read: "Management has the right to run the city." Barnes remarked, "that sounds like plenty of rights." He continued in another section: "Management shall have the sole right" to take action to run the city. Barnes said he wanted to know whose idea it was to use Senate Bill 5 to send a message to all the city governments that they are incapable of running their cities. "Is that the reason that we have not been able to produce jobs in Ohio?" he asked. "If you can't negotiate a contract, is that why we are losing people across this state every day? If you can't negotiate a contract, why are you there?" Tossing the contract on the table, he said loudly and with exasperation, "If you can't negotiate a contract, why don't you just sit down and get out of the way? Because evidently you don't know what you are doing if you are saying that public employees are not giving you the authority to act." Criticizing Ohio's city governments that were lobbying in favor of Senate Bill 5, he went on: "Isn't that interesting, they come down here with all that we have to deal with, a host of issues, yet they come down here and say 'We can't do it.' Well, they need to get out of the way and let some people who can do it."

"This bill is not about policy," emphasized Michael Foley (D-Cleveland). "This bill is about raw political power. That's why we are so upset, and that's why our friends in the gallery are. This has nothing to do with balancing budgets." Instead, he said, it was all about "consolidating Republican power," the same as it had been with House Bill 159 (a voter suppression bill), which the GOP had pushed through a week before. Foley said he understood there would be changes with the Republican sweep in November 2010, but that this was "consolidating power to the detriment of the middle class." He said his son had become very interested in politics and had come across a definition of what was going on in the Ohio legislature. The word was "Plutocracy: government of, by, and for the rich," an observation that drew approving laughter and applause from the crowd and a pounding gavel from Batchelder. "That's what I fear we are heading for," Foley said, and recited a list of indications of the growing disparity between the rich and poor. He mocked the governor's recent statements about "shared sacrifice." Kasich was not talking about the wealthy, Foley pointed out; instead Kasich was asking for sacrifice from the poor and the middle class and "the people who fight fires and teach kids" and provide security.

"Ohio is polarized because of Senate Bill 5," Alicia Reece (D-Cincinnati) observed, saying that real leadership would lead to rejecting the whole bill and starting over. Ohio's shareholders are not just the rich, she said; they are everyone, including public workers. "We work for them, too, and the people that sweep the floors in the capitol." She said that she had spent a lot of time in the hospital with her mother, who had succumbed to breast cancer. "Thank God for those nurses. The nurses were wonderful," she said. "So, who am I to say that you are good enough to take care of me and my mother but not good enough to negotiate better wages and not good enough to have health care yourself?" Reece said she had come to the legislature to move Ohio forward but that this bill "takes us a hundred years backwards." She said she had been thinking of her grandfather, a Navy veteran who had served in two wars but who, as a young African American male, could only find work shining shoes when he came home. Thanks to the unions, who had created a fair employment process, her grandfather was able to get hired at the post office. "He was able to build his house, his piece of the American dream," she said. "The people in the labor movement, they got our backs," Reece said.

"And we show our gratitude by introducing Senate Bill 5 to stab them in the back. My grandfather would turn in his grave if he thought his granddaughter would support something like this."

Like Rep. Barnes, Reece referenced Martin Luther King. On Martin Luther King Day, she said, Americans are now quick to quote and praise the civil rights leader. But, she noted, "we should remember that not everyone was on his side [when he was alive]." The question facing the House that day, she said, was, "Which side of history are you going to be on? I want to be on the right side of history." She said she wished the public employees and their unions had been brought in as the bill was being written, rather than only being allowed to comment as it was being imposed upon them. She talked about the huge crowds from all over Ohio that had turned out at the capitol to oppose SB 5. "I see this as a David and Goliath movement—little Davids, the nurses, the teachers, the janitors, the custodians, the little Davids, firefighters, the police officers, the correctional officers, the little Davids, the bus drivers, the social workers, the sanitation workers." She paused for emphasis before concluding, "I urge a no vote on this bill. But I will tell you, the little Davids are in this fight to the end. And there will be a time, when we take this to the ballot, that the government Goliath will be challenged."

Rep. Armond Budish (D-Beachwood) gave the last anti-Senate Bill 5 address. The House minority leader also cited the Triangle Shirtwaist fire and then listed the several specific aspects of the bill that would be detrimental to public workers. Looking across the chamber, he said, "Listening to Representative Wachtmann today, I could picture him giving that antiworker speech a hundred years ago, and Representative Wachtmann, I also hope there were no schoolchildren here to hear your speech."

Loud cheers and applause broke out, and in addition to pounding his gavel, Speaker Batchelder growled sharply, "That's enough! The gentleman is instructed to make no personal references to another member of this House." Of course, when Rep. Wachtmann had attacked another House member, Speaker Batchelder said nothing.

Budish maintained that "collective bargaining levels the playing field between workers and their employers. It is only a question of fairness." Budish ridiculed what he saw as the main conception behind Senate Bill 5—that government officials, at both state and local levels, are too weak and incompetent to negotiate contracts. "Is that really your argument? Seriously?" Budish asked. "Governor Kasich and many of you say Senate Bill 5 is needed to give government tools to control their costs," he said, noting that it appeared that Gov. Kasich had built his whole budget on that concept. Kasich, Budish observed, planned to cut more than a billion dollars from local governments and more than $3 billion from school districts, but was telling them they should not worry because SB 5, by crushing the unions, would allow governments and schools to control costs. "That sure sounds a lot better than telling them the truth," Budish said, and the truth was that "the draconian budget cuts means slashing jobs and salaries." He further declared, "We should honor and respect our public servants. Your vote for Senate Bill 5 insults and demeans them and undermines the middle class." But, he said, this would be only a first step, because attacks on private sector unions were sure to be next.

The last two House members to speak on Senate Bill 5 were Republicans who supported the bill and were both members of the ALEC Civil Justice Task Force: Rep. Bill Coley of Middletown and Rep. Matt Huffman of Lima. They repeated the largely unfounded Republican arguments in different ways and added little of substance.

At the conclusion of Huffman's statement, Speaker Batchelder called for the vote. The panel lit up in red and green, and Batchelder announced the total: 53 in favor and 44 against, a nearly perfect party-line vote. Four Republicans had joined the Democrats in voting no, and two Republicans were not present for the vote.

Howls of protest erupted from the gallery. "Will the patrol clear the hall," Batchelder called. As the din grew louder and angrier, he asked that House members remain seated. Many Democrats, however, wandered the floor taking video on their cell phones of what they knew was an historic moment.

Jeers and shouts of "Ohio hates you" filled the air in the House chamber. A large banner was unfurled from the gallery, saying in big bright letters, "Your Corporate Owners Thank You," with a reference to the Koch brothers. Another banner read, "Thanks for Corporate Welfare." As the crowd very slowly left, their defiant chant echoed loudly in the chamber, making normal conversation impossible: "Shame on you, shame on you, shame on you."

On Thursday, March 31, the amended bill quickly flew through the Senate in the concurrence vote by the identical 17–16 margin. The expectation was that Kasich would act quickly and sign the bill on Friday. But, reflective of the extremist nature of the process and ideology behind SB 5, Kasich scheduled a special Thursday evening signing.

Gov. Kasich had said that when the bill passed, there would be no celebratory signing event and that he might sign it privately. That certainly was not true. Instead, Kasich gathered in an ornate room with his Republican allies in the union-busting drive to sign the bill with fanfare. With a full contingent of cameras and journalists, Kasich signed the bill with, at his elbow, Senate President Tom Niehaus, House Speaker William Batchelder, Rep. Louis Blessing, and the bill's sole sponsor, Sen. Shannon Jones.

Kasich even used the hours before he signed SB 5 to try to fundraise with the legislative victory. Shortly after its passage, Kasich sent out an email to his supporters, asking them to back his "ongoing efforts to fight for Ohio taxpayers" by donating $5, $10, or $20. Talking about people like me, who, as a "boss," served in an unpaid position with the AAUP, Kasich wrote, "There is a reason that the union bosses opposed these changes, because it strips power from the union leaders and returns it to the taxpayers and workers." Such a comment suggests that he never did understand what the fight over Senate Bill 5 was really about.[8]

The signing itself was broadcast live on the Ohio News Network and provided plenty of film for late-night news across the state. Kasich, enthused by his apparent victory, explained the same talking points that all supporters of the bill had parroted: "gives tools to control costs," "provides flexibility," "unsustainable costs," and so on. Kasich continued that this was an effort to provide a balance between government employees versus "those folks in the private sector."

"Let me be clear about a couple of things,' Kasich said, going on to deny criticisms that many had leveled at the union-busting drive. Kasich maintained that the bill would not cut anybody's salary, would not take away anybody's pension, and would not destroy anybody's healthcare. However, he neglected to say that it would create the probability of all that happening. "This is an effort to provide balance," he said about a bill that made collective bargaining a sham. He then went on to misrepresent, once again, the fact that public worker's compensation is demonstrably less than that of those employed in comparable work in the private sector. Kasich then pointed out how the economic collapse had hurt so many Ohioans. Since as an investment banker on Wall Street Kasich had taken part in the profession that had crippled the economy in 2008, there was much irony—apparently lost on the governor—in his suggesting that now he was trying to help Ohioans whose livelihoods had been shattered. Anticipating that his own budget bill was going to hurt local governments and school districts, he said SB 5 would allow them to deal with fewer resources. He then went on to suggest that his SB 5 and its union-busting impact were part of his "growth agenda."[9]

"I'm proud of the members of the legislature," Kasich said. "They have been my partners since I was inaugurated as governor." He went on to point out a couple of other controversial bills he had pushed through the legislature, specifically mentioning his JobsOhio program, which had privatized the economic development arm of the state government and, as seems obvious, made it easier to funnel public money into wealthy private hands. Much of the news conference was an opportunity for the Republican leadership to congratulate themselves on a job well done.

President Niehaus, saying "this was a good day for Ohio," repeated many of the same maxims. But Niehaus particularly praised Sen. Jones for sponsoring the bill. "This is kind of an amazing evening," Speaker Batchelder said, "for those of us who served here in 1983 when the original bill was passed . . . Tonight, we will know that the people of this state will be treated equally." Like Kasich, Batchelder repeated the misinformation that public workers were paid more than their private sector counterparts, but he went further, to perfectly explain the flaw in the argument: "When you have a lady working at McDonald's, who doesn't really have much to take home to her kids, to tax her to subsidize those who are paid a great deal more and given better benefits, it's not fair." Batchelder suggested that busting the unions would give "inspiration for those who work very long hours, for very little pay, almost no benefits. Now they know they are just as important in Ohio."

Batchelder, of course, was endorsing a race to the bottom where, no matter how many college degrees or how much experience or what kind of expertise a school teacher or a government engineer or scientist had, they should be in exactly the situation of the fast food worker that he described: "long hours, very little pay, almost no benefits." Obviously, McDonald's workers and others in the fast food industry deserve better pay and benefits, but Batchelder and the Republicans never proposed that in any legislation.

Saying that Speaker Pro-Tem Louis Blessing of Cincinnati had been "integral" to the passage of SB 5, Kasich praised Blessing for his important role, equating Blessing's work on SB 5 to the Cincinnati Reds hitting a walk-off home run. "Thank you, Governor," Blessing said with a broad smile. The long-term legislator then praised Shannon Jones for her courage. Saying that all the leadership was "spectacular," he said he had never before worked with a governor who would say "Let's do this" without considering the political consequences. In time, Blessing said, union contracts were going to "compress"—an artful way of saying that salaries and benefits would shrink for middle-class Ohioans.

Calling Shannon Jones a "friend," Kasich introduced the sponsor of Senate Bill 5 to the assembled media. "I think a handful of thank-yous are appropriate," Jones said. She thanked her family, Niehaus (for his "resolve"), the entire leadership team of the Senate, especially Sen. Kevin Bacon (who was a "rock"), Speaker Batchelder and Rep. Blessing (for some really "smart work"), and "obviously," Gov. Kasich for his "unwavering commitment."

"But mostly," Jones went on, "I would like to thank all those brave constituents all across Ohio, really dedicated and committed public servants . . . under difficult circumstances, who came to the statehouse to show how they need the flexibility to turn their communities around." She concluded by thanking the governor again and saying she looked forward, "maybe, for what's to come."

"Well, you ain't seen nothing yet," Kasich quipped.

It would turn out that Gov. Kasich was right about that—but not in the way he expected. Soon the smug confidence expressed at the signing and the ruthlessness demonstrated in the passage of Senate Bill 5 would be shattered by a historic groundswell of resistance to union busting and to attacks on the middle class that would reverberate far beyond Ohio's borders.

Chapter 7

The Real Fight Begins

Even before the House vote, we at the UC-AAUP had begun making plans for the next step in the struggle. In a message to our membership on March 29, signed by Deborah Herman, Jana Braziel (our vice president), and me, we noted that we were preparing for Round Two. In collaboration with We Are Ohio, the Ohio Conference, and the other AAUP chapters statewide, we would be joining in the drive to get more than 231,000 signatures collected in 90 days so that we could place on the November ballot an issue to repeal Senate Bill 5. The bill would be barred from going into effect by our signature-gathering campaign.

We emphasized that this would be a complex undertaking. It was necessary that We Are Ohio propose language for the referendum, which would need to be approved by the Secretary of State's office. That language needed to be submitted along with 1,000 signatures. Once the language was approved, we would have 90 days to collect 10 percent of the number of votes cast for governor in the most recent election. In this case, that meant over 231,000 signatures. We told our members that the scale and challenge of this effort was why the labor coalition would be hiring professional staff to make sure the drive was managed effectively.

We also explained that even if Senate Bill 5 went into effect, our contract at UC would continue until it expired on June 30, 2013. Thus, we wrote, even in a worst-case scenario, we had some security until then and could focus our efforts entirely on repealing the legislation. What we did not talk about publicly was our fear that if we failed to repeal Senate Bill 5, given the radical nature of Gov. Kasich's strategy, that he would take advantage of another feature of the legislation.

If SB 5 went into effect, he would have the right to declare a state of fiscal emergency and abrogate all existing union contracts. Given the behavior of Kasich and his allies so far, we suspected that this was exactly what would happen. Yet, even barring the possibility of this worst-case scenario, we had plenty to worry about in defending the university and our profession. "Between now and 2013," we wrote to our colleagues, "all AAUP Chapters across Ohio will be putting full effort into securing our collective bargaining rights for the future—for our own sake, but also for the sake of UC students, their parents, and the future of truly *public* higher education."

In retrospect I must emphasize, as well, the activity and leadership shown by AAUP state conference executive director Sara Kilpatrick, President Dr. John Cuppoletti, and the entire conference board. The board's communications committee, led by Professor Dave Witt and Professor Steve Aby of the University of Akron and Professor Marty Kich of Wright State, had really stepped up their work to inform all the chapters of the joint efforts around Ohio to stop SB 5. Their work to coordinate our statewide efforts was invaluable.

Locally, I cannot say enough about the faculty on the UC-AAUP executive council. They were, from a variety of academic disciplines, Jana Braziel, Lynn Davis, Robin Dennison, Ron Jones, Andrea Kornbluh, Greg Loving, Rick Paul, Stephen Pelikan, Helen Meyer, Stephen Mockabee, Jennie Russell, Debbie Tenofsky, and Alan Vespie. It was not easy for faculty members who are mainly accustomed to calm, reasoned argument within the confines of a university environment to realize that they need to engage in a bitter political battle with forces that really wish to see their undoing. Former staffer Dave Rubin provided invaluable advice.

In our first meeting after the Kasich visit, we considered a new policy. Surprised at the use of UC security against faculty, and now knowing just how bad things might get as the struggle went on, we discussed a policy about proper conduct during demonstrations, what the limits of the chapter's liability would be, and how best to maintain the image of the faculty and the AAUP under such trying circumstances. Tempers had been frayed by the experience and the stress we were under, and it was only the beginning. Good people could simply disagree about some of the strategy, but we shared a common bond in working for the good of the university.

I heard from both students and our state executive director Sara Kilpatrick that a student mobilization workshop was being held in Columbus on April 3 at the International Brotherhood of Electrical Workers union hall. The students wanted some faculty to attend, and so I joined several other AAUP leaders from other universities at the workshop. The topic was Senate Bill 5 and several voter suppression bills. It was a great experience and another opportunity to be impressed by the smart, capable, and creative students who came to the fore during this crisis.

About 50 student leaders were in attendance from various colleges and universities around the state, including Ohio State, UC, Miami, Akron, Shawnee State, Wright State, and Ohio University. Aliya Rahman of Miami and Elizabeth Anthorp of UC gave an update about the efforts in the Cincinnati area. For faculty, the important aspect of the meeting was to make contact with many of the students who would be key allies in our campaign in the months ahead. It was encouraging to see that many of the students had a more sophisticated understanding of the threats Ohioans were facing than did some of our faculty who, absorbed in their research and teaching, had not paid much attention until now to the growing political threats to higher education.

Communication was going to be central for us from this point forward, and social media played a major role in connecting many disparate groups. Several Facebook sites were developed, including Stand Up for Ohio, Defend Ohio, Students Opposing SB 5, No SB5 for Ohio, UC Defend Ohio, Defend UC, and Students Opposing SB5. Additional Facebook sites focused on other damaging aspects of legislative activity, such as Save Our Turnpikes and Stop Selling/Leasing Ohio Assets (including privatizing prisons to turn them into corporate profit centers). All of these and others contributed to creating a statewide dialogue that united the resistance against many extremist initiatives.

In an effort to keep the momentum moving and kick off the signature-collecting campaign, rallies across the state were planned for April 4. The goal was not to bring protesters in their thousands again to the statehouse but instead to focus on the local communities for grassroots demonstrations that would tie the movement closely to local issues. I was contacted by Bill Dudley, a local organizer for the United Food and Commercial Workers (UFCW) to participate. Dudley had already generated his own contacts with student groups, though I tried to help with those efforts. He asked whether I could speak briefly at a rally in Dayton, and naturally I said yes. Dudley was to be one of those people who stood up during the campaign and worked very hard to ensure our joint success.

I rode to the Dayton rally, which was held at the Teamsters hall, with a busload of students in the pouring rain. As we entered the building, we found about two hundred people and their families waiting for us, and a good number of students from Wright State and Miami

University. I was glad to see that Rudy Fichtenbaum, chief negotiator of the Wright State AAUP chapter (and future AAUP national president), was there as well. Various Dayton-area labor and political leaders, as well as several students, spoke about the importance of defeating SB 5, and then Fichtenbaum and I had a chance to speak.

A labor economist by discipline, Dr. Fichtenbaum laid out a careful and detailed argument. He minced no words, listing Senate Bill 5, voter suppression bills, bills to undermine public pensions, and efforts to create "charter universities" as "all part of a well-financed concerted effort by the Republicans and Wall Street to undermine the standard of living for working Americans. Wall Street and their lapdogs in Washington have declared war on America's working families." He went through the various damaging aspects of Senate Bill 5 and ridiculed the idea that anything fair had been provided to replace binding arbitration to resolve disputes: "Calling this a dispute resolution procedure is like claiming that a bank robber, with a loaded gun, is negotiating a withdrawal from the bank."[1] Laughter and cheers filled the hall.

Noting that he was a college professor, he said, "let me give you a little test. Will SB 5 and the governor's budget create more jobs for Ohioans?" "No," came the roaring reply. Fictenbaum continued, asking in sequence, "Will SB 5 improve education in our public schools? Will SB 5 and the governor's budget give us better emergency and fire protection services? Will SB 5 and the governor's budget help care for the sick, the abused, and the elderly? Will SB 5 and the governor's budget and his support to privatize our universities . . . give our children a better college education?"

"No," the crowd roared in answer to each of these questions. "You all get an A," said Prof. Fichtenbaum, but he added, "Our governor, the governor from Wall Street, who worked for Lehman Brothers, who helped bring us the worst economic crisis since the Great Depression, and the Republican-dominated legislature, get an F." He went on to poke holes in the flawed Republican arguments, demonstrating, for example, that for comparable jobs with comparable education, public workers earn less than their private sector counterparts.

Fichtenbaum then went on to explain how Senate Bill 5 particularly targeted college professors. Backers of the bill called professors managers because "we make recommendations about who our colleges and universities should hire to teach your children, because we have the temerity to demand that we make recommendation on the selection of administrators," or recommendations regarding planning, budgets, educational policies, curriculum, as well as on hiring and retention of faculty. "We make recommendations," Fichtenbaum emphasized, "based on our knowledge and professional expertise, these are *not* decisions. They are recommendations!" He added, "Anyone who doesn't know the difference between a recommendation and a decision needs to back to school because they are not qualified to be voting or to be signing legislation."

"I've been a professor of economics at Wright State for 31 years," Fichtenbaum, gray-haired and bespectacled, said. "Do I look like an administrator?" he asked, to loud laughter. "Do I sound like an administrator?" He concluded,

> I am not a history professor, but that last time I looked there was still a document called the Constitution of the United States of America, and if I recall correctly, it doesn't start out "We the Corporations" or "We the Wall Street Bankers." It starts "We the People." Let's take back our country and our state. Let's start by repealing SB 5 and fighting for a budget that puts people before profits.

It was my job to follow this tough act. Although we had not planned this, Fichtenbaum had set me up. "Well," I said, "I am a history professor, and I'm going to talk to you about some history." The crowd chuckled, and I started by noting that the hundredth anniversary of the Triangle Fire on March 25 had just passed and remarking on the obvious irony in the timing of this attack on unions by the state legislature. I detailed some of the events surrounding the fire, especially the brave work of the International Ladies Garment Workers Union (ILGWU) and the irresponsible behavior of the business owners that led to the deaths of 146 workers, most of them young immigrant women.

I particularly credited FDR and the New Deal for creating a legal framework, with the Wagner Act, in which workers could stand on a level playing field with corporations to fight for fair treatment, fair wages, and reasonable benefits. I then quoted the well-known statement by President John F. Kennedy:

> Those who would destroy or further limit the rights of organized labor—those who would cripple collective bargaining or prevent organization of the unorganized—do a disservice to the cause of democracy. Employees, represented by free and democratic trade unions of their own choosing, participate actively in determining their wages, hours and working conditions. Their living standards are the highest in the world. Their job rights are protected by collective bargaining agreements. They have fringe benefits that were unheard of less than a generation ago. Our labor unions are not narrow, self-seeking groups.

> They have raised wages, shortened hours and provided supplemental benefits. Through collective bargaining and grievance procedures, they have brought justice and democracy to the shop floor. But their work goes beyond their own jobs, and even beyond our borders. Our unions have fought for aid to education, for better housing, for development of our national resources, and for saving the family-sized farms. They have spoken, not for narrow self-interest, but for the public interest and for the people.[2]

Naturally, these words brought loud applause from the crowd. I concluded that in this drive to defeat SB 5, our movement represented all kinds of Ohioans, including college professors. "I think I can speak for the AAUP, that we are in this with you to defend our way of life in Ohio, to defend our universities, and we are in this to win." The Teamsters roared their approval. Afterward, Fichtenbaum and I had the chance to marvel at what had just happened. Two college professors, local political and labor leaders, and students—all speaking in a Teamsters union hall, and to great enthusiasm. That kind of united purpose, we hoped, could not be defeated.

Another huge rally was planned for Columbus on Saturday, April 9. Buses left Cincinnati from the United Auto Workers hall on Reading Road and the AFSCME hall on Tennessee Road at 9:30 in the morning. Announcing the rally, Sara Kilpatrick's message explained that the point of the rally was to continue the kickoff of the referendum drive: "Because the fight has just begun! We need all hands on deck for the referendum effort. This is the fight of our lives!"

About fifteen thousand people turned out in Columbus on April 9 to show their opposition to Senate Bill 5. From all reports, it was a raucous rally. Prof. Fichtenbaum again addressed the multitude. But I was thousands of miles away in Dublin, Ireland, at a conference. Something I have not mentioned much until now is the obvious fact that, as a faculty member, I have many responsibilities at the university. Most importantly, I had four sections of the year-long world history survey to teach. My first responsibility is always for about a hundred students each term. Not only did that entail preparing lectures for the classroom and meeting with students in my office over their reading and especially their term papers, but I had exams and quizzes to prepare and grade. As a multidisciplinary department at our regional college in Blue Ash, where we work to teach critical thinking, the faculty in our department have taken a writing-intensive approach. That means essay exams, a term paper, and other short writing assignments. Teaching, preparing, grading, and working with students and meeting with them on the weekends for History Club or for study sessions before exams, all involves the meat and potatoes of my career and the things I love about it.

Naturally, like other academics involved in the SB 5 fight, I could not allow my outside activities to interfere with my core responsibilities. Part of those ongoing responsibilities includes my research agenda. As a Cold War historian, I've published books, articles, and reviews on the period, and my work is always continuing. Thus, the weekend of the big rally in Columbus, I was off to give a paper at the William J. Clinton Institute for American Studies at University College Dublin. The conference, "History, Memory and American Foreign Policy," featured many international historians. Prominent historian Jay Winter of Yale University gave the keynote address. I spoke on the Ulster background of Truman's Secretary of State Dean G. Acheson and the impact that had on his foreign policy design in the early Cold War. Because of my pressing responsibilities, I flew to Ireland and back on the weekend. Interestingly, many of the historians at the conference, from several European countries, knew about the struggle we were waging in Ohio and wanted a firsthand report. I was happy to provide the story over pints of Guinness.

The AAUP's Ohio Conference had its annual meeting in Columbus on the weekend of April 15–16, which, coincidentally, was ideal timing because we were able to focus on issues connected to Senate Bill 5 and how we could best organize to defend Ohio's faculty. Probably most importantly, the staff, particularly UC's Debby Herman, designed a workshop to teach all of us how to properly and legally collect signatures for the referendum campaign. They were meticulous in training us how to do this, with the goal of ensuring that none of our signatures would be turned away as illegitimate. We anticipated that the Republicans, who had done whatever was necessary to pass SB 5, would also do whatever they could to disqualify our signature-gathering. We had to gather booklets of signatures so perfect that they could not be thrown out.

After the state conference, we quickly scheduled a series of workshops across our three campuses to educate more faculty and students about how to collect valid signatures. Dozens of faculty and students took part in the workshops as we geared up for what we knew would be a challenging drive to collect thousands of signatures. In the meantime, we had passed another hurdle in the drive.

On Friday, April 15, the Ohio Attorney General approved the petition ballot language, and the Ohio Secretary of State certified that about 2,500 of the 2,800 signatures submitted (only 1,000 were needed) were valid. We Are Ohio now began printing the first batch of petitions to be distributed to various points around the state. The campaign leaders made it very clear that what we needed was exactly 231,149 valid signatures to get the referendum on the ballot so we could repeal SB 5 at the polls in November 2011. The petition booklets would have about 70 signature lines, yet they would be over 100 pages long, since Ohio law requires that the entire bill be attached to the petition. Further, each petition booklet could only have signatures of registered voters from a single county.

"We must take seriously our responsibility to preserve the integrity of this process," Sara Kilpatrick of the Ohio Conference emphasized in a message to the leadership. "We don't want to be the ones handing in lots of petition booklets that are subsequently disqualified, or lose any of them!" Outlining the strategy, she emphasized that, first, each collector had to go through one of the training sessions. She said she was willing to go to any chapter to do a training session and noted also that the UC chapter staff had also been trained and was able and willing to do training sessions as well. Second, each chapter needed to name a lead organizer who would be responsible for the booklets. Each of the booklets would have a tracking number, and the individual signing out the book would be responsible for returning it. The lead organizer in each chapter would be Kilpatrick's direct contact for delivering and collecting booklets and dealing with any problems. Third, no collector could keep a booklet longer than two weeks. This was in part to make sure they weren't lost, but also because We Are Ohio needed to keep track of the speed with which we were gathering signatures.

In April, our UC executive council also adopted a new policy. I have to emphasize what a groundbreaking moment this was. As I've pointed out before, for decades the chapter had been apolitical and, until the Strickland donation, had never contributed to a political campaign. But now for the first time in our history, forced by the political attack on our existence, we wrote, debated, and adopted a Labor Solidarity Donations and Endorsements Policy. This was a clear sign that we were gearing up for the fight to defend our profession and our university.

The signature-gathering in Cincinnati got off to a strong start on April 23, when a jointly sponsored signing event was held at University Ministry Baptist Church, sponsored locally by the AFL-CIO Labor Council and We Are Ohio. "Join Cincinnati firefighters, nurses, teachers, clergy, students, and other citizens," the announcement stressed, "and be among the first to sign a petition to place SB 5 on the ballot in November." Hundreds of people showed up for that first signing, perhaps demonstrating a pent-up desire to strike back at the legislation. The turnout at this event boded well for the future. The actual scale of the organization as it developed was extraordinarily impressive. By early May, We Are Ohio announced that they had more than ten thousand people gathering signatures across the state, and clearly the overwhelming majority of those people were union members like us, who were committed to defeating this attack on Ohio's way of life.

One factor that became clear during this early period of the campaign was that religious groups in Ohio—at least the Catholic Church and mainstream Protestant churches—were opposed to gutting collective bargaining rights. On March 2, a coalition of nearly one hundred clergy released a statement expressing their opposition to SB 5. On the other hand, a handful of politically right-wing evangelical churches were much less forthcoming, but undoubtedly their membership was made up of many Republicans who were philosophically, even theologically, against unions. But the religious groups that went public were unequivocal in their support of collective bargaining rights.

Recognizing that it was the season of Passover, Tom Choquette, director of the Cincinnati Interfaith Workers Center issued a statement that read, in part, "The human values of respect for the dignity of persons and the right to economic security, spiritually affirmed through these religious rites, appear to the Cincinnati Interfaith Committee for Worker Justice to be put at risk by recent legislation passed by the Ohio General Assembly and signed by the Governor." Senate Bill 5, in particular, "causes grave concern." The impact of such legislation, Choquette wrote, will be to "increase the economic vulnerability of families of public sector workers, especially those on the lower end of wage scale. With their purchasing power reduced and their confidence in their economic future diminished, the participation of these workers economically and socially in the life of their community will likely decline." In addition, he asked, "What happens to workers' self-worth and morale when through the curtailing of collective bargaining rights they are told your voice, your point of view, your experience on a whole range of issues will no longer be listened to or considered in the contract negotiation process?" Choquette asked group members to attend a meeting sponsored by the AFL-CIO at the International Brotherhood of Electrical Workers hall on Fishwick Drive on April 25, "to become involved in this vital campaign to insure economic and social balance."[3]

Led by Bishop Dennis Schnurr of the Archdiocese of Cincinnati, the Catholic bishops of Ohio had weighed in early on the issue. In a statement on February 28, the bishops wrote that they "encourage leaders in government, labor, and business to pursue changes that promote the common good without the elimination of collective bargaining." While the debate at that point was continuing, they urged good-faith negotiations. "In our faith tradition," the bishops wrote, "defending the human dignity of every person, born and unborn, includes promoting economic justice." The bishops emphasized that people "are at the center of all things and the economy exists for them, not people for the economy. This social doctrine has long recognized that all people have the right to economic initiative, to productive work, to just wages and benefits, to decent working conditions, to organize and join unions or other associations, and to engage in collective bargaining."[4]

By contrast, politician and evangelical preacher Mike Huckabee made a stop in the Cincinnati area late in the campaign on October 14 to make a pitch for SB 5. "Make a list" of your friends, Huckabee told his audience in Mason, a Cincinnati suburb. "Call them and ask them, 'Are you going to vote on Issue 2, and are you going to vote for it?' If they say no, well, you just make sure that they don't go vote. Let the air out of their tires on Election Day. Tell them the election has been moved to a different date. It is up to you how you creatively get the job done."

Of course there was a good deal of laughter surrounding such comments, but faith leaders and NAACP leaders wasted no time in criticizing the comments. "Huckabee's disgusting comments show that Building a Better Ohio and its corporate-funded supporters will do anything, even advocate for illegal tactics, to keep Ohioans from voting against Issue 2," said NAACP Ohio Conference President Sybil Edwards-McNabb.[5]

On April 25 the Women's City Club, a historic organization founded in 1915 in Cincinnati, sponsored perhaps the first public forum on Senate Bill 5 and other controversial legislation passed by the Republican legislature. Representing the pro-SB 5 and Republican side would be local Tea Party founder Mike Wilson and attorney Gary Greenberg. Representing the Democratic and labor side would be Tim Burke, head of the Hamilton County Democratic Party, and Julie Sellers, president of the Cincinnati Federation of Teachers. I attended the event at Mount Auburn Presbyterian Church's social hall to represent the AAUP.

After both sides had made initial statements, the floor was opened for questions. Most of the pro-SB 5 commentary had been inaccurate about the preservation of collective bargaining and how this was necessary for governments to reduce expenses. I pointed out what had already been said—that to eliminate binding arbitration and create a system where the administration simply got to impose its will did, in fact, eliminate any meaningful collective bargaining. But the heart of my comment was to point out that the faculty unions, without question, were specifically slated for elimination in SB 5. I identified myself as president of the UC-AAUP and said that elimination of my union was exactly what SB 5 aimed to do and explained why. Since it was the faculty who were the real bulwark protecting excellence at any university, I noted, this was a direct attack on the quality of higher education in Ohio.

Greenberg attempted to make the old flawed comments about the principle of shared governance being the reason that faculty were really managers and thus should not be union members. "You can't have it both ways," he said. Before I could weigh in again, Tim Burke, who was clearly on top of the issue, pointed out clearly how ridiculous it was to bar professors from union membership simply for doing their jobs.

Surprisingly, after some vigorous back-and-forth about the legislation, the conversation turned to a series of Republican voter suppression bills, especially House Bill 194. The senior citizens in the audience were especially irate at the obstacles being put in the way of voting. An older woman, who had volunteered to work the polls for years, was especially vehement in her denunciations of the legislation. Noting that she was a Republican, she said she had never seen anyone try to vote who was not eligible. The problem, she said, was that not enough people voted, and that was the issue that should be addressed, not trying to reduce the number of people who vote. The audience loudly murmured their agreement.

On balance, I thought that when both arguments about Senate Bill 5 were put side-by-side for the people to decide, as they were at this Women's City Club forum, SB 5 looked like just what it was—an extremist effort to disarm ordinary people and make it much easier to exploit them. It left me feeling hopeful that we could win but all the more certain that opponents of the bill genuinely had to continually and loudly lay out our arguments about the legislation so that people could fairly judge the impact of such a law.

In an effort to do this, through the UC-AAUP we mobilized faculty around a "teach-in" on Senate Bill 5, other damaging legislation, and some national trends. Dr. David Stradling, a professor of history, had been a student of William Cronon's and gave a talk about Cronon and his work, and about the attacks that he faced for speaking out about the actions of the Wisconsin legislature. For my part, I gave a review of several important books written about the radical turn that has taken hold of the Republican Party, in order to explain the roots of the extremism. Part of the teach-in was a film series about various movements around the world for economic justice. Although we did not have a great turnout for the event, we nonetheless communicated our concerns to dozens of students who perhaps had not thought through the consequences political decisions have on their lives.

Once again I have to credit the students that I worked with for their self-organization and awareness of the importance of these issues to their lives. On April 28, we heard from Kate Beltramo, one of the student organizers who was such a joy to work with. "Hello, Professors," she wrote. Noting that she was serving with Organizing for America, she informed us that the "UC Democrats, Defend Ohio, Students Opposing SB 5, and other progressive groups on campus have teamed together to get this bill on the ballot. I have been trained by We Are Ohio to circulate the petitions, and I have developed a medium-sized team to circulate petitions." She continued:

> It would be wonderful to work together on this! I have reserved McMicken Commons (and indoor space inside TUC in case of rain!) for the entire month of May, but volunteers have stated that Mondays, Tuesdays, and Fridays (10 a.m. to 3 p.m.) would be best for tabling. This is still being solidified, so I will email you as soon as I know what days we're going to table. The days will be consistent throughout the month of May, and we may even add more depending on availability and interest.

She concluded her note: "Thank you for everything you do for both the referendum efforts and for education." She ended with a cheerful smiley face.

Of course, this was a perfect opportunity for faculty and students to work together, and we jumped at the chance. By this time, thanks to our staff, we had at least two dozen faculty members properly trained to collect signatures. Having received our first shipment of booklets on April 26, we began to fan out through the university and the community to begin gathering the signatures. At my college in suburban Blue Ash, we organized tables three or four days a week, staffed by faculty, to collect signatures.

While we were gathering signatures across the university to allow students and faculty the opportunity to sign the referendum, other unions were working through the various Cincinnati neighborhoods. At the state level, our executive director Sara Kilpatrick was traveling to campuses throughout the state, training people to properly collect signatures. During the last week of April, for example, she traveled from our office in Columbus to Kent State, the University of Akron, Cincinnati State, and the University of Toledo, where she consulted with leadership and trained at least 55 more faculty members to collect signatures.

One of the most interesting experiences during the signature drive was Saturdays at historic Findlay Market in the Over-the-Rhine area of downtown Cincinnati. Very busy with shoppers from all over the metro area, the weekend market is highlighted by music, wine tastings, and people just generally enjoying the city atmosphere. We worked in teams just in case anyone ran into any particular trouble, but in fact, other than a few comments like "I think SB 5 is a good thing," there were no problems. We collected a lot of signatures, and many people signed enthusiastically.

The counties that we were mainly concentrating on were Hamilton County, where Cincinnati is located, as well as Butler, Clermont, and Warren, which surround the city. Butler, with the towns of Hamilton, Fairfield, and Oxford (home to Miami University) has a more diverse political mix than do heavily Republican Warren and Clermont counties. Nonetheless, as we learned during the campaign, there were plenty of Republicans who disagreed with their party's attack on public workers. For example, one afternoon at a table where some students on McMicken Commons were collecting signatures at the UC main campus, one young woman came up to talk to the students at the table. She had noticed that the students had put out a "UC Democrats" sign as well as the SB 5 signs. "I'm a Republican," she told them. "I'm against SB 5. A lot of Republicans are. Having your sign up discourages people from stopping and signing the petition." The students took down the Democrats sign.

On Monday, May 9, members of the executive council held sessions in the afternoon with Brian Rothenberg from Progress Ohio, a Columbus-based think tank that dealt with media communication, messaging, and events. As a former print journalist, I already knew much of what we discussed regarding the media, but I learned some things about the way the television media worked, including the different deadlines and the need for a visual opportunity. This was all part of our effort to be prepared in the future for any problems or opportunities that might arise.

A very public attack occurred from an unlikely direction in the Sunday *Enquirer* on May 6. Dale Schaefer, a professor and former dean in UC's College of Engineering, wrote a scathing critique of the UC Chapter of the AAUP for the newspaper, a column that also, not surprisingly, appeared in the right-wing *Washington Times* in the nation's capital. I knew Dr. Schaefer from Faculty Senate meetings where, as a Senate member, he would occasionally stand up and rail against the AAUP about some usually misperceived problem. The hostility in his newspaper column was not surprising, but what was surprising was the repetition of so many well-worn right-wing falsehoods about unions as well as outright misstatements of fact.

I was, of course, unhappy that a faculty member would so deliberately distort the role of the AAUP at UC. Common sense would demonstrate that much of what Schaefer said was not true. After comparing the AAUP to Communists in Eastern Europe during the Cold War, Schaefer said that the "AAUP bargains on its own behalf with the administration. Neither the faculty nor its elected leadership, the Faculty Senate, is part of the process."[6]

I admit that my response to such willful inaccuracy was much tempered by consultation with staff and colleagues. Because of the rampant distortions in Schaefer's piece, I asked the *Enquirer* for an opportunity to respond, and they published my piece the following Sunday with the headline, "Faculty Integrally Involved in AAUP at UC, and in Contracts."

"It is untrue," I wrote, "that neither taxpayers nor the faculty are present at contract negotiations. UC faculty members form the AAUP-UC's negotiating team and always have, since 1975." I noted that I was a member of the 2007 team and that the negotiating team is supervised by a 13-member elected executive council made up entirely of UC faculty members. And, of course, everyone on both sides of the negotiating table are taxpayers, too. "And," I continued, "if anyone thinks the UC team does not represent the employer's interests strongly, then you have not faced them across a negotiating table."

It was also untrue to suggest that UC faculty do not approve the contracts. "All faculty members," I noted, "are routinely kept informed throughout the process by email and newsletter about the course and content of negotiations." When it seems we have reached what is the best deal possible, then we schedule meetings of faculty at all of UC's campuses to explain the contract and answer questions. Then, active UC-AAUP members vote on the contract. The current 2010–2013 contract had been approved by 87 percent of the voting members. "Only twice since 1975 has a contract been rejected and resulted in a strike, the last time being 18 years ago," I wrote.

"Contrary to the impression given by Schaefer," I continued, "the AAUP is a faculty-controlled and faculty-driven organization, both at the local and national levels." I emphasized that no one is "forced" to be a member, as Schaefer had stated. I explained that "fair share fees" are just nonmembers' fair share toward services and benefits they receive and are based on an annual audit by an independent auditing firm. Those nonmember fees cannot be used for any political issues.

Since 1975, I wrote, the AAUP at UC has contributed to exactly one political campaign, that of Gov. Ted Strickland in 2010. "This rare and exceptional action was taken because chapter members predicted back then how disastrous a Kasich administration would be for public education in Ohio, and it certainly seems that is being proven true." Shared governance is a key AAUP principle, and I pointed out the irony of Schaefer serving on a Faculty Senate that has real influence because that is guaranteed by Article 27 of the UC-AAUP contract. I concluded that the UC chapter's membership had grown by 24 percent in the past seven years, "in large part, we believe, because of this increased level of advocacy for preserving America's higher education system. We will continue to fight for these principles because it is what is best for Ohio's citizens."[7]

The column created a stir among the faculty. Not only did I hear personally from several faculty members, but I began to see the column tacked up on doors and bulletin boards. A senior faculty member in a science department, whom I had never met, sent me a very supportive note. Saying he was quite "incensed" by Schaefer's letter, which was "entirely misrepresentative of the collective bargaining process as it has worked at UC," he thanked me for writing my column. "I've always regarded [collective bargaining] as an open, non-coercive, and participatory process involving the faculty—members and nonmembers alike." In closing, the professor wrote, "I hope we can weather these difficult challenges and maintain the active role the faculty have had in contract negotiations as well as in shaping the broader mission of providing the best possible academic environment for our students."[8]

We had some good news about this time: a Quinnipiac poll reported on May 18 that if the referendum were held at that point, Senate Bill 5 would be heavily defeated. It is important to keep in mind that, despite the uproar that had occurred thus far, the public debate had not really begun in earnest yet. "The measure to strip many collective bargaining rights from state and local government workers," *The Columbus Dispatch* reported, "would be rejected by 18 points, 54 percent to 36 percent." In language that described what would, in fact, be close to the final result, the *Dispatch* noted that independent voters, crucial to the success of any statewide candidate or issue, opposed the controversial measure by 19 points and that it was losing by a large margin in nearly every region of Ohio. Central Ohio voters were turning thumbs down by a whopping 26 points. "Although it is a long way until November when opponents of SB 5 hope to ask voters to overturn it, at this point there is strong support for repealing Gov. (John) Kasich's signature plan," Peter Brown, assistant director of the Quinnipiac University Polling Institute, said in a news release.[9]

Though obviously we were encouraged by the poll, and would continue to be by subsequent polls over the coming months, we never allowed it to slacken our fervor in killing the legislation. Although perhaps we never said this in so many words, I think many of us believed, as I did, that the issues at stake were so important, not just to us but to the nation's future, that it was necessary to defeat Senate Bill 5 badly enough to send a message that this kind of attack on working people was really beyond the pale.

One sign of the collaborative nature of the fight against the bill was that we were contacted by some area public school teachers who wanted to know if they could help gather signatures with us at the university. I'd already seen crowds of public school teachers at intersections in the city and suburbs, waving signs of protest against SB 5, so I was happy to enlist their help. Some of them joined students and faculty at the main campus tables on McMicken Commons and in the Tangeman University Center, and some of them joined us at tables at my regional campus in suburban Blue Ash. Many of our students had been their students, and it was great to see the young people stopping to talk with their former high school teachers.

Our student activists were busy as well. The statewide organization began to create student press captains at each university to try to boost coverage of student opposition to Senate Bill 5. At Ohio State, students organized a rally with popular local bands and speakers—both politicians and union leaders—about SB 5. "Live Against 5," set for May 26 at the Columbus campus, was billed in a news release as "an open event for ALL Ohio State students, and all Ohioans who want to come out and have a great time for a great cause! And make sure to SIGN A PETITION!"

One newspaper that did some very fair reporting on the Senate Bill 5 battle was *The Toledo Blade*. On May 31, *The Blade* reported who was backing the pro-SB 5 movement. The paper announced the creation of a pro-SB 5 committee headed by Vaughn Flasher, a longtime statehouse lobbyist and Senate Republican political director. Flasher's reputation among Democrats as a dirty campaigner led us immediately to expect that we would face a barrage of misleading, underhanded, but hopefully ineffective campaign advertisements. Sen. Majority Leader Niehaus and House Speaker Batchelder, *The Blade* reported, were also expected to be on the committee. This group would eventually become known as Building a Better Ohio, which we promptly dubbed "Bitter Ohio."

Rebecca Heimlich, state director of the very conservative Americans for Prosperity, said—in classic double-speak—that her organization would be "working together but not technically together" with the pro-SB 5 forces. Americans for Prosperity was the Washington-based organization founded by the right-wing brothers Charles and David Koch to fund extremist causes like SB 5, corporate schools, and voter suppression laws. Heimlich said that the campaign was raising money in-state at this early point but would be happy to take checks from out-of-state sources. Because of new campaign finance laws, Americans for Prosperity would have to report expenditures during the campaign but not sources of revenue, which could remain secret.[10]

During this period of the signature gathering, we at the AAUP had a minor dustup, an incident in which a professor used his college—not university-wide—listserv to report that he and another faculty member would be in a particular hallway with signature booklets for the SB 5 referendum if anyone wished to come by to sign. A right-wing blogger got wind of this and organized phone calls to the UC administration with overblown concerns about "liberal" professors brainwashing students. The UC student newspaper, *The News-Record*, learned of the issue and gave us a call. I responded to James Sprague, an excellent student journalist, and tried to provide a commonsense perspective.

"We do not believe professors should use their positions to pressure students to take a particular political position in the classroom—that's contrary to AAUP principles," I wrote to Sprague. "But this announcement didn't do that; it made graduate students aware of a ballot petition and the opportunity to vote. Listservs are basically high-tech announcement boards. I think university students are smart and independent enough to ignore announcements if they're not interested, no matter who sends it to them." This had been an independent action by the faculty and not on the advice of the AAUP. But we encouraged faculty after this to not use college listservs, to avoid any misperceptions. My response seemed to resolve any issues locally. On right-wing blogs, however, the response was, "Professor McNay is being intellectually dishonest."[11]

In the midst of all this, like clockwork, we returned our first wave of signature booklets to the AAUP office, where they would be forwarded to We Are Ohio headquarters in Columbus. We then picked up new books that we would have for two weeks before we would have to turn those in again as well. Our goal was not to be concerned about whether the books were full or not but instead to keep a steady flow of valid signatures moving to Columbus, where an unofficial count would be kept so the campaign could measure our progress toward the more than 231,000 signatures we needed.

On June 17, the AAUP received great and surprising news from We Are Ohio. We carried the news in our chapter newsletter with a big headline: "SB 5 Repeal Signatures Hit Astounding Number: 714,137!" In the accompanying article, Dr. Herman and I focused on just what we had accomplished so far: "Since February of this year, the Chapter has been involved in political battles as never before in its history. Within weeks of taking office, Gov. Kasich introduced, with Ohio State Senator Shannon Jones, Senate Bill 5, legislation that declared all faculty 'managers' and stripped all other municipal and state employees of any real bargaining rights." We outlined how We Are Ohio had been formed as a great coalition among labor organizations, faith groups, and others who wanted to work together to defend the middle class in Ohio.

"The signature campaign has been successful beyond anyone's wildest imaginations just two months ago," we wrote. The Ohio AAUP had done its part and delivered more than the 10,000 signatures it had committed to the campaign (a large number, considering the collective size of our chapters across Ohio). In Cincinnati alone, AAUP staff trained 56 petition collectors: faculty members from UC and Cincinnati State, UC students, and community volunteers. "Team UC" had gathered a total of 2,298 signatures just from the UC campuses.

Although most faculty were about to break from their regular schedules for summer research and writing projects, working on developing new courses, attending conferences, or even getting some well-deserved rest, we urged them to stay engaged. "This summer we cannot rest . . . We cannot cede the summer to legislative activity that is, potentially, a grave danger to affordable, accessible education for Ohio students. Or which might strip us of our bargaining rights and eliminate the obligation to respond to open records requests at one or more of Ohio's public universities." Clearly, the extremist behavior of the Ohio legislature had us on guard. We warned our faculty: "This summer we must stand up. Stay tuned, watch your email, and be ready for action!"[12]

Now that Senate Bill 5 was definitely going to be on the ballot in November, Gov. Kasich and the Republicans, in desperation, tried another tactic. The Ohio Ballot Board, which arranges for the presentation of issues on the ballot on Election Day, was controlled by the GOP and was being pressured by Republicans to split the complex bill up into several separate ballots, with the hope that some individual issues would not be defeated. But Secretary of State Husted ruled that Senate Bill 5 could not be split up and had to be voted on in its entirety.[13]

As part of an ongoing research project on the career of George V. Allen, the American Ambassador to Iran from 1946 to 1947, I traveled to Washington DC and spent a couple of weeks at the National Archives and the Library of Congress in June. Ensconced in the archives, deep into the burgeoning Cold War in the 1940s, I was unable to attend the parade that was planned on June 29 to deliver our signature booklets to the Secretary of State's office in Columbus. I caught the stunning news on the internet.

"1,298,301 signatures," announced Melissa Fazekas, the spokeswoman for We Are Ohio. Led by a police escort with lights flashing, a parade of thousands of people—bagpipers, motorcyclists, a fire truck, church members, and large groups of union members—moved through downtown Columbus accompanying a semi truck loaded with petitions for delivery to the Ohio Secretary of State's office. Fun fact: the Secretary of State's office had to bring in a structural engineer to ensure their floor could hold the estimated 26 tons of petitions being dropped off by We Are Ohio. The office had 60 staff members waiting to process the petitions, which would soon be sent off to each of Ohio's 88 counties for each board of elections to validate the signatures.

Complete with overhead photographs of the huge crowd, *The Columbus Dispatch* headlined their story "SB 5 Opponents Make a Statement in a Big Way." As the story noted, "They dubbed it the 'million signature march' and then delivered, literally." The paper noted that the amount was equivalent to one out of six of Ohio's eight million voters. State Rep. Matt Szollosi (D-Oregon) marched in the parade and told the *Dispatch*: "From the standpoint of workers, Senate Bill 5 was a declaration of war. It's kind of hard to put the lava back in the volcano."[14]

"Record 1.3 Million Back Vote to Torpedo Senate Bill 5," reported *The Toledo Blade*, noting that it was the largest signature drive in Ohio history. "Politics are politics and [politicians] are going to do what they want to do. Fortunately, there's a checks-and-balances system to make sure that they do hear our voices," Mike Haynes, a member of the Toledo police, told *The Blade*.[15]

"We are public servants," said Mahoning County Sheriff's Sgt. T. J. Assion, president of the Fraternal Order of Police Lodge 141, who had marched with the parade. He told *The Youngstown Vindicator*, "We are public employees [and] the governor has trampled all over our rights—the governor and his cronies—with this new law commonly referred to as SB5. We've collected . . . over 1 million signatures on petitions, and it's time to turn those in and show the governor that he's not as popular as he thinks he is, he's not as smart as he thinks he is, and that he's dead wrong."[16]

Filing five times the number of required signatures needed seemed to ensure that even the most devious activities could not now prevent Senate Bill 5 from appearing on the November ballot for repeal. On July 21, Republican Secretary of State Jon Husted announced that our campaign had enough valid signatures, more than four times the necessary amount, to put SB 5 to the people for a vote. Of the signatures submitted, 915,456 were found to be valid, a nearly 70 percent rate, which is very good for such a signature campaign and evidence of the effectiveness of our planning and determination.

After We Are Ohio delivered the massive number of signatures, Sen. Shannon Jones, the Springboro Republican who had introduced the bill, said that she expected the voter referendum on the fall ballot. "If it is," she said in a statement reported by *The Cleveland Plain Dealer*, "I'm confident there will be a broad, grassroots campaign in support of the reasonable reforms we're asking of our public employees." Jones would be wrong, once again.[17]

Chapter 8

War on Many Fronts

It is not possible to really explain the crisis we faced in 2011 without noting that it was coming on multiple fronts. In addition to union busting, the conservatives in the legislature launched destructive initiatives in two other areas: voting rights and privatization of higher education. Not surprisingly, they were helped in these efforts by ALEC, the conservative legislative bill mill.[1]

One strategy introduced was to turn Ohio's universities into "charter" institutions by weakening their bonds to state oversight and state funding, in return for more autonomy. Throughout the struggle on this issue, we were baffled as to why—given the demonstrated failure of charter schools in elementary and secondary education—lawmakers would want to undermine our public universities as well.

The first word that we had about charter universities came to us with a thunderclap in an excellent piece in *The Cincinnati Enquirer* on February 24, 2011. "Ohio Gov. John Kasich is promoting a plan for 'charter universities' that would exempt colleges from multiple state regulations as long as they meet certain conditions, while continuing to receive taxpayer money," the *Enquirer* reported. The newspaper had talked to David Creamer, vice president for finance and business services at Miami University, who told them that Kasich had not yet formally proposed the restructuring plan. But he said that relief from regulatory burdens would help colleges control costs. "In trying to make sure things don't get mishandled, we create a lot of red tape," he said. "That's a decision every institution would have to make, whether the tradeoffs are worth it."[2]

But the best part came from a letter, obtained by the *Enquirer*, that UC President Gregory Williams had written to Kasich. In the letter to

Kasich, Williams listed several other areas where "charter universities" could be relieved of administrative burdens, including civil service, purchasing, state budget regulations, and "collective bargaining." Williams also asked Kasich to consider further reforms, including allowing universities to self-insure or purchase their own workers' compensation insurance; allowing universities to directly acquire land through eminent domain; limiting required responses to public records requests; and reducing reports to the Board of Regents.

To be fair to Williams, we subsequently learned that these were not exactly his personal requests. But perhaps even worse was that all of the state's university presidents, acting together through the Inter-University Council and its Kasich-appointed director Bruce Johnson, had put together this laundry list of issues, including their desire to undermine their faculty unions. The letter was evidence that Williams was, to a great extent, joining with the other presidents on the Inter-University Council in this attack on the faculty.

Each of these issues individually is controversial and bad policy. The desire, for example, to allow universities to refuse to respond to public record requests creates pockets of secrecy where corruption can thrive. Although university presidents tend to buy into the mythology that they are CEOs of corporate entities, they are not. They are managers of public institutions, and thus their records and operations are and should remain a matter of public record. Similarly, too many university presidents become focused on being real estate managers or behaving like the owners or managers of semi-pro athletic teams, and spend a disproportionate time away from the central and most important reason for the university's existence—its instructional and research mission.

But that Williams, in a private letter to the state's right-wing governor, would suggest that he wanted relief from his collective bargaining obligations came as a blow to the faculty at UC. We struggled with this issue in the months ahead. Knowing the likelihood that Kasich would punish any president and university who did not support his initiatives, some faculty members were willing to give Williams a pass on this letter. This position has some added legitimacy, given the fact that Williams subsequently issued a couple of heavily nuanced letters trying to soften his position in the weeks afterward, including one to the Faculty Senate cabinet.

The popular Ohio political blog Plunderbund seemed to echo faculty sentiments in a commentary headlined, "Because Charter Schools Worked Out So Well, Kasich Says, 'Let's Try Charter Universities.'" Plunderbund went on to opine, "Yep, yet another group that Kasich is thinking he needs to give them 'flexibility' from public accountability regulations because of the massive cuts Kasich is planning to make. Yep, austere times [are] *precisely* when we should get rid of our fiscal safeguards, right folks."[3]

Triggering the push for charter universities was the selection of Jim Petro, a former Republican attorney general, as chancellor of the Ohio Board of Regents. Charter universities "need to be examined carefully," Petro told the *Akron Beacon Journal* on March 2, 2011. He told the newspaper that he was not certain exactly what such an institution would look like, but "we have to look at best practices, what has worked elsewhere, how we can redesign it."

University of Akron President Luis Proenza was enthusiastic about the possibilities, the newspaper reported, adding that the state's controlling board had stopped Proenza's plans to buy two properties for future development in February 2011 on the grounds that money was tight. That kind of rebuff could be a thing of the past, the newspaper noted—but the report did not observe that perhaps the university ought to stick to the business of providing an affordable and quality education rather than operating like a property development company. "I would find it extremely valuable from a number of perspectives," Proenza said. "Many regulations add 10 to 20 percent to the cost of doing business. Program approvals sometimes take months or a year or more. Sign me up."[4]

At Kent State, the *Beacon Journal* reported, President Lester Lefton seemed cautiously optimistic about whether charter universities could work in Ohio's second-largest campus system. KSU "is supportive of the notion of charter status to universities that meet certain criteria or make progress toward accountability, accessibility and financial stability," Lefton said in an email. The "freedom from many state regulatory ordinances" would allow KSU to operate more efficiently, the newspaper reported. The paper also observed that in 2010 then-Chancellor Fingerhut had rejected KSU's plan to raise student fees to fund $250 million in renovations to the Kent campus. In theory, "that obstacle would be history if KSU had more autonomy."[5]

Petro was fond of implying that wonderful things would happen if government just got out of the way of public universities. Petro, who first raised the idea of creating charter universities in 2005, confessed to *The Columbus Dispatch* that, while not knowing yet what such a school would be like, he was certain something needed to be done so that Ohio's state schools could cut costs and spend money more efficiently. "If we free our schools from these constraints, we can build the reputation of our system, increase access to Ohioans and begin to draw the best and brightest students from across the country," Petro told the *Dispatch*, repeating the frequent conservative error of overestimating cost savings produced by deregulation.[6]

The canard of "flexibility" was effectively destroyed by Sara Kilpatrick in a powerful column in *The Columbus Dispatch* on March 12, 2011. "This is not an accurate portrayal of the potentially dramatic and dangerous turn the charter university idea would be for Ohio's citizens," Kilpatrick wrote. "Rather, it would be another taxpayer-funded privatization scheme that will ultimately hurt Ohio's students and future economic growth." For generations, Kilpatrick argued, Ohio's taxpayers and elected officials have made a commitment to providing a high-quality, affordable, and accessible public-college education to the next generation. "In fact," Kilpatrick observed, "our current governor and at least 82 out of the 132 members of the 129th General Assembly have enjoyed the benefits of an Ohio public-university education." But now, "under the pretext of the state's current fiscal crisis, flexibility and a private-sector-knows-best attitude, Republican leadership wants to abandon this commitment and dismantle Ohio's public university system," Kilpatrick observed.[7]

Kilpatrick went on to note that Virginia Tech had recently become a charter university in that state and had seen tuition rise 24 percent in one year. But Kilpatrick said that the problem was greater than the harsh impact on students—though that was very serious. It would also mean a lack of accountability and oversight. "Taxpayer dollars would be spent, yet taxpayers would have no means of holding these institutions accountable," Kilpatrick wrote, since the universities could easily conceal their operations. "Our public colleges would become for-profit business instruments rather than a public investment in all Ohioans' educational attainment and prosperity."[8]

Further, she noted, given the revelations in Cincinnati and elsewhere, "charter universities would serve as another union-busting tool against unionized faculty and staff on campuses. This will mean far fewer people will have the ability to speak up if they see corruption or theft of taxpayer money." The real problem, she observed, with Ohio's public university system was not collective bargaining or a lack of flexibility—it was that "too much money is spent on unnecessary administration. Even conservative think tanks like the Goldwater Institute have found that 'administrative bloat' is the largest factor behind rising tuition costs and waste in higher education." Kilpatrick concluded that "Kasich, Petro, Johnson and our university presidents cannot successfully provide solutions when they keep misidentifying the problems. Ultimately, Ohio's students will suffer from these misguided policies."

Gov. Kasich didn't waste much time in presenting his radical budget. A bizarre aspect to the announced budget was the way that Kasich intended to take presentation of the budget out of the hands of journalists. Rather than announcing the budget at a press conference and answering questions, "Kasich is spending about $5,000 to rent the 900-seat [Capitol Theater] for an 'Ohio Town-Hall Meeting' tonight and broadcasting on satellite television and the Web," Bloomberg news reported. Asked in an interview the week before why he had decided to announce the budget in the theater, Kasich replied, "I thought it was a cool idea. We want to explain it all to people."[9]

Kasich's budget was a complex package of gifts to the governor's political allies. Every pet Republican project was represented in some way. Inaccurately called by Kasich "The Jobs Budget," the budget in fact promised to undermine employment in the state by eliminating public sector jobs and the service infrastructure that support private sector employment. The budget proposed to sell five state prisons, privatize the Ohio Turnpike, eliminate seniority for teachers, and slash local government funding by 49 percent. For local schools, K–12 funding would be cut 11.5 percent in 2012 and another 4.9 percent in 2013, but Kasich would also expand the opportunities for vouchers that would further undermine low-income schools. For higher education, Kasich proposed at least a 10.5 percent cut in 2012. And for faculty in the State Teachers Retirement System, a 4 percent increase in the employee's contribution was planned.[10]

"This budget is woven with one reform after another. It is, I would guess, the most reform-oriented budget in modern Ohio history," Kasich said, using "reform" where the words "cut" or "elimination" should more accurately be used. The budget immediately had many critics: "This is a shell game which will bring upon local governments and towns the most devastating tax increases or job cuts that they've ever faced. It's an assault on teachers, police, firefighters, librarians and even your local school cafeteria worker," said Brian Rothenberg of Progress Ohio, a left-leaning organization.[11]

Buried deep in the budget was language addressing the creation of charter universities:

> The Chancellor of the Ohio Board of Regents will submit a report to the General Assembly and the governor containing findings and recommendations for developing the appropriate policy, administrative rule

> and statutory changes necessary to implement a charter university program. The plan will define the manner in which an institution of higher learning can receive increased freedom from state regulations in return for less dependency on state financial subsidies. Universities' eligibility will be determined by certain performance measures determined by the chancellor.[12]

In their analysis of the situation, the Ohio Conference AAUP communications committee of Marty Kich, Dave Witt, and Steve Aby observed that the specifics of what the concept of a "charter university" meant were absent from the budget bill. Instead, the budget legislation empowered Chancellor Jim Petro to define it, and then submit it to the legislature for final enabling legislation. However, Governor Kasich and Inter-University Council President Bruce Johnson had already suggested that many items could be connected to "charter universities." These possibilities included limiting or completely eliminating collective bargaining rights for some or all campus employee groups; little or no oversight by the board of regents with regard to local administration decisions; and allowing university administrations to avoid compliance with Ohio's open records laws. It would be our job to continue to monitor the plans for charter universities as they unfolded.[13]

On March 22, Jim Petro, as the newly nominated Ohio chancellor of the Board of Regents, testified before the House Financial and Appropriations Committee.[14] For someone who had advocated for charter universities for years, he was remarkably nonforthcoming during the testimony, which suggested to faculty members across Ohio that perhaps the plans were still being put together and that we still had an opportunity to influence them. "I really don't know" was a common Petro response to questioning. We joked that we could probably make this into a tag line in our campaign against the privatization of our universities. "They really don't know what they are doing" would be one version.

We were impressed by some of the representatives' questions, which revealed that legislators had been reading the letters faculty across the state had been publishing in newspapers and had paid attention to testimony that Sara Kilpatrick had given on the charter concept as well as to a publication we had circulated, entitled "Looking for Savings in All the Wrong Places." Rep. Denise Driehaus (D-Cincinnati) particularly pressed Petro about the role of the faculty in the planning for charter universities. Was he meeting with faculty? Petro avoided answering the question for quite a while but eventually said he would be willing to sit down with a group of faculty and talk about the concept. Of course, he never actually arranged to do this.

In a discussion on April 4, faculty members gathered a better idea what the process would be for creating "charter" universities. We feared that somehow Kasich would insist that the charter legislation would be wedged into the budget bill or simply imposed through some administrative process, since our presidents unfortunately seemed in favor. But it became clear in a meeting of the House Subcommittee on Higher Education that legislation would be required. Subcommittee Chair Randy Gardner (R-Bowling Green) noted that the budget bill required Chancellor Petro to announce the plan by Aug. 15 and that the legislature should implement it on July 1. Gardner asked whether the chancellor had authority to implement it or whether the legislature would need to pass legislation. "I believe it is intended," Petro said, "and it would be my intent, to come back to the General Assembly for adoption of legislation that would specifically create the category of 'charter university.'" Petro also noted that they were now calling it a plan for "entrepreneurial universities"—obviously an effort to escape the negative connotation of the widespread failure of charter schools.[15]

On April 7, Sara Kilpatrick was able to testify for the AAUP before the House Finance Subcommittee on Higher Education. After explaining the prominent and historic role of the AAUP in higher education, she went on to describe the charter university proposal in the budget bill. "Proponents of charter universities describe the idea as a simple one," she said. Public universities would receive less money in state subsidies in return for less state government regulation. This "flexibility" would then supposedly lead to cures for all of higher education's ills. "Beyond this vague description," she said, "different parties continue to describe the concept of charter universities in different ways—so at this point, the legislature is being asked to endorse a general concept without knowing exactly what it means."

Kilpatrick continued her testimony: "If we look at past comments on what 'charter university' means," it becomes clear that "the idea would undermine the whole concept of *public* universities—and instead make them semi-private institutions that still take taxpayer monies, but have little or no accountability to the public." Such a drastic change would ultimately hurt Ohio's students and undermine future economic growth, she said.

Kilpatrick argued that for generations Ohioans have made significant investments in the state's public universities. "Now," she said, "under the pretext of the state's current revenue crisis and the purported need for 'flexibility,' the governor is proposing that we all abandon this commitment and, in quite real terms, begin the process of dismantling Ohio's public university system."

She argued that it is possible to look around the country for evidence of the damage that a move to such privatization has done. In Virginia, for example, she noted Virginia Commonwealth University's sharp increases and that the University of Virginia had increased its tuition by 50.5 percent over the last five years.

In Ohio, Kilpatrick argued, the charter university strategy "would make it even more difficult than it has already become for the average Ohio family to send their children to college." Students would either choose not to attend college or would graduate with a huge amount of debt—both of which would equate to less spending potential in Ohio's future. Further, the high cost would serve as a bar to adults who wish to return to college to upgrade their skills and compete in new industries.

Kilpatrick went on to comment on another element extolled by the "charter university" proponents—the abandonment of open records rules and much of the reporting required to bodies such as the Ohio Board of Regents. "This inevitably means a lack of accountability and oversight," Kilpatrick noted. Taxpayer dollars would be spent, yet taxpayers would have no means of holding these institutions accountable, because citizens and the news media would have no means by which to shed light on decisions about how taxpayer money would be spent—and who was really making those decisions and benefiting from them. "Cronyism, favoritism, nepotism, and in some cases even corruption," Kilpatrick said, "all are likely to creep back into our university system when no one has the right to ask questions and examine documents." The call from charter proponents to not have to do competitive bidding for construction projects could generate many of the same problems, she said.

Kilpatrick said that various press organizations had reported that proponents of "charter universities" also clearly see them as union-free zones. She acknowledged that was at least consistent with charter university strategy to prevent any questioning of their decisions, since unions are often among the most vocal on-campus critics of administrative financial decisions and priorities. "Without unions and without open records law requirements, who will be left to safeguard the taxpayers' money?" Kilpatrick asked.

Kilpatrick also noted that since there is a national market for university professors—perhaps the most mobile members of the American workforce—this continual attack on faculty collective bargaining might mean Ohio would lose some of its best and brightest professors. "AAUP contracts have been, for decades," Kilpatrick said, "one of the only mechanisms by which faculty can fight to ensure that salaries and benefits keep pace with national markets." Without the contracts, it would be all too easy for "administrations to continue to redirect funds toward ever-expanding administration apparatus and administrator salaries," she said, and as a result, "we will not be giving our students the best education possible."

"The real problem with Ohio's public university system," Kilpatrick emphasized, "is not a lack of flexibility or collective bargaining" but that "it is woefully underfunded by the state." And of the funds the system receives, "too much money is spent on unnecessary administration." Kilpatrick said in conclusion, "The charter university idea is at best a Pandora's Box that the legislature is being asked to endorse, with details to come later. At worst, it is the first step toward semi-privatization of one of Ohio's most precious public assets and a betrayal of this generation's access to an affordable college education—something that previous generations were able to count on."

The AAUP expected legislation to be proposed rapidly on the charter university idea. Being bad and destructive policy had not stopped Senate Bill 5 from being quickly adopted, but this time it appeared that a number of stakeholders—namely the university presidents—were uncertain about the ramifications of the plan. As a result, public discussion of the concept declined sharply. But we could not sit back thinking that saner heads would prevail. It was necessary for us to keep pounding home to the public what the privatization of their university system would mean to them.

"The problem with all this optimism about deregulation and freeing the creativity of charter universities," I wrote in a column that appeared in the Hamilton *Journal-News*, "is that the legislature is being asked to sign off on a Trojan horse right now, as part of the budget bill, without any concrete explanation as to what these charter universities would mean for Ohio or its citizens."[16] I expressed great concern that the proponents of the concept were asking us to hold off on criticism until they introduced the plan, which they expected to do in mid-August. But then they wanted to pass legislation rapidly so that the new concept could be actually implemented in July 2012.

"Exactly when is a public debate supposed to take place?" I asked. "We have to make our voices heard now," I insisted, "not wait until the end of the summer when the legislature will likely be trying to railroad through a proposal." I was particularly critical of the way the Republican legislature seemed determined to impose this radical legislation without consulting with faculty or students about the dramatic change.

I recounted some of what we knew about charter experiments in other states. It was not comforting. In Virginia, the often-touted example of charter success, the University of Virginia had just announced an 8.9 percent tuition hike, this after increases of more than 50 percent already imposed since 2006. The College of William and Mary was not far behind, having announced a 7.7 percent hike in 2011.

In the state of Washington, where Gov. Christine Gregoire had been touting a similar charter university model, I warned that the universities might be seeking as much as a 16 percent hike in each of the next two years. In Texas, tuition has increased by an astonishing 63 percent since the state universities were deregulated in 2003. The Texas legislature has been so alarmed at the trend that it is trying to re-regulate the state universities to rein in these runaway tuition increases.[17]

The problem extends beyond just high tuition for the state's residents, I explained. Universities have begun to pursue the more lucrative out-of-state residents who pay a much higher cost for their education without claim on the state subsidy. Out-of-state students and foreign students must pay much more for tuition, and so places that might have been reserved for in-state residents are increasingly reserved for those who come from outside the home state. "Abandoned, financially and otherwise, by state legislatures, entrepreneurial universities must inevitably chase cash that out-of-state students bring," I wrote, but meanwhile "soaring tuition costs create an ever-increasing obstacle to the state's own residents who wish to attend their so-called state 'public' university."

One of the principles that the AAUP most enthusiastically supports is the idea of shared governance. There was a fine example of shared governance at its best at the University of Cincinnati during the struggle over the charter university model. Faculty Senate Chair Dr. Richard Harknett, associate professor of political science, in collaboration with the Faculty Senate Cabinet created a committee, chaired by Dr. Frank Wray, a professor of biology, to examine the implications of the charter university concept. The committee was called the DAIR Committee, short for Deregulation, Autonomy, and Internal Restructuring. I must emphasize the independence of this faculty investigation. Dr. Harknett worked diligently to isolate the task force from influence either from the AAUP or from the administration, although both were encouraged to provide the task force with information. Like the administration, AAUP representatives provided a good deal of documentation to the task force, but its independence was jealously guarded.

Naturally, I was somewhat concerned about this process. My AAUP colleagues and I had examined the charter university concept thoroughly and were certain it would have a damaging impact on our institution. But I was well aware of the possibility that another given group of professors might come to a different or more complicated conclusion. Then we would be in the difficult situation of being on different sides of the issue, and it was hard to understand how that could contribute to a positive outcome. In the end, we just had to be confident that a group of intelligent people looking at the same evidence with the best interests of the university at stake would come to the same conclusion that we had.

One of the most valuable initiatives that we launched was in collaboration with students at UC. Because the huge hikes in tuition connected to the charter concept are likely to punish students and their families above all, we developed a series of videos that circulated widely on YouTube. Staff member Eric Palmer worked on the videos featuring UC students. Common themes were the importance of their university education, their attachment to UC, and their desire not to be driven away from college by exploding tuition costs. One particularly effective video had the theme of musical chairs: as the state continually cuts funding and hikes tuition, some students would be left without seats.[18]

We were contacted by students at Miami University who, like students all over the state, were doing what they could to preserve their university as a truly public institution. The Miami students had a meeting with their university president, David C. Hodge, to address their concerns about the charter concept. They wanted someone from the AAUP to be with them. Their experience was not unlike those of other students trying to generate a dialogue with their administrations. Too often, administrators talk down to students and suggest they do not know what they are talking about. To prevent this, the Miami students wanted someone from AAUP to back them up. I happily agreed to join them. It is worth noting that the faculty members at Miami are not unionized. Shared governance is undermined by a University Senate made up of administrators, staff, and faculty, a situation that effectively muffles and dilutes the voice of the faculty. So it is no surprise that the students looked to the AAUP for assistance.[19]

Over about a three-month period, I twice went with the Miami students to visit President Hodge. They were positive and productive meetings. The first meeting was a bit tense, the second more comfortable. The presence of an AAUP president did raise some eyebrows on my first visit. But on both occasions the students were clear and assertive in arguing that they feared damage would be done by converting to a charter university. The real difference in the two meetings was that the university presidents had actually seen the charter plan by the second visit. Most of the presidents became less enthusiastic when they realized how much money they would lose from the state and how little they would gain from so-called "flexibility."

Finally, in August, Chancellor Petro came out with the report on what he now preferred to call the "entrepreneurial" university concept. Although the plan was introduced with fanfare, there were also voices of concern. The universities favored relief from bureaucratic government mandates, said Bruce Johnson of the Inter-University Council, "but we think the state needs to invest more, not less, in higher education." He speculated that easing of regulations could create savings but asserted that the money should then be plowed back into the university system and not spent elsewhere.[20]

As proposed, the plan included all the issues that we had been concerned about. Boards of Trustees would be able to have secret meetings with internal auditors behind closed doors, buy and sell property with less state oversight, and set tuition based on the cost of an academic program. On our state conference website, the Ohio AAUP announced our continued opposition: "Don't let the names fool you. Regardless of what they are called, charter universities undermine the whole concept of public universities and instead make them semi-private institutions that still take taxpayer monies but have little or no accountability to the public. This is an approach that will ultimately hurt Ohio's students and future economic growth."[21]

There ensued a good deal of silence on the side of state officials. In order to accomplish this major change, some legislator was going to have to step up and sponsor the bill. Given the turmoil already surrounding the Senate Bill 5 fight, the now-lukewarm support of the university presidents, and the widespread criticism of the plan by faculty and students, it appeared that no legislator wanted to touch this hot issue.

In early September, the UC-AAUP leadership began to hear some rumors that the DAIR committee was heading toward the same conclusions we had about the damage possible from the charter idea. But we could not be sure that was the case until the report was formally presented at the All-University Faculty Meeting on September 27. With President Williams and our board of trustees in attendance,

DAIR Committee representatives reported their findings. Though couched in diplomatic language, the conclusions were clear:

> To summarize, the consensus of our committee is that the Enterprise University plan, as currently presented in the Chancellor's initial report, would not produce a net benefit to UC or its stakeholders. While the committee finds several of the ideas in the report conceptually appealing, including the desire to unburden universities from costly regulations as a means to make the universities more cost efficient, and the effort to enhance the universities' role in workforce development, the Enterprise University plan, as currently proposed, is unlikely to produce actual savings that could enhance academic programming or affordability for students. In fact, it likely will lead to higher tuition.[22]

At the AAUP, we, of course, read this with delight. This report became an important tool in the months ahead. The well-researched and well-reasoned 25-page report did more than just dismantle the argument for the charter university concept. Entitled "UC: An Ohio Preeminent 21st Century Public University," the report also emphasized the strength and value of the University of Cincinnati as a truly public university and worked to present the university's assets in such a way as to make a strong argument for special attention from the legislature. In the months ahead, Senate Chair Harknett had the opportunity to put the report in the hands of the chancellor and legislators. This was not, after all, a report coming from the faculty union, which would have been easily dismissed by Gov. Kasich and his allies; it was from the representative body of all the faculty at the state's second-largest university.

In the months ahead, we kept pursuing the argument, but we heard nothing from the advocates of the charter university concept. As of this writing, the idea seems to have been abandoned by the administration while they pursue other objectives. In the spring of 2012, several Ohio newspapers ran stories that the idea was "stalled."

The Cleveland Plain Dealer explained on April 22, 2012, how several issues had sidetracked the attack on the universities represented by the charter concept. First, when initially developed, the proposal had a system of tiers. Naturally, Ohio State was the top tier, given the enormous influence of OSU President Gordon Gee. Other university presidents were unhappy with having OSU, with its size and resources, appear to be driving the concept in a way that would provide it with financial advantages. Further, all the presidents were unhappy with giving up money in return for "freedom," and thus none of their area legislators would support the legislation.

Finally, many legislators did not want to give up control over tuition increases. Nevertheless, Sloan Spaulding, general counsel for the Board of Regents, told the *Plain Dealer* that the charter university plan might reappear in a very different form in the future, perhaps in Gov. Kasich's next budget.[23]

It would be unfortunate if the charter concept reappears. The concept is no answer to the widespread problem of administrative bloat and diversion of funds away from basic education and research missions. Semi-privatization is not a solution to misplaced priorities. A re-examination of our corporate tax policies and tax policies for the very wealthiest Ohioans in addition to a real jobs creation plan are what are needed from the governor and the legislature. As of this writing, the Ohio legislature is, astoundingly, once again considering another large cut to the income tax that will represent yet another windfall to the wealthy and further cuts to public education. Ohio must establish a reasonable tax policy that requires corporations and individuals who've benefited so tremendously from the boom years of the economy to pay their fair share and to help invest in the future so Ohio and the United States can continue to be the places of opportunity they have always been.

CHAPTER 9

DEMOCRACY UNDER ASSAULT

While faculty across Ohio were trying to fend off the charter university initiative, the Republican legislature launched an attack on yet another front. This time the target was the people's right to vote—confirmation that there were few ideas so bad that the Republicans in the Ohio legislature would not embrace them.

The Republicans passed several bills in 2011 that were designed to suppress the vote under the guise of eliminating fraud that did not exist. Chief among these was House Bill 194, introduced on April 12, 2011, which was a sweeping assault on voting rights. So seriously did we take this threat that progressive groups in Ohio created a new coalition, Fair Elections Ohio, to launch yet another petition drive. This drive would put HB 194 on the ballot to repeal, just like Senate Bill 5. The long and bitter struggle to defend voting rights in Ohio would carry on right through the 2012 election, as Republican Secretary of State Jon Husted gained a reputation for being the "Secretary of Suppression" because of his untiring efforts to suppress the vote in our presidential battleground state.[1]

Senate Bill 5 was, then, not just a one-dimensional fight to defend collective bargaining but a major battle in a war launched by right-wing ideologues to create a state as the chamber of commerce or multinational corporations would wish to have it.

Veteran House Republicans and ALEC members Rep. Louis Blessing and Rep. Robert Mecklenborg, both of the Cincinnati area, were the cosponsors of House Bill 194, which became popularly known as the "voter suppression act." Readers will already know Rep. Blessing as one of the chief proponents of Senate Bill 5. Perhaps there is a certain consistency between trying to deny Ohioans their right to organize as well as their right to vote.

House Bill 194 was a sweeping reduction in the opportunity of Ohioans to vote. It would have cut early voting from 35 days before the election to 21 by mail and 17 in person. Most seriously, it also limited in-person voting before the election by barring it on Saturday afternoons, Sundays, and the three days before the election—the times most people tend to vote early.

A little background is useful to understand why Ohio had expanded the opportunities to vote after the 2004 election and just how ruthless was the attempt by the Ohio Republicans in 2011 to limit those opportunities. The expanded voting in Ohio was created specifically to address the rampant problems of the 2004 presidential election. George W. Bush won the state narrowly in an election filled with delays, extraordinarily long lines, and irregularities—many of which are directly traceable to the biased actions of Republican Ken Blackwell, who was then both Secretary of State in charge of the election and the head of the Bush-Cheney campaign in Ohio. Drawing on a detailed congressional report titled *Preserving Democracy: What Went Wrong In Ohio*, Mark Crispin of *Harper's Magazine* did a careful evaluation of the 2004 election in the Buckeye State.[2] Every Ohioan should own a copy of the report and commit to memory the offenses to fair elections committed in 2004. Too detailed to cover extensively here, a few excerpts from Crispin's article make clear the scale of the problems generated by the Republicans in that election:

> On September 7, based on an overzealous reading of an obscure state bylaw, [Blackwell] ordered county boards of elections to reject all Ohio voter-registration forms not "printed on white, uncoated paper of not less than 80 lb. text weight." Under public pressure he reversed the order three weeks later, by which time unknown numbers of Ohioans had been disenfranchised.

Blackwell also targeted provisional ballots:

> The Help America Vote Act—passed in 2002 to address some of the problems of the 2000 election—prevents election officials from deciding at the polls who will be permitted to cast provisional ballots, as earlier Ohio law had permitted. On September 16, Blackwell issued a directive that somehow failed to note that change. A federal judge ordered him to revise the language, Blackwell resisted, and the court was forced to draft its own version of the directive, which it ordered

Blackwell to accept, even as it noted Blackwell's "vigorous, indeed, at times, obdurate opposition" to compliance with the law.

Further, Crispin argues that the required recount of Ohio did not really take place because there so many irregularities in so many counties, including the suburban Cincinnati GOP stronghold of Warren County:

> Blackwell did manage to ban reporters from a post-election ballot-counting site in Warren County because—election officials claimed—the FBI had warned of an impending terrorist attack there. The FBI said it issued no such warning, however, and the officials refused to name the agent who alerted them. Moreover, as the *Cincinnati Enquirer* later reported, email correspondence between election officials and the county's building services director indicated that lockdown plans—"down to the wording of the signs that would be posted on the locked doors"—had been in the works for at least a week. Beyond suggesting that officials had something to hide, the ban was also, according to the report, a violation of Ohio law and the Fourteenth Amendment.

In response to the embarrassing debacle that was the 2004 election in Ohio, the state legislature in 2005 passed laws dramatically expanding early voting opportunities. Republicans were firmly behind enhancing the opportunity to vote—until the election of Barack Obama in 2008. Obama carried the Democratic centers in northern Ohio, and he also won Columbus. But a key to the victory was that, for the first time since the election of Lyndon Johnson in 1964, the Democratic presidential candidate won Hamilton County, where Cincinnati is located. And Obama won the usually Republican county by a good margin, 53 percent to 46 percent (a margin that he repeated in 2012).

The Republican voter suppression effort is rooted in the fact that, with high registration and turnout, the Republican Party is likely to lose statewide elections in Ohio. This was the lesson the Republicans learned in 2008, and it caused the GOP to go from support of expansion of voting access to restrictions on voting access. House Bill 194 was one of many bills that appeared in 2011 and 2012, not just in Ohio but across the country. The bills are linked to model legislation promoted by ALEC.[3]

House Bill 194 was adopted by the Republicans on May 18, 2011, by a strict party-line vote after a vigorous debate. The bill was introduced by Blessing, and Mecklenborg led the charge as chair of the

Committee on State Government. Mecklenborg argued that there was nothing new in House Bill 194 and that the issues it covered had been "vetted" thoroughly. Rep. Ron Gerberry (D-Austintown) then rose to attempt to amend the bill. He noted that the new bill would make the provisional ballot form more complicated, since it would now be necessary to complete five places on a ballot rather than two, and he wanted to amend the bill to say that the information provided would be used only to identify the voter and not to invalidate the ballot if a mistake was made on the form.[4]

"We were told today that we were going to hear a lot of mistruths," Gerberry said, adding, "Well, we started right out of the gate" referring to Mecklenborg's comments. Gerberry denied that there had been an open process for House Bill 194, remarking, "There is a difference between 'listening' and 'hearing.'" He noted that the day before, the committee had received 19 amendments to the bill that "we [the minority] didn't know anything about." The previous week, he noted, the Democrats had brought forward 21 amendments that "we felt were very, very important" and discussed them openly with their Republican colleagues. They were all rejected. The Democrats had offered seven or eight more amendments the day before the vote; "All of them were dismissed," he said. "Now we will be criticized for standing on the floor and saying what this bill really does."

"I find it ironic," Gerberry said, "how the United States is so proud of its involvement in the building of democracies across the globe and how we stood proudly when we saw the Iraqis vote, but here in Ohio we are about to pass legislation that will make it more difficult to vote, will discourage people from voting." He ridiculed the Republican use of the term "reform": election reform, he argued, should make voting easier.

"What HB 194 says is that we want more participation, but only from certain people," Gerberry said, referring to the fact that the restricted voting hours would reduce voting among traditionally Democratic voters—the elderly, the poor, and working people. "This bill is not about making it easier to vote," he said, "but about finding ways to throw out ballots, lengthen voting lines in our urban centers, and further complicate the right to vote." Now, he said, the legislature was creating a situation in which "if every voter does not cross their T's and dot their I's on the ballot, 'We gotcha!' because your vote won't be counted." Warning that this bill would likely lead to the same kind of election fiasco that Ohio had gone through in 2004, Gerberry concluded that he asked for the acceptance of his amendment and the defeat of House Bill 194.

Mecklenborg countered that some Democratic ideas had been put into the bill, and he argued against Gerberry's amendment because it linked voting and registration. Part of the Republican bill would eliminate "Golden Week," that period in which voters can register and vote at the same time. Mecklenborg and other Republicans were strongly opposed to same-day registration and voting.

Rep. Ted Celeste (D-Grandview Heights) spoke next about what he called "the voter disenfranchisement bill," a bill in sharp contrast with legislation considered earlier in the legislative session that sought to make business regulations and rules more simple and to promote common sense. A brother of former Democratic Ohio Gov. Richard Celeste, Rep. Celeste criticized one of the more ridiculous requirements of the bill, which said that poll workers did not need to provide help to voters at the polls. Imagine a business, he said with bewilderment, where employees were ordered not to help the customers. With all the talk from Republicans that government should be more like business, he said, this was an "amazing contradiction. That's not like business."

Rep. Matt Huffman (R-Lima), an ALEC Civil Justice Task Force member, introduced the thoroughly discredited arguments about voter fraud. As is true elsewhere in the country, voter fraud is not a problem in Ohio. Nevertheless, Huffman argued that the bill was designed to eliminate fraud that "occurred particularly in the election of 2008 that we know about"—of course, referencing President Barack Obama's historic victory in Ohio. He also said that the amendment contained language that would allow Ohioans to vote anywhere in Ohio, not just in their precinct. On this basis, Huffman urged a no vote on the amendment.

While trying to discount the criticism of the amendment, Gerberry and Rep. Michael Stinziano (D-Columbus) denied that the bill established same-day registration. "Well, it doesn't matter," Gerberry said in exasperation, "You're going to table it anyway." Sure enough, Speaker Batchelder soon called for a vote, and the amendment was defeated, 54–38.

Rep. Kathleen Clyde (D-Kent) introduced another amendment. "Let's call this bill what it really is," Clyde said, "voter suppression." Election reform, she said, should be a careful deliberative process with input from both sides of the aisle, and any election should be about the issues and the strongest candidate winning "with as many people participating in their government as possible."

But House Bill 194 "seeks to accomplish just the opposite," Clyde said. It changed the "rules of the game" to especially hurt certain groups of voters: elderly voters, urban voters, low-income voters, young voters. "That's voter suppression," Clyde emphasized. The bill was especially disturbing, she said, for two reasons. First, it obviously makes it harder for Ohioans to exercise their fundamental right to vote, by reducing the number of days one can vote early in-person from 35 to as few as 6. And eliminating the three days before Election Day is especially bad because they have been the biggest days for early voting. She also criticized the aggressive stripping of voters from the voter rolls. "Is it more important that we have a squeaky clean database or that we defend the fundamental right to vote," she asked?

The second major problem with the bill, Clyde pointed out, is that fewer votes will be counted because HB 194 purposely puts obstacles in the way of voters. It eliminates the requirement that poll workers direct voters to their correct precinct, and it makes the provisional ballot form more complicated, thus increasing the possibility of mistakes that would disqualify the vote. Moreover, poll workers would be prohibited from assisting with filling out the form unless voters could prove they are disabled. "I shudder at the thought of this provision," Clyde said shaking her head, adding the question: "Will there be literacy tests on hand?" She was referring to the racist Jim Crow laws used in the South during the segregation era to deny African Americans the right to vote.

"In the spirit of compromise, even though that has been totally missing from this process," Clyde proposed an amendment to expand in-person voting (though not back to the original days) to a much less drastic reduction in "something that has proved to be very successful." Her amendment would also have allowed local boards of election to determine their hours rather than imposing reduced hours statewide.

Rep. Jim Buchy (R-Greenville) said that in recent weeks he had talked to the legislative chamber about history and about economics. "Today, I want to talk about civics," he said, though he provided no evidence of expertise on these subjects. Buchy, an ALEC member, praised the "astute leadership" of Chairman Mecklenborg, whose committee had "vetted" the bill. "Voting is a sacred right, but with rights come responsibilities," Buchy said. He harkened back to the days of his youth when voting by provisional ballot was rare and there were no early voting days. He voted for the first time in 1961. "It was your civic responsibility to make arrangements to vote on Election Day," he said. But now, he argued, it has been made so easy to vote that "we have created a lot of opportunities for mayhem at the polls." Like other Republicans, Buchy went on to incorrectly claim the existence of widespread voter fraud.

"We have the best system in the world to vote," he said. "And here we are nitpicking on the false guise of disenfranchisement and suppression. That is not true," Buchy said adamantly, arguing that it is voters' responsibility to register correctly and vote correctly. "That is one of the precepts that we have as free Americans," Buchy said, urging defeat of the amendment and passage of the bill. More than one African-American representative during the debate pointed out that in 1961, the year Buchy fondly remembered voting for the first time, millions of African-Americans were denied the right to vote by "the best system in the world."

Committee chair and cosponsor Mecklenborg urged that Clyde's amendment be tabled. Huffman moved to table the amendment. Like Gerberry's, the amendment was tabled by a 54–38 party-line vote.

"When we get these responses to our amendments, we get a little window into what went on in committee," Rep. Matt Lundy (D-Elyria) said. He was especially critical of the process in Mecklenborg's committee. Proponents of voter suppression were given all day to sing its praises, he said, but opponents who had traveled from all over the state were interrupted in their testimony and told to "just wrap it up." Mecklenborg's committee, Lundy maintained, could not even "demonstrate a reasonable and democratic process," so it should come as no surprise that the committee had produced a bill that undermined voting rights.

"This bill should actually come with a warning label: 'Warning: This is not about election reform. It is about voter prevention. Passage of this bill is hazardous to your vote counting in Ohio,'" Lundy said. He noted that if Ken Blackwell were still secretary of state—referring to Blackwell's notorious involvement in the flawed election of 2004—he would have understood the motivation behind HB 194. "Let's call this the 'Back to Blackwell' bill," Lundy said, because it would produce long lines on election day and make it more difficult for votes to count. "Maybe we won't go back to 1961, but we will certainly go back to 2004," he observed.

Lundy noted that House Bill 194 followed right on the heels of what was known as the "poll tax bill." Lundy was referring to House Bill 159, another nasty piece of Republican legislation that required Ohioans to acquire a photo ID in order to vote. An estimated 887,000 Ohioans did not have one of the government-issued IDs (which would not include college or university IDs). Of course only the rarest of the very rare examples of voter fraud involve in-person voting so, as critics of the bill pointed out, this bill was in search of a nonexistent problem and designed only to reduce the number of people voting. Given the likely unconstitutional nature of House Bill 159 and the widespread opposition on many fronts, including even Secretary of State Husted, the "poll tax bill" stalled in the Senate.

Rep. Bob Hagan (D-Youngstown) said, similarly, that House Bill 194 was a "weapon of mass deception." He emphasized that there was no existing problem with voter fraud for HB 194 to fix. No board of elections in Ohio had sought this legislation, he emphasized.

"How can you pretend with a straight face that this is about election reform?" he asked directly of his Republican colleagues. "Who are you kidding? You know what this is about. All you are thinking about is the next election. Look in the mirror tonight and say, 'I did it for the people of Ohio.'" He encouraged Republicans to be honest with the people who had elected them. Worried about the 2012 election, Hagan said, Republicans want fewer and fewer Democrats to vote. "Your history on the Republican side is real clear. This is happening in three or four states right now. You are getting this from on high. It is the [Karl] Rove issue. You are getting this from somewhere else. You should be ashamed of yourselves," Hagan said, although he did not mention ALEC, the real source of these voter suppression bills. Hagan went on to cite the low numbers of Ohioans who actually vote, something the legislature should actually be concerned about.

"Subjugation, enchainment, and serfdom," are words Rep. Tom Letson (D-Warren) used as dictionary synonyms for "disenfranchisement," to describe the impact of House Bill 194. He proposed an amendment that would prevent ballots from being thrown out because of technicalities with the way they were filled out. Boards of elections could agree on the voter's intent, he said. The Republicans promptly defeated this amendment.

"This is the Voter Suppression Act of 2011," said Rep. Matt Szollosi (D-Toledo), and it was clearly an attempt to reduce voting in densely populated urban areas where many Democratic voters lived. From a policy standpoint, he maintained, it makes no sense to reduce in-person voting from 35 days to as little as 6 days or to bar in-person voting during the busiest time on the weekend before the election. But from a "political standpoint, it makes perfect sense," especially in light of the other radical bills that were being introduced by the Republicans. "This is purely an attempt to suppress the vote and consolidate political power. This bill is bare-knuckled, in-your-face, political hardball, and has absolutely no place in Ohio law," Szollosi concluded.

A series of African American legislators then attacked the bill and Republican motivations for pushing it through the state house. "I've tried to come up with a rationale for this bill but have come up with nothing," said Rep. Sandra Williams (D-Cleveland). In fact, a thorough examination of the last several elections reveals no problems with voter fraud and no corruption at the polls. Indeed, despite the huge turnout, the election of 2008 had been one of the smoothest on record. "One of our most important duties is to approve bills that improve the lives of Ohioans. These [voter suppression] bills don't even come close," Williams said. "This is a blatant tactic to take away the constitutional rights of poor, low-income, elderly, and minority voters," she said. "No matter how you look at it, this bill will set back equality, and voting rights, and social justice by 50 years," she said.

Williams noted that while the Republicans had been passing voter suppression and union-busting laws since the session began, more than a quarter million Ohioans had filed for unemployment. "What happened to all the talk about jobs, jobs, jobs," that got the Republican majority elected in 2010, she asked. "You've done nothing about jobs."

Rep. Alicia Reece (D-Cincinnati) said she needed to voice the concerns of her constituents in Hamilton County because thus far only Rep. Mecklenborg and Rep. Blessing had spoken from the Cincinnati area. Reflecting back on comments about the responsibility to vote, she said that the new process made it likely that those who had fulfilled their responsibility to vote could still have their votes thrown out because of incorrectly filling out a form or some other technicality. And poll workers would no longer be required to help voters find the right place to vote. "We call them irresponsible. We say they are not worth being counted," she said of those who might need help at the polls, ridiculing the idea. "I am for more access. I am for every eligible vote being counted."

Rep. Bill Patmon (D-Cleveland) looked back to the Fifteenth Amendment to the U.S. Constitution that guaranteed former slaves the right to vote. Holding up the text, he read that the right to vote could not be "denied or abridged" by any state. "This bill goes a long way toward denying and abridging" the right to vote, Patmon said, and suggested that the courts would eventually rule against HB 194.

Rep. James Barnes (D-Cleveland) remarked that his family comes from a small town in the Deep South, Aliceville, Alabama. His experience with segregation as a small boy was humiliating. At the root of overcoming such a system, he said, is the idea of one person, one vote. "How unreasonable can we be," he asked. "We all took the same oath of office. Whatever happened to the notion of equal justice, equal opportunity?" He especially took aim at the bill's provision that no longer required poll workers to help voters. "That is rigging an outcome," Barnes said.

Rep. Terry Boose (R-Norwalk), ALEC member Rep. Ron Young (R-Leroy Township), Rep. Andrew Brenner (R-Delaware), Rep. Jarrod Martin (R-Beavercreek and member of the ALEC Public Safety and Elections Task Force), and Rep. Cheryl Grossman (R-Grove City and member of the ALEC-Commerce, Insurance, and Economic Development Task Force) all defended the bill by focusing on voter responsibility and minimizing the obstacles presented by House Bill 194.

Rep. Boose, an ALEC Tax and Fiscal Task Force member, said the urban legislators had no monopoly on poor people. His rural district had plenty of poor and unemployed. "I'm tired of hearing that it's you guys and your districts getting abused by this," he said. "You've said twice that the current system favors the Democratic vote," he said, countering that Republicans were only making the system fair. "This bill is not discriminatory. It makes us equal," he said, apparently not recognizing the concept of "one man, one vote."

Rep. Michael Stinziano (D-Columbus and member of the ALEC Communications and Technology Task Force), a director of the Franklin County Board of Elections, noted many flaws with the bill. He suggested an amendment allowing counties that wish to, to mail out absentee ballot applications. It has been a proven winner in counties that do it, he said. Elections are already not equal county by county, so this local option would not change that situation. Among those who spoke against Stinziano's amendment was Terry Boose, who, bizarrely, suggested that asking all counties to mail out applications was imposing a "poll tax" on rural areas. Apparently agreeing with Boose's strange suggestion, the Republican majority tabled the Stinziano amendment by the same party-line vote.

Later amendments proposed by Rep. Reece (D-Cincinnati), Rep. Charleta Tavares (D-Columbus), and Rep. Theresa Fedor (D-Toledo) that aimed to reduce some of the worst abuses of the bill were also defeated by a party-line vote. Debate was closed by a nearly party-line vote, and a final vote was taken to approve the voter suppression bill, 53–39.

On June 23, 2011, the bill was introduced to the Senate. As Sen. Mark Wagonner (R-Toledo) said as he introduced the bill, the version considered now by the Senate included some minor adjustments and reflected the will of both GOP-dominated bodies.

Sen. Shirley Smith (D-Cleveland) minced no words. "We all know this bill is discriminatory, racist, and disingenuous," she said, and continued in a powerful statement that deserves to be quoted in full:

> The oppressive language is without cause and totally unnecessary because there is no evidence of widespread voter fraud. This bill is part of a national Republican agenda, and Ohio is caught in the crosshairs The Republicans are stacking the deck in order to deliver a 2012 win to their party by, what Malcolm X would call, "any means necessary." Diehard Republican operatives are working hard to conjure up ways to disenfranchise poor minority voters and pimp the political process for their own gain. I cannot say enough how ashamed I am to say that I am a member of a body that engages in such shenanigans to keep control of a mess of our government that, in fact, they created and continue to perpetuate by the same types of public policy that it is proposing today.

She concluded:

> The fight for equal rights began long ago, and it continues today. We don't care how many beads you make us count, we don't care how many bubbles we have to count in a bar of soap, and we don't care what kind of literacy test or poll tax you subject us to, we will prevail. What you've done is awakened a sleeping giant. And we will do whatever we need to do. We'll rise up to the occasion. Poor people, black people, Latino people, will show you that no matter what you do, your tricks and games will not triumph. They have not in the past, and they will not now. I urge a no vote on this bill.

Sen. Nina Turner (D-Cleveland), after dismantling the bill piece by piece, said that partisanship is part of politics, but it should not be part of drafting election laws:

> Partisanship on these issues erodes confidence in our democracy. How can there be a partisan way to approach elections laws? Well, in Ohio, we've found out today . . . Over the course of a few months, we've dealt with bills that take away people's rights to collectively bargain, unfair budget bills that take away people's jobs, and now today we are dealing with election regressions that will take away people's voices. This new reality in Ohio is not only unfortunate, it should be unacceptable.

The Senate approved House Bill 194, passing it by a party-line vote of 23–10. It was sent to the governor's office on July 1, 2011, and Gov. Kasich signed it the same day.

Organized by Fair Elections Ohio, in a replay of our successful Senate Bill 5 drive, thousands of volunteers fanned out across the state in an effort to defend voting rights. This time we had the advantage of already having many trained volunteers. Nevertheless, the campaign against the union-busting legislation and the charter university concept was inducing some fatigue in our volunteers, and signature-gathering this time went a bit more slowly than before. I have to admit being among those who thought: "What? We have to do this again? And to protect something so basic as our access to the vote?" Nevertheless, once again the massive signature-gathering drive kicked off and gained momentum.

At the University of Toledo, supporters of both repeals, SB 5 and HB 194, rallied together on Oct. 12, 2011. "We wanted to make a connection between Issue 2, which attacks democratic rights, such as the right to have union representation, and House Bill 194, the voter suppression act, which damages democracy," Mark Sherry, a professor of sociology, told *The Toledo Blade*. The story featured a photograph of a UT custodian giving a "No on 2" button to a student.[5]

On July 18, the first one thousand signatures were submitted, and ten days later, the secretary of state's office certified those first thousand signatures, which gave our organization until September 29, 2011, to gather enough signatures to put the bill on the ballot for the November 2012 election. Importantly, this meant that House Bill 194 would not be able to restrict voting in either the 2011 or 2012 general elections. Not surprisingly, we were successful in gathering enough signatures to put House Bill 194 on the November 2012 ballot. Secretary of State Jon Husted announced on December 9, 2011, that our coalition had submitted 307,358 valid signatures, more than the 231,150 needed.[6]

Clearly, the Ohio GOP feared that another referendum in 2012 would bring out Democratic, and independent voters angry with the actions of the Republican legislature in restricting voting access. Early in 2012, rumors began to spread of a bizarre plan forged by Ohio Republicans trying to prevent a—to borrow a Bushism—"thumping" at the polls. There ensued a very confusing effort that would generate a battle over access that would continue right through the 2012 election.

Republicans introduced Senate Bill 295, which would repeal House Bill 194, except for one of its most egregious restrictions, the ban on early voting during the three days before the election—perhaps the most crucial time, when a high percentage of early votes are cast. In a perceptive editorial, the *Akron Beacon Journal* correctly called this a "sneak attack." The paper went on to encourage a "clean repeal" of House Bill 194 so that Democrats and Republicans could get a fresh start on potential reforms.[7]

Finally, on May 8, 2011, Ohio Republicans accomplished an historic first: for the first time in Ohio history, the legislature repealed a bill that was up for a vote of the people on a referendum. Democrats were outraged and unanimously opposed the repeal, which nevertheless passed by a 54–42 vote. "By taking the action that we're proposing to take today, we discourage people in the future from taking advantage of the initiative and referendum right," Rep. Dennis Murray, a Democrat from Sandusky, said on the House floor, as *The Cleveland Plain Dealer* reported. "This goes fundamentally to the question of who it is in this state that holds the power of government. I think that's the people of this state, and I think the action we're taking today violates the constitution."[8]

Although confusion reigned at the time, in the end House Bill 194 did not appear on the 2012 ballot, but the impact Republicans had in attempting to restrict the vote for those Ohioans who make up the Democratic Party base, the urban voters, undoubtedly spurred the high voter turnout for the 2012 election, when President Obama won reelection in large part because of his victory in Ohio.

One aspect of this episode should be shared before moving on. It was revealed during the campaign against HB 194 that Rep. Robert Mecklenborg, cosponsor of the voter suppression bill and the man who chaired the committee that introduced it, would soon be gone from the Ohio legislature. Although the news only became public in July, on April 23, just days after the introduction of House Bill 194, Rep. Mecklenborg had been arrested for DUI. He resigned in the wake of the incident.[9]

This is not to focus on the troubles of a particular individual. It does, however, shine a bright light on the flawed judgment of those who would try so ruthlessly to deprive thousands of Ohioans of their Constitutional right of access to the polls. Ohioans expect and deserve better judgment from those who occupy seats in the legislature.[10]

Chapter 10

"Stage Is Set for Battle"

"Great news from Ohio," wrote Prof. Howard Bunsis, chair of the AAUP's national Collective Bargaining Congress, in a message to AAUP members. Noting that Sara Kilpatrick, state executive director, and Rudy Fichtenbaum, a leader of the Wright State chapter, were in Columbus for the delivery of the massive number of signatures to get SB 5 on the ballot as a referendum, Bunsis wrote, "We are so proud of our members and leaders in Ohio who worked so hard on this campaign. What is encouraging is how the entire labor movement in Ohio has come together, and how the AAUP is an important part of that movement."[1]

"SB 5 Makes Ballot; Stage Is Set for Battle," the headline in *The Columbus Dispatch* reported on July 22. "This is really a historic moment for us. We're kicking off a campaign for social rights and justice," National AFL-CIO President Richard Trumka told *The Cleveland Plain Dealer* at a gathering of union leaders and other SB 5 opponents in downtown Columbus. "This is about defending the middle class," Trumka continued; "This is about saying what kind of state we will be and what kind of nation we will be." For her part, Pierrette "Petee" Talley, secretary-treasurer of the Ohio AFL-CIO, told the *Plain Dealer*, "We're headed into a very bad campaign. We're up against interests that have a lot of money."[2]

Evidence of the powerful forces backing Senate Bill 5 was clear when one of Gov. Kasich's closest allies, Newt Gingrich, announced his support for the legislation. The conservative group backing SB 5, Building a Better Ohio, produced a video of Gingrich with his statement of support. In the video, as *The Cleveland Plain Dealer* reported, the former House Speaker repeated the central—and flawed—argument made by supporters of the bill, that it would give local governments tools to better manage themselves without raising taxes. "Gingrich, who appears a bit sluggish in the video, offers high praise for Gov. John Kasich, mentioning his name three times," the *Plain Dealer* reported. The writer then speculated, "Perhaps Gingrich is hoping to snag Kasich's endorsement," in a reference to Gingrich's presidential aspirations. Near the end of the video, Gingrich states, "This is a chance to be involved and strengthen what Gov. John Kasich is doing."[3]

This renewal of the Gingrich–Kasich partnership was just a piece of the conservative coalition that was targeting Ohio's working people. In addition to Building a Better Ohio, other groups that contributed large sums of money and brought in outside organizers included Alliance for America's Future, with Liz and Mary Cheney, daughters of Dick Cheney, in its leadership; FreedomWorks, a creation of former Republican Sen. Dick Armey; the Ohio Liberty Council, a coalition of Tea Party organizations; the Ohio branch of Americans for Prosperity, chaired by David Koch and funded largely by Koch money; and Make Ohio Great, a creation of the Republican Governors Association and funded by several wealthy conservatives, including Rupert Murdock. All of these groups would spend millions in out-of-state money mainly bankrolled by wealthy plutocrats whose primary objective was to crush the union movement in Ohio.

On August 3, I attended the local kickoff event of the campaign at Laborer's Local 265 in Cincinnati. The large meeting room was packed with union leaders and members from the area, several politicians, and a handful of university faculty like myself. Several speakers, including AFL-CIO Executive Secretary Doug Sizemore, spoke confidently, even defiantly, about how we were going to fight these attacks on unions and working people, and we would win. But in talking with people and looking around the crowd, I saw many anxious faces, and there was fear, and there was anger. I was, nevertheless, encouraged by the meeting, not because of the rhetoric, but because there was a unity in the fear and the anger and the defiance. I began to believe that such unity might be able to overcome the powerful and wealthy forces that opposed us.

At the AAUP at UC, we sent a message to our membership on August 10, titled "It's Time to Roll Up Our Sleeves." Executive Director Deborah Herman struck the right tone. Informing UC faculty of We Are Ohio locations for phone-banking and canvassing in the city, she wrote that polling seemed to show that the people were on our side. However, she emphasized, that would not matter if we did not get people out to vote—and to accomplish that would require months of get-out-the-vote activities. Herman wrote that with the Wisconsin recall elections now over, national conservative organizations could focus on stopping the repeal of Senate Bill 5. "They may outspend us," Herman wrote, "but we have the edge in people-power and we're right on the issues. We just need to do the work."

We were very much aware of events in Wisconsin. The recall elections held between July 19 and August 16, we believed, were a victory for the Democrats, since two Republican legislators were defeated in districts that were traditionally held by the GOP. But they had failed to recall a third senator, which was the magic number to gain control of the state Senate. Still, winning two of those three seats was a huge accomplishment. What this meant in the Ohio context was more uncertain. Our repeal and Wisconsin's recalls were two very different animals. We believed that it would actually be easier to repeal bad legislation than it would be to recall bad politicians, and that idea would be borne out later when We Are Wisconsin failed to recall Gov. Scott Walker. But we also saw that Walker's conservative allies outspent We Are Wisconsin by a 2–1 margin. As one of my colleagues earlier noted about the legislative races, "Wisconsin was a win for truth and beauty, and now it is our turn to nail down a victory."

We were realistic about our chances. Faced with such powerful opponents and masses of misinformation, we could lose the repeal. So we began to make contingency plans if that should occur. We were aware that the UC-AAUP chapter, for example, had existed before the legislation that SB 5 was eliminating. We talked about ways to collect dues if our universities were barred from doing so through payroll deduction. Our union, after all, had existed for more than 30 years without fair-share fees. We talked about continuing this grand coalition with other unions to try to force our employers to respect and work with us. We talked about hanging on until we could get the legislation reversed in the future. But as I look back on these conversations, we seemed to have been driven by a need to have some kind of future to look forward to if we failed to repeal SB 5. In reality, as I see it now, as contracts expired, we would increasingly be cut out of an important role in our universities, especially with the special provision SB 5 contained to eliminate the AAUP and other faculty unions. Like other union employees, we would certainly lose our voice in the workplace.

As it became certain that SB 5 would be on the ballot, that its opponents had assembled a formidable coalition, and that the public was on our side, murmurs of discontent with the initiative campaign began to reach us from the Republican side. First to voice this discontent was Brent Larkin, editorial page editor, at *The Cleveland Plain Dealer* on June 25. He wrote that there were "many thoughtful people on both sides of this issue. It's time for them to push aside those who view Senate Bill 5 through a purely political prism and to explore the possibility of a compromise." Then on August 7, *The Columbus Dispatch*, which had given a ringing and enthusiastic endorsement of SB 5, editorialized, "Ohio is about to tear itself apart. No matter which side wins the impending war over State Issue 2, the state will suffer deep and long-lasting wounds that will threaten its already fragile economy. At a minimum, labor-management relations will be set back years." The *Dispatch* then went on to urge a compromise in the interest of all Ohioans.[4]

Our coalition did not take such talk about compromise seriously, since Gov. Kasich and his allies had been determined from day one to force this radical legislation through no matter how much damage was done. But then we got some interesting news. Gov. Kasich and his Republican allies now appeared to want to avoid the fight they had precipitated. "As a critical deadline approaches," *The Toledo Blade* reported on August 17, "Gov. John Kasich on Wednesday formally offered to negotiate over Ohio's controversial new law weakening public employee collective bargaining in exchange for a promise from labor to pull a politically divisive referendum from the ballot." Kasich made the announcement at a press conference, flanked by House Speaker William Batchelder and Senate President Tom Niehaus, both of whom by this time had become symbols of the ruthless attack on unions.[5]

On first hearing of Kasich's offer, we at the AAUP were concerned that such talk might undermine the unity of our coalition and that some groups—perhaps one of the big unions or perhaps one of the public safety unions—would feel it was safer to try to work with the Republicans on SB 5 than to gamble on the repeal. It appeared that some union leaders were actually talking behind closed doors with Kasich and his allies about a compromise. At the AAUP, we felt that we had been completely rebuffed as the bill went through the legislative process while actually being made more destructive. We did not believe that the people who had demonstrated such ideological extremism had suddenly become reasonable. We were relieved when we heard We Are Ohio's response.

"These politicians who passed Senate Bill 5 have the ability to come back and repeal the law, and that's what they should do—repeal the entire law," We Are Ohio spokesperson Melissa Fazekas told Ohio's assembled media. "Or they can join us and vote 'no' in November on Issue 2 . . . We're saying that if you repeal the bill—and that's what you should do, then there's really nothing left to talk about, is there?" Under questioning at a news conference, Fazekas stuck to her guns: "We stand together with the 1.3 million Ohioans who signed the petition and want a no vote on Issue 2." When reporters suggested to her that the public might view the unions as the side that didn't want to compromise, she replied, "I think that Ohioans are very smart, they were very involved in the process going through the legislature where they were literally locked outside in the cold and their voices were not allowed to be heard. It is awfully funny to now be standing here and talking about coming to the table when this entire bill takes away their rights to do so." She also made clear that whatever communications had taken place between the governor and his allies and any union representatives, no such discussions had taken place between the two sides in any official capacity and that We Are Ohio had never been contacted by the governor.[6] Since that time, no union leader has come forward to admit to participating in such a meeting with the governor and his allies.

Among the factors that made the Republican gambit untrustworthy was the public letter itself. It contained all of the tired false statements we had now been hearing for months. It attempted to portray the Republican effort to undermine the middle class as a reasonable and valiant attempt to save Ohio from a terrible fate, consistent with the GOP effort to manufacture a crisis context. Signed by Kasich, Batchelder and Niehaus, the letter began,

> Without a doubt, Ohioans have made it clear that they believe our state is headed in the wrong direction. The status quo has failed us and certain policies of the past have led only to unprecedented fiscal shortfalls, historic double-digit unemployment rates and economic recession.

This passage, like the rest of the letter, was a political statement and not a rational analysis. The first sentence made it sound as though Gov. Kasich's very narrow victory had given him a mandate. This was not true, of course, but the governor always acted as though it was. In the letter—which was oddly addressed to "Government Employee Union Leaders of We Are Ohio"—the Republican authors of the letter admitted no responsibility for the fiscal shortfalls, nor any recognition that Ohio had been caught in a crushing national recession upon which state policies could have had little impact. The letter went on, "While we passionately believe in the reforms of Senate Bill 5 and stand ready to vigorously—and successfully—defend them, we ask you to consider this option and join us in working with determination for a compromise for the benefit of the taxpayers we all serve." The advocates of SB 5 then asked union leaders to cooperate with them to "avoid the bitter political warfare that so many have come to detest." Of course, their own attempt to crush the unions was a perfect illustration of "the bitter political warfare" that those being targeted by SB 5 certainly "detested."

Perhaps the only completely accurate statement in the letter was about the unnecessary conflict that Gov. Kasich and the Republicans had created: "In a matter of days, Ohioans will be thrust into a costly political battle that will likely result in lasting scars and bitter divisions at one of the most fragile moments in our state's history." Citing the public's growing concern with the "political brinksmanship," that has consumed our national political debate, the Republican leaders closed with a request that a delegation of ten union leaders from the We Are Ohio decision-making authority meet with them 10:00 a.m. Friday morning in the Riffe Center, a government building in downtown Columbus. In other words, they were proposing a classic exercise in political brinksmanship.[7]

It was almost certainly the We Are Ohio coalition's inability to trust Gov. Kasich and his allies that led to the united front. Republican Sen. Timothy Grendell of Chesterfield, who had been an eloquent critic of SB 5, told the *Plain Dealer* that he had urged his fellow Republicans to slow down and reexamine portions of the bill he and others considered problematic. "We had union people willing to have discussions, but nobody who was leading the charge from the legislature wanted to have those meetings," Grendell said.[8]

On Friday, August 18, in a staged scene that outraged union members across the state, Gov. Kasich, Speaker Batchelder, and Senate President Niehaus sat at a long table in the Riffe Center, a government building in downtown Columbus. Across the room were empty seats with name cards for Ohio's unions. Headlined "Kasich Stages 'Talks,' Assails No-Show Unions," *The Columbus Dispatch* reported: "With no union leaders in sight yesterday, Gov. John Kasich and Republican legislative leaders welcomed a horde of reporters into a Riffe Center conference room arranged to prove their point." Kasich told the *Dispatch*: "Ninety-nine percent of life is just showing up. Obviously, they flunked the test."

Kasich objected to We Are Ohio's position that there would be opportunity to talk once SB 5 was repealed by the legislature, which the governor called an "ultimatum, not a negotiation," wrote *Plain Dealer* Columbus Bureau Chief Reginald Fields in a political analysis. Kasich used the event as an opportunity to ramp up his rhetoric, Fields reported: Kasich blasted the unions for not negotiating and accused union leaders of misleading their members. Noting that the "governor's approach is clearly aimed at painting the unions as stubborn and unyielding as campaigning for Issue 2 kicks off," Fields observed perceptively that there were risks involved, too. "The tactic could backfire," he wrote, "if voters think the governor is bullying unions and caving at the last minute on his own collective bargaining law while trying to silence voters who may want to have their say on Nov. 8."[9]

"Why now, Gov. John Kasich?" asked *Plain Dealer* columnist Phillip Morris on August 19, in a powerful piece.

> Why now does this tough-talking governor, who came into office and immediately set about to disembowel Ohio's public unions, suddenly pretend he's in the mood for tea, crumpets and compromise on Senate Bill 5? . . . Why now does he feign that his political gamesmanship is a form of statesmanship with unions that have united to wreak what appears to be certain havoc on the measure at the polls in November?

Morris went on excoriating the governor:

> This is a war that Kasich started without discussions. This is a war that he should have the commitment to finish without belated discussions . . . He awoke the sleeping middle-class labor giant, and he should have the courage to face it head on, even though polls show that his measure will be devastated in the fall election.

The fight over Senate Bill 5 was a defining moment in Ohio history, Morris said: "We as a state are now in the necessary process of finding out a lot about ourselves. The referendum war on SB 5 is a just war that will provide answers to a host of moral, social and economic questions." Morris went on to say that there are legitimate questions to be asked about the state's powerful public unions, but that the issues had been clouded by distortions Kasich and his allies promoted about jobs and savings that would be created by undermining the unions. "That was a falsehood," Morris wrote, referring to the administration's claims, and "union leadership, which had shown signs that it was willing to compromise on certain economic issues, responded with a line in the sand. It gathered 1.3 million signatures on a petition to let voters decide the fate of SB 5." Morris labeled the governor's offer of compromise "cheap idle talk." "It wasn't that long ago," Morris pointed out, "that the governor was famously quoted as saying, 'If you're not on the bus, we'll run over you with the bus,' in regard to lobbyists who would oppose his efforts to rein in government spending. Well, don't bail now, tough guy."[10]

In Columbus, Sara Kilpatrick, AAUP's executive director, was straightforward in her evaluation of Kasich's strategy. "It was very clear," she wrote to Ohio AAUP members, "that this was a publicity stunt in order to position Building a Better Ohio, the pro-SB 5 campaign, going into the fall battle." She noted that Kasich "was sure to assert that the lack of labor leaders at the meeting was reflective of the uncompromising nature of unions. We Are Ohio was sure to remind the Governor that there is nothing stopping him from doing the right thing on his own." She made clear to us that, barring a repeal from the legislature, SB 5 would be on the ballot in November: "We Are Ohio continues to ramp up its staff, garner volunteers, and raise the money necessary to run an effective campaign."[11]

Any large-scale political campaign like the fight to defeat Senate Bill 5 requires more than just the enormous quantities of personal time and effort being committed by thousands of people across Ohio. It also requires money. The big unions were in the process of committing millions of dollars. The AAUP, for the first time, also contributed a significant amount of money to the cause. Most of Ohio's AAUP collective bargaining chapters contributed—often tens of thousands of dollars. The state and national organizations dug deep for money that could be invested in the campaign. And perhaps most moving to us was the money voluntarily contributed by out-of-state conferences and chapters, even from individual AAUP members across the country. But we needed to do more, as Cary Nelson, then-president of the AAUP wrote in a national message to all AAUP members. "The AAUP's chapters and its national leaders have contributed half a million dollars to the cause," Nelson wrote on August 25. "Our members and our staff are on the ground waging this battle. We urge you to contribute now to help repeal this legislation."[12] In the end, the AAUP, its state and national organizations, the Ohio chapters, and chapters from all over the country, contributed more than $700,000 to We Are Ohio to, in our view, protect higher education and the principles the AAUP represents.

It was obvious that the unions were pouring in money to defend themselves. On the pro-SB 5 side, however, where the money was coming from was purposely much more difficult to identify.

As *The Cleveland Plain Dealer* reported in September, Building a Better Ohio would announce in late October who had donated to the campaign but was not required by law to say how much the donations were, and that would remain "a secret." While Building a Better Ohio was hiding its finances, We Are Ohio was not. We Are Ohio's Melissa Fazekas criticized the makeup of the Republican organization and said that Ohioans have a right to know who was behind the campaign to pass Issue 2. "While We Are Ohio . . . is publicly releasing our campaign finance reports, our opposition is hiding their donors," Fazekas told the *Plain Dealer*.[13]

It was a "mystery," the *Dayton Daily News* reported on October 25, which corporations and individuals were contributing, and how much they were giving, to the campaign to defend SB 5. Building a Better Ohio spokesman Jason Mauk, who had said that in late October his group would list their donors but not the amounts, was eager to point out that the secrecy was legal. The *Daily News* explained why: "The limited disclosure requirement is a result of how the campaign committee was set up. Building a Better Ohio is a separate PAC from the 501(c)4 nonprofit Building a Better Ohio Inc. The nonprofit can take unlimited, undisclosed donations and then write a check to the PAC." For those interested in following the money, this was not good enough. "We're missing one of the most essential parts of the puzzle, which is how much money did they invest. Some disclosure is better than nothing, but just barely," Catherine Turcer of Ohio Citizen Action, a nonpartisan nonprofit group that tracks campaign money, told the *Daily News*.[14]

When the finance reports were released, the stark difference was clear. We Are Ohio listed its donors by name and amount. It had raised \$30.5 million, in both cash and in-kind donations. Donations had come to the cause from more than two hundred unions, including locals and chapters all over the country, with the Ohio Education Association, AFSCME, and SEIU leading the way, the *Daily News* reported. The unions contributed \$18.6 million of the \$19 million in cash and 98.8 percent of the \$4.6 million in in-kind help. Roughly \$5 million in cash came from the national offices of labor organizations. Also, showing the grassroots nature of the campaign, We Are Ohio received contributions from more than 7,100 individuals whose average donation was \$46. By contrast, Building a Better Ohio received \$5.97 million. Fifty-one organizations contributed, including the Ohio Chamber of Commerce, Owens Corning, the Ohio Automobile Dealers Association, the Ohio Farm Bureau, and Motorists Mutual Insurance. No amounts were included. Even the list of contributors and the total was misleading, because several conservative groups were spending on their own separately. For example, Alliance for America's Future (AAF)—a Virginia-based and GOP-friendly non-profit—spent millions of dollars mailing to voters millions of fliers urging a yes vote on Issue 2. AAF's fliers contained such misleading information that the *Plain Dealer*'s fact-checker generously judged them "problematic." AAF's principals include Dick Cheney's daughters Liz and Mary, and Barry Bennett, a former top aide to former Rep. Jean Schmidt, a Republican from southwest Ohio. "Alliance for America's Future," John Nichols of *The Nation* reported, "is one of the most aggressive of the out-of-state special interest groups that have elbowed their way into the referendum fight. Cheney's group is part of a shadowy network of campaign organizations in which Dick's daughter [Liz] serves as a principal operative."[15]

The Cincinnati Chamber of Commerce was a powerful player when it entered the fight. "We recognize that this change is not without discomfort, but this reform is long overdue," chamber CEO Ellen van der Horst said in a news release that clung closely to Republican talking points. "Senate Bill 5 is another strong step in tackling the current fiscal crisis and making long-term, transformational change. It puts Ohio in a better position to create more flexible governments that can allocate resources based on market conditions, provide maximum value to the taxpayer and, ultimately, grow jobs."[16] Van der Horst's statement, of course, misrepresented the manufactured fiscal crisis and repeated inaccurate statements that union busting created jobs. What it would certainly do would be to increase corporate profits at the expense of all other social concerns in Ohio.

The Ohio Chamber of Commerce produced a similar statement. It came as no real surprise, since the chamber's attack on union workers was in sync with Gov. Kasich's position and with the chamber's long-term policy of support for lower wages. The chamber had also been on the wrong side of the minimum wage fight in 2006. A Constitutional Amendment that had indexed the minimum wage to inflation was adopted by a statewide vote of 57 percent to 43 percent, over shrill opposition from the chamber of commerce. Thus, the minimum wage in Ohio would be increased to $7.85 per hour starting January 1, 2013. Tipped employees were to be paid a minimum hourly rate of $3.93. Ohio's minimum wage in 2011 was $7.70 per hour for nontipped employees and $3.85 per hour for tipped employees.

In late August 2011, we also learned that the Cincinnati USA Partnership, an economic development organization directed by the Cincinnati Chamber of Commerce, had been awarded $2 million by Gov. Kasich through his controversial new JobsOhio agency, an attempt to privatize the state's economic development efforts. Several other economic development agencies, almost all with some ties to their local chambers of commerce, had also been part of Gov. Kasich's giveaway of a total of $14.9 million in taxpayer's money. These funds had been generated by the innovative economic development program Third Frontier, initiated in 2002 and designed to help fund new high-tech jobs in the state. Since the state's high-tech research centers are largely in the universities, much of the money invested through Third Frontier found its way into university research programs. It was never intended to be a giveaway to the state's chambers of commerce. But during the 2010 campaign, Kasich had been clear that he planned to use the program to funnel public money into private hands. He said that Third Frontier should be restructured so business executives controlled more of the money. "I'm also not really thrilled with the idea of universities running it because I've seen glaciers move faster at decisions than universities," he said.[17] An interesting observation from someone with broad experience at Lehman Brothers, where flawed decisions seem to have been a specialty.

This tax giveaway to the Cincinnati chamber, which came only weeks after the chamber announced its support for Senate Bill 5, certainly had the appearance of a political payoff. However, finding creative ways of channeling Ohioans' hard-earned tax dollars into the pockets of corporate interests, not economic development, has been a primary objective of the Kasich administration, so the transfer of funds might have occurred without SB 5. But what we wanted at the time was a promise from the chamber that it would not use the windfall of taxpayer money to campaign for SB 5 or to free up other funds to do so. The people of the Cincinnati region never received such a commitment.

We did learn more about where this newfound wealth might be directed. In the fall of 2010 the Ohio Chamber of Commerce, in conjunction with the Cincinnati organization and other metropolitan chambers of commerce, produced a report called, "Redesigning Ohio: Transforming Government into a 21st Century Institution." It has reissued this badly flawed report in subsequent years with slight changes.

"Redesigning Ohio" is mainly filled with proposals based in right-wing ideology that arguably do not serve the middle class, and seems to have as its primary purpose the reduction of tax contributions for the state's corporate heavyweights. This is no surprise, since nearly all of the substance of the chamber's plan has one source: the conservative group ALECs "State Budget Reform Toolkit." Much of the language and argument contained in both plans are strikingly similar, pushing something called "Budgeting for Outcomes," or BFO. The argument embracing BFO in both the ALEC report and the Ohio Chamber proposal is surrounded by much verbiage that makes it sound both new and harmless. It is neither. Essentially, making use of zero-based budgeting, it is budget planning based not on what needs to be done but on how much money will be expended. Much of this approach requires the existence of a crisis so that people will make decisions they ordinarily would not. David Osborne, a principal in Public Strategies Group, provided many of the ideas behind the chamber's proposal. "Crisis as Opportunity" is the title of an article that he coauthored on his organization's website. He and his coauthors argue that "we all know that crisis brings opportunity. During a crisis, the politically impossible becomes possible."[18]

In reality, BFO suggests to policymakers that they can be justified in slashing government expenditures to some undetermined lower level based on ideologically driven choices because of the many supposed positive benefits that will ensue. Cutting funding, for example, will make state government services more "creative" and will actually "improve" public services. There is no mention of layoffs, of important work not accomplished, or of the heavy tax burden passed on to local communities. It is all gently covered in a smoke screen of happy talk about "improvements." As noted earlier, much of this approach relies on the existence of a budget crisis, so that people will be willing to make decisions they would ordinarily reject. "Ohio is facing an unprecedented fiscal crisis," the Ohio Chamber website states breathlessly. "Although we're not alone, we would be remiss in not taking this opportunity to transform our state government to one that is sustainable and provides greater value to our citizens." Clearly, in tandem with a legislature purposely reducing revenues, BFO is a tool for conservatives of the Grover Norquist "starve-the-beast" school of undermining government services.[19]

Not all Ohio chamber members simply accepted this radical political approach by the state and local chambers of commerce. When the Youngstown Chamber announced its support for Senate Bill 5, Tom Byers, general manager of A. B. Crane & Steel Service Inc., withdrew his membership, as did others. "I just wish they would've stayed neutral on [SB 5]," Byers told the local newspaper. "I don't see how it helps to support it so strongly." Fireline, Inc., a manufacturer of fire rescue and safety equipment, also withdrew its membership.[20]

My whole experience with the chamber in Cincinnati and Ohio has been a puzzle to me. In my newspaper years in Montana and Idaho, I had found that the chambers of commerce that I covered were a friendly bunch of small business owners who were devoted to their neighbors and their communities. They liked union workers because they earned good wages, which they could then spend in the stores. And union members' decent benefits gave them the kind of stability that contributed to prosperous neighborhoods. However, in the 1990s, while I was in graduate school, the chamber changed into a very different kind of organization.

Thomas Donohue began the transformation when he took over as president of the national office in 1997. The U.S. Chamber of Commerce "has become more brazenly pro-Republican" under Donohue's leadership, Britain's *The Economist* newsmagazine reported in April 2012. "Its ranks of lobbyists, strategists and flacks bristle with former Republican congressional attack dogs. Its people are said to meet periodically with Republican-supporting groups to share intelligence, such as polling data, and to co-ordinate ad spending. It has ties to Karl Rove's American Crossroads political action committee, whose president is the Chamber's former chief lawyer."[21]

SourceWatch, which monitors right-wing organizations, has, with other public interest organizations, done a good deal of work on tracking the Chamber of Commerce's activities. In the wake of President Obama's victory in 2008, the chamber ramped up its political efforts. "We plan to build a grass-roots business organization so strong that when it bites you in the butt, you bleed," chamber President Tom Donohue told the *Los Angeles Times.* Reacting to what the chamber sees as a potentially hostile political climate, Donohue told the *Times* that the organization would seek to punish candidates who target business interests with their rhetoric or policy proposals, including congressional and state-level candidates. In rhetoric more appropriate to the robber barons of the nineteenth century, Donohue said, "I'm concerned about anticorporate and populist rhetoric from candidates for the presidency, members of Congress and the media . . . It suggests to us that we have to demonstrate who it is in this society that creates jobs, wealth and benefits—and who it is that eats them."[22] This belief that only the people in suits in the corporate board rooms generate wealth has become a central concept of the contemporary Republican Party.

Not surprisingly then, the chamber was determined to crush the union movement in Ohio in 2011, through its ardent defense of Senate Bill 5. And the chamber could be a front for the corporate interests behind SB 5. "Under a system Donohue pioneered," the *Times* reported, "corporations contribute money to the chamber, which then finances attack ads targeting individual candidates without revealing the name of the businesses involved in the ads."[23] The chamber is, after all, an organization driven primarily by the nation's largest corporate interests. In 2008, for example, only 45 huge multinational corporations contributed nearly half of the chamber's $140 million in donations. In 2010, Dow Chemical gave $1.7 million, Prudential Financial gave $2 million, and Rupert Murdock of News Corp. gave $1 million.[24] With activities closely paralleling Karl Rove's American Crossroads group, the chamber on the national level has lobbied against climate change regulations and against regulations of business, even after the Deepwater Horizon oil spill and the corporate malfeasance that brought on the Great Recession. Another relationship that draws it very close to the Senate Bill 5 battle is that U.S. Chamber of Commerce was a member of ALEC in 2011. Its deep involvement with the organization is evident in its membership in ALEC's Civil Justice Task Force, the Education Task Force, the International Relations Task Force, and the Telecommunications and Information Technology Task Force. Several prominent chamber leaders, including Vice President Page Faulk, were prominent speakers at ALEC's meetings in recent years.

I have spent a good deal of time examining the Chamber of Commerce's role in the Senate Bill 5 campaign, because it was the largest and most visible in-state organization that advocated for the union-busting legislation within the large group of national conservative groups that entered the fray in 2011. In Ohio, small business owners who are members of their chambers of commerce should ask themselves, in the wake of SB 5, whether the chamber is really supporting the kind of state they want to live in—and whether vilifying the police who protect our streets, the firemen who protect our homes, the teachers who educate our children, and the many ordinary union members who are customers of businesses around the state, is really the road Ohio should take.

These important issues were at the center of public debates that were held all over the state in September and October of 2011. One of the most important of the debates pitted two local Cincinnati-area legislators against one another: Sen. Shannon Jones, SB 5's Republican sponsor of the bill, and Rep. Connie Pillich, an outspoken opponent of the legislation. Held in suburban Cincinnati on September 22, during the debate Jones repeated the inaccurate central talking points behind SB 5: that there was no money left, that it would leave bargaining intact, and that it leveled the playing field between private and public sector workers. Pillich countered that it was interesting to hear that the public sector had created the recession. She emphasized that SB 5 was no modest reform. "The deck is stacked in the favor of management from the beginning to the end of the process, there is no bargaining," Pillich told the audience. "It is like going to divorce court and finding out your spouse is the judge."[25]

One of key televised debates was carried on NBC affiliates statewide with a panel of journalists from Cleveland, Columbus, and Cincinnati, and moderated by White House correspondent Chuck Todd. It featured Republican Sen. Keith Faber on the pro-SB 5 side and former Democratic congressman Dennis Eckert on the anti-SB 5 side. Both men traded heavy verbal blows during the debate, but the strongest message coming out of it was Eckert's argument that any of the reforms the Republicans and others wanted to make could be made within the context of collective bargaining—change could be accomplished best through negotiation. But crushing the unions through SB 5 was an objective driven by national Republican political goals, Eckert pointed out, not Ohio's budget issues.[26]

"Seldom in the history of Ohio," Eckert said, "have the people had such a unique opportunity to stand and be counted. The citizen's veto of Senate Bill 5 gives us one of our most cherished opportunities and responsibilities."

As the bruising campaign went into its final months, it would soon be clear just where the people of Ohio would stand.

CHAPTER 11

THE MIDDLE CLASS DEFENDED

By September, We Are Ohio had regional field directors and organizers set up all over the state. In Hamilton, Butler, Warren, and Clermont counties (that is, Cincinnati and the surrounding counties), there were at least ten people assigned to the job of organizing many more volunteers. Over the course of the campaign, the AAUP at UC had interactions with several of them and found them young, enthusiastic, and professional. Already quite well organized, we did not need their help the way other groups did, but we collaborated with them and often directed them where their efforts would be most effective. There were also other groups active in Ohio and the Cincinnati area, including Organizing for America staff and volunteers—often the continuing presence of the 2008 Obama campaign in Ohio, who would still be in place for Obama's 2012 campaign.

But the key for our coalition's dynamic and effective drive toward the November election was the thousands of people who simply volunteered. Often union members or church members, they were always people with a conscience and concern for the kind of state and country we were becoming. For our part, at the UC AAUP, we were trying to block Gov. Kasich and his conservative allies from ending our 40 years of collective bargaining at the University of Cincinnati. As the election neared, I was constantly concerned that there was something more we could do to protect the university and preserve our right to have a say in our workplace. I didn't want to leave anything undone that might help us.

I received a message from Catholics United on September 7, illustrating my fear: "Don't wake up on Nov. 9th wishing you did more." Noting that there were only 63 days left before the vote, the Catholic organization emphasized that there was not a single minute to waste: "Every added day, our opponents lie to Ohioans about the effects of Senate Bill 5 . . . We may be outspent by our opponents but with your help, we will not be out worked or out volunteered. Now more than ever we need to be talking to voters about the facts and the harmful consequences of Issue 2." Catholics United beseeched people to volunteer to go door-to-door asking for people to "vote No on 2."[1]

In early September, I met with Hollie Hinton, a mayoral candidate for the city of Chillicothe who was planning a We Are Ohio rally/fundraiser event for the Cincinnati area. She asked me to be on the organizing team, and, of course, I agreed. Shortly after the meeting with Hinton was the annual Labor Day Picnic at Coney Island, on the edge of the city along the Ohio River. The UC's AAUP chapter faculty had for years sponsored a booth at the picnic, and our signature effort at the picnic is hauling in a couple of helium tanks so we can blow up balloons, stamped with the AAUP logo, for the hordes of children who throng the event. While I was handing out balloons with my colleagues at the 2011 picnic, I encountered Bill Dudley of the UFCW. We talked, and it occurred to us that we should combine Hinton's We Are Ohio rally and fundraiser with an event Dudley was arranging for the same day, October 11, with the Teamsters. Hinton and I took the idea to our organizing team, and we agreed to put the two events together. The next few weeks would involve planning for this event as well as many other efforts to try to build the momentum we needed for victory in November.

We Are Ohio offered a workshop at this point that we thought particularly useful, the "Friends and Family" program. Held the evening of September 12 at the IBEW Hall in Cincinnati, the program appealed to those who were uncomfortable approaching strangers to convince them to vote against SB 5 but would feel better talking with friends and family. Not only did the program offer a lot of useful strategies for broaching the issue, but it also helped the campaign in another way. By taking their friends and family off the lists to contact, participants would reduce the number of people that We Are Ohio volunteers would have to contact. This was one more way that the campaign to repeal SB 5 was innovative and comprehensive in its strategy.

In early September, I had published in several places a long essay entitled "The War on Higher Education." It was initially written for *Passport*, the newsletter of my professional organization, the Society of Historians of American Foreign Relations. After its initial publication, I shared it widely. In the essay, I summarized the attacks that unions and higher education were facing in Ohio and several other states, and reviewed the problems with Senate Bill 5, House Bill 194, and especially the charter university concept. The piece was useful in spreading the knowledge of just how extensive, systematic, and potentially damaging to society were these concepts being promoted by conservative forces, largely through ALEC. Some of the most interesting comments on the essay came from faculty in Europe, who had been fighting their own battles against politicians and trustees working to impose corporate models and micromanage their universities to the detriment of higher education. "I just read your piece on 'The War on Higher Education' with alarm, but also with gratitude for your efforts in bringing these fast-moving stories to broader attention," wrote Professor Howard Hotson, a historian of early modern intellectual history at England's University of Oxford. "Unfortunately, what you are describing appears to be taking place right around the world—not least here in Britain—though as usual the U.S. is setting the pace in many respects."[2]

"A primary focus of any faculty union," I wrote in the piece, "is on the twin issues of academic freedom and shared governance, and these are issues particularly under fire by the conservative movement. Faculty unions have been expanding in Ohio and elsewhere, largely in response to university budget decisions that have taken place without faculty input and without regard for the instructional mission of the universities." I reviewed the recent unionization victories at Bowling Green State and at the University of Illinois at Chicago (and since that time, the University of Oregon). "Questionable resource allocations by university administrations," I noted, "were key motivating factors in both the BGSU and UIC certification drives."[3]

Our battles on multiple fronts began to come to a head during this period. The charter university plan had been announced in mid-August, the deadline was approaching for signature collection for House Bill 194, and the campaign was well underway for Senate Bill 5. While we had great support from a significant portion of the student body, we felt it necessary to seek specific statements of support from the two student representative bodies, the Graduate Student Assembly and the undergraduate Student Senate. To do this, I made appointments with Paulette Penzvalto, president of the Graduate Student Assembly, and Alan Hagerty, undergraduate student body president.

I met with these students leaders on September 26 in the graduate student offices. We had a productive meeting. I introduced the issue to them and explained to them how much this mattered to UC's faculty and to the future of education in Ohio. Faculty members do a great deal of service for students by advising and assisting student clubs and organizations. I explained that while this service may not be specifically barred by Senate Bill 5, many faculty, including myself, would simply stop doing service if the state were to dictate to us that we could do some important forms of service but not others. I also pointed out what a flawed concept it was to block faculty from taking part in decisions about hiring, promotion, and tenure. Both Paulette and Alan asked good and perceptive questions, and said they would bring the issue to their groups and get back to me. The undergraduates invited me to speak to them, which I did on September 28, and the graduate students on October 5.

The Student Senate meets in Tangeman University Center, room 425. Interestingly, there is a plaque on the wall recognizing longtime librarian Les Vuylsteke's devoted service as an advisor over many years to the Student Senate. Now retired, Vuylsteke had been devoted to the AAUP and had recruited me to the executive council years ago. I provided the student senators with some history of the AAUP, both nationally and at UC. I explained how SB 5 would undermine faculty rights at the university, how the issues we had struggled so hard to defend—academic freedom and shared governance—would be at the whim of the university were it not for our contract. I emphasized how this was not just about us but about the campus police, the food service workers, the people who sweep the halls, cut the lawns, and shovel the snow. Further, it was a sweeping attack on all workers across the state. Finally, I emphasized the problems that SB 5 would create for faculty in doing service. I was asked whether this meant that faculty would be barred from their important role as advisors to student groups. I said we could not be sure how this would be applied in the end, but that the students should put themselves in the shoes of the faculty who would certainly be barred from the important advisory role in curriculum decisions and hiring and promoting other faculty. How would they, the students, then feel about cooperating with an administration that would do this to them? I asked that they consider passing a resolution opposing Senate Bill 5 and urging a no vote on Issue 2. The undergraduates clearly took their responsibility seriously, and I was, once again, impressed with the maturity and ability of the students.

Not surprisingly, university administrations all over the state began to attempt to take advantage of the crisis facing their employees before the November vote. At Wright State, the administration agreed to begin negotiations, but then began to stall. Late in the spring, even though all previous contracts had been for three years, the administration proposed that only a one-year contract be negotiated, a proposal that caused the faculty's negotiating team to walk out of the negotiating session. Shortly thereafter, as it became clear that the effort to repeal Senate Bill 5 had considerable momentum and was likely to succeed, the administration began real negotiations for a new three-year contract with the WSU faculty. That contract was then approved by the university's Board of Trustees and the membership of the bargaining unit in October 2011, ahead of the November referendum on Senate Bill 5.

Much more aggressive behavior occurred at Youngstown State University and Cincinnati State Technical and Community College. The Youngstown State faculty union, part of the Ohio Education Association, came very close to going on strike. They were the subject of harsh and unreasonable editorial attacks by the local newspaper, *The Youngstown Vindicator*.[4] As at many other universities, the Youngstown State administration and board of trustees were making bad choices about its financial resources. Stan Guzell, chief negotiator for the faculty, was clear about the university's misplaced priorities: "It's not that they don't have the money, it's that they want to spend it on things that don't include [the faculty]," he said. The administration remained intransigent, and the faculty, for the good of the students, eventually agreed to the concessions being demanded.[5]

Cincinnati State, an AAUP chapter representing about two hundred faculty, did go on strike for a week in protest over a workload issue that faculty pointed out would require them to teach 20 percent more than their peers at other Ohio community colleges. The administration disagreed. It was the first labor strike in the school's history. Along with several other AAUP faculty and staff from nearby universities and our state office, members from UC walked the picket lines with our Cincy State friends.[6] Our view was that, once again, faculty members were having to make a stand for quality in the face of an administration whose focus was primarily on production. As at Youngstown, the Cincinnati State faculty eventually accepted the concessions rather than punish the students.

While opposition to SB 5 was strong in the polls—including one in late July that showed the public behind us in defeating SB 5, 56 percent to 32 percent—we became concerned when another Quinnipiac poll that showed that our lead had dwindled to 51 to 38 percent. Although this was still a significant margin, the numbers were moving in the wrong direction. "This is a wake-up call, as well as a call to action," Sara Kilpatrick wrote to the AAUP statewide leadership.

"Issue 2 is not in the bag for us, and we need to mobilize and educate everyone we know about what this law actually does." She noted that she feared that the pro-SB 5 forces were being successful in their misrepresentations of the bill as just a moderate "common-sense" reform. She added that she had personally donated money and had signed up for canvassing shifts with We Are Ohio. Despite the great activity we were already generating, we had to do more. "Issue 2 is ours to lose," Kilpatrick said, "but luckily, we still have six weeks to get the job done. So let's do it!"[7]

Our strategy continued to be to correct the misinformation being generated by the pro-SB 5 side—and one group, of course, that they targeted with particular venom was the public school teachers, college faculty's allies in education. So, in collaboration some public school teachers and with a group students that called themselves Concerned Students of the University of Cincinnati and Miami University, we jointly sponsored a showing of *The Inconvenient Truth of Waiting for Superman* on October 24. This film was produced by a group of New York City teachers who were being targeted by "reformers"; it was a response to the controversial and distorted film *Waiting for Superman*, which vilifies teachers and teachers' unions. In May, Gov. Kasich had brought former Washington, DC, school superintendent Michelle Rhee, a darling of the right-wing set, to Cleveland for a special showing of *Waiting for Superman*. We showed *The Inconvenient Truth* because it corrected many of the misrepresentations in the original film and proposed using the advice of the teachers and parents themselves to improve the schools, rather than high-priced paid consultants who have never taught. We had a good audience at the Esquire Theater near the university, including faculty, students, neighborhood residents, some families, and politicians, including Rep. Denise Driehaus (D-Cincinnati). There was a rewarding discussion in a Q&A period afterwards.

On September 1, A. J. Stokes, campaign director for We Are Ohio, sent a communication to the coalition. It said in part that the advertising campaign would start that day. "We didn't choose this fight," Stokes observed, "but we know that the people of Ohio will be with us if we continue to run a strong campaign and communicate our message." We Are Ohio opened the advertising blitz with an ad featuring Doug Stern, a 15-year veteran of the Cincinnati Fire Department.[8] Stern pointed out that Senate Bill 5 made it illegal for his union to negotiate for enough equipment and manpower to safely and adequately do their job.[9] The resulting slower response times could mean the difference between life and death, he said. The pro-Senate Bill 5 side quickly produced an ad by Toledo Mayor Mike Bell, a former Toledo firefighter, who discussed his own experience. He noted that he had been laid off as a firefighter early in his career because of city finances (he was later rehired) and said that he believed that Senate Bill 5 would provide officials like him with the tools necessary to prevent doing that again or raising taxes. Mayor Bell, who had been elected in 2009 in Toledo as an independent, was rare among those who appeared in pro-Senate Bill 5 advertisements, which rarely featured real people; they usually used actors or no one at all. Meanwhile, Jason Mauk, a former chief of staff for Senate Republicans and spokesperson for Building a Better Ohio, spent time denying that the ad was a response to We Are Ohio's firefighter ad.[10]

One after another, real Ohioans pounded home the destructive aspects of Senate Bill 5 in We Are Ohio's ads during the months of September and October. In one very effective advertisement, Shawna Turner, a nurse at Ohio State University's Heart Hospital, noted that—as for the firefighters—SB 5 would make it harder for nurses to negotiate for adequate staffing levels. In response, Building a Better Ohio spokesperson Mauk once again tried to inaccurately soft-pedal Senate Bill 5 as a modest reform. And a *Plain Dealer* fact-check column was simply incorrect in claiming the BBO advertisement was "mostly false." The column argued that hospital administrators would not reduce staffing once nurses could no longer negotiate to defend staffing. This perspective is much too naïve and ignores the corporate influence infiltrating all areas of medical care.[11]

"Thousands of teachers across Ohio oppose Issue 2 because we care about the kids we teach," said Courtney Johnson, a school teacher in Hilliard, near Columbus, in an ad about SB 5's impact on schools. "Issue 2 would restrict teachers' rights to bargain collectively for smaller class sizes, for up-to-date textbooks, even negotiating on school safety issues." She went on to note that Issue 2 could mean even more standardized testing and less time spent on classroom learning. "Teachers know what our students need to succeed. Don't let the politicians take away our rights to speak up for Ohio's children," Johnson asked. Because SB 5 was designed to muzzle professors, we particularly identified with this advertisement.

And just before the November ballot, one of the most famous Ohioans stepped forward. "Here in Ohio, we rely on everyday heroes to teach our children, take care of the sick, and keep our community safe," former astronaut and Ohio Senator John Glenn said in an ad. "Issue 2 will make it harder for teachers, nurses, firefighters, and other public employees to protect and serve us." After a brief pause, he concluded: "Here in Ohio, we don't turn our backs on those who watch ours. That's why I'm joining millions of Ohioans who are voting no on Issue 2."

So desperate did the backers of Senate Bill 5 become in trying to craft some legitimate advertisements that would actually feature Ohioans that it led the organization into making a huge advertising mistake. Perhaps the most powerful advertisement produced by We Are Ohio was one called "Zoey." It was about a little girl in Cincinnati whom firefighters had saved from a burning home, and it featured the girl's gray-haired great-grandmother, Marlene Quinn. "When the fire broke out, there wasn't a moment to spare," Quinn explained in the ad. "If it was not for the firefighters, we wouldn't have our Zoey today," she continued, as film of a happy Zoey at play filled the screen. Quinn went on to note that Issue 2 would make it illegal to negotiate for enough firefighters to do the job. "How many of those politicians in Columbus have fought a fire?" Quinn asked and then, in a powerful statement, looking directly into the camera, went on: "Those politicians don't care about the middle class. They've turned their backs on all of us. I don't want the politicians in Columbus making decisions for the firefighters, the police, teachers, nurses, or any organization that is helping the people. Fewer firefighters could mean the difference between life and death, and that's why I'm voting no on 2."

What Building a Better Ohio did next is little short of baffling. But consider their position. The Republican arguments for crushing the public unions lay in tatters. The state was in an uproar. No one had ever stepped up to cosponsor Senate Bill 5. The polls were badly against them. They were unable to find any Ohio citizens to appear in their ads, except for the Toledo mayor. And because of all of this, the money that national right-wing groups had promised to them was not forthcoming on the scale they had expected.

On the morning of October 11, I was getting ready to leave for class when I caught what I thought was the Zoey ad running on television, with Marlene Quinn featured prominently. But the voice was wrong; it was another woman, not Quinn, and at the end of the ad was the statement, "That's why you should vote yes on 2." And then there was a note that the ad was paid for by Building a Better Ohio. What had I just seen? I could not replay it, of course, and I had to hurry to class. That afternoon was the joint rally-fundraiser that our coalition had been planning for a couple of months. There was a festive atmosphere, with hundreds of people from different unions, especially the UFCW, and other groups at the Teamster's Hall, Local 100, that afternoon. A stage had been set up, Teamsters national president Jimmy Hoffa, Jr., would speak later, and hamburgers, hot dogs, and soft drinks were being served. In a room inside the hall, I had a chance to speak to union members, students, and donors about how SB 5 was a special attack on the unionized faculty at the universities and would cripple our ability to defend academic freedom and shared governance. At the end, I brought up the ad I had seen that morning, which had apparently stolen Marlene Quinn and used her words for the opposite purpose. "These are the kind of people we are up against," I said, stressing the dishonesty of the act. People were in disbelief, saying that could not be. But others spoke up who had also seen the ad that day.

A firestorm of criticism spread across the state as the ad was continually replayed. As *The Columbus Dispatch* reported:

> Last week, Marlene Quinn was starring in a television ad explaining how Cincinnati firefighters saved her great-granddaughter, and urging Ohioans to vote against Issue 2 so firefighters could continue to negotiate for proper staffing levels. Yesterday, the 78-year-old Quinn was startled to learn that she also was starring in a new ad by the Republican group Building a Better Ohio, her image and words swiped from the Issue 2 opposition ad and spliced to sound like she is a supporter of the anti-collective-bargaining law.[12]

"I think it's dishonest and downright deceitful that they would use footage of me to try to play tricks and fool voters," Quinn said in a statement released by We Are Ohio. "It's insulting to the brave firefighters that saved the lives of my grandson and my great-granddaughter Zoey. I'm outraged. They did not ask my permission. I feel violated."[13]

As the *Dispatch* pointed out, Building a Better Ohio had taken the original ad, splicing Quinn's statements with the words of a female narrator who said instead that failing to pass Issue 2 would force firefighter layoffs, which would threaten safety, because communities have to pay for "excessive benefits" of public workers. The ad ends with Quinn's statement about "life or death."

Donald McTigue, an attorney representing We Are Ohio, sent "cease-and-desist" letters to television stations that served Ohio's markets, including a letter from Quinn: "I demand that all television stations or other forms of media immediately stop airing this misleading advertisement by Building a Better Ohio," Quinn wrote. "I also request that Ohio media outlets refrain from accepting any future advertisements in which my likeness is used to advocate in support of Issue 2 or Senate Bill 5."[14]

Shockingly, Senate Bill 5 backers supported the blatantly dishonest ad. Far more serious than an ad that simply shades the truth, Building a Better Ohio's enthusiastic embrace of this dishonest action was appalling but really was reflective of the entire story of Senate Bill 5 since the first day it was introduced. The brazen attitude was nevertheless stunning.

"That's the kind of stuff you just don't do," Jack Reall, president of the Columbus firefighters union, said of the ad. "This is a group that wants us to believe our politicians are going to do the right thing when it comes to safety, staffing, training. Then you turn around and make a decision like this."[15]

Jason Mauk, spokesman for Building a Better Ohio, stood his ground in the face of the criticism. "Opponents of Issue 2 chose to use a personal story to make a political argument, but the same story makes an even more powerful case for supporting the reasonable reforms we're asking of our government employees," he told the *Dispatch*, again misrepresenting SB 5 as a moderate reform. "Without Issue 2," he maintained, "our communities will continue to lay off police officers and firefighters because they can't afford to pay them."

Reall, however, in a more accurate observation to the *Dispatch* cut through Mauk's rhetoric by pointing out that the layoffs were not about collective bargaining: "We're laying off public safety workers because we've cut local government funds, and we've decreased taxes on the wealthy."

"We're certainly not taking the ad down," Mauk told the *Plain Dealer*. "We absolutely stand by it and our right to air those arguments."[16] While Building a Better Ohio would not back down in the face of the facts, Ohio television stations did. Reluctantly at first, but then rapidly, television stations stopped running the ad. So heated was the controversy that the *Plain Dealer* editorial board weighed in on October 13: "Building a Better Ohio has a right to its predictions about the consequences of a failure of Issue 2, but it has no right to mislead viewers about where Marlene Quinn stands. The group should pull the ad off the air—something a number of TV stations already have done—and move on."[17]

As for the anti-SB 5 campaign, we were, of course, delighted about the impact such disreputable behavior would have on public opinion. True to my initial reaction, it did reveal to the public just what kind of forces we were fighting against: people who would do anything to crush unions, to eliminate workers' rights, and, in our case, to eliminate our faculty union.

The proponents of Senate Bill 5 had two other sets of advertisements. One was based on using Gov. Kasich as a spokesperson. This was funded by Make Ohio Great, a front group for the Republican Governors Association (RGA). The RGA had spent at least $9 million to get Kasich elected and so poured more money into Kasich's campaign to pass SB 5. A spokesman for RGA told *The Columbus Dispatch* that Make Ohio Great is "connected to the RGA and was formed to support all of Gov. Kasich's agenda" not just SB 5. Jason Mauk, spokesman for Building a Better Ohio, said that he knew nothing about the new group and that they were not affiliated with BBO: "Asked if Make Ohio Great was an organization set up for secret cash to flow into the defense of Senate Bill 5, Mauk said, 'I don't know, but it's not a vehicle affiliated with this campaign, I can tell you that.'" The trick, the *Dispatch* explained, was for the ads to support Kasich and his fellow Republicans' efforts to promote Senate Bill 5 without actually mentioning the bill or ballot issue by name. An ad done that way can skirt the law and maintain that it was not a political ad—and thus would not have to reveal details about its organization to the Secretary of State's office.[18]

Another set of pro-Issue 2 ads were based on a study by the right-wing American Enterprise Institute and funded by the conservative Ohio Business Roundtable. Predictably, AEI's work provided right-wing talking points with scholarly apparatus. Its arguments were thoroughly discredited in the months of the campaign. The plan, for example, exaggerated the benefits that union members receive and even argued against all other studies to say that public employees were paid more than their private sector counterparts. Finally, it further inflated the numbers by calculating a dollar value for "job security," an idea that economists found very dubious. Saying this ad was "misleading" and left out "critical facts," *The Cleveland Plain Dealer*'s fact-check column ruled the ad "mostly false."[19]

At the beginning of October, the AAUP at UC announced to our faculty our three-pronged plan to get out the vote. First, we feared that the confusion surrounding HB 194 would prevent county boards of elections from doing their job. So we had earlier mailed out a registration card and an application for an absentee ballot to every UC chapter member; they would have received that material in early September. Second, we continued to emphasize the need for people to use the "friends and family" strategy. We noted that too many union members failed to "vote union," and that was only self-destructive. We hoped that the way the backers of SB 5 had attacked union members would change that situation and open more eyes to the real problems facing the state and nation. An effective way do that would be by talking to friends and family. Third, we created a member-to-member phone bank, organized largely by the chapter's Political Issues and Academic Freedom Committee, chaired by Dr. Andrea Tuttle Kornbluh, a professor of history. Even if we could not get all of our friends and family to vote no on Issue 2, surely we could talk to our colleagues. The phone bank consisted of about 50 faculty and librarians, who called hundreds of our faculty union colleagues to make sure they were going to get out and vote. Our list of questions included asking them whether everyone in their household was registered and whether they had talked to their family members about SB 5. Finally—and this was perhaps the most important question—we asked whether they were willing to volunteer for phone banking or canvassing with We Are Ohio. In doing the phone banking myself, I was struck by the anger and determination that continued to be obvious among the faculty. Even all these months later, the manner in which Senate Bill 5 was passed still appalled people, and the fact that our union was being singled out for elimination remained deeply offensive. And there was fear of what would happen to higher education in Ohio if faculty were silenced.

In the newsletter the UC-AAUP provided to members on October 4, we noted that the campaign was now in its final stages. "It's simply not true that TV ads win elections," we told our faculty colleagues, because, "especially on issues like this, what really makes the difference is person-to-person contact." We needed to spend a few hours each week helping to turn out the "no" vote among our friends, neighbors, and family members—and among those who had no social relationship with a professor or any other union member. "By reaching out to our friends, family, and neighbors and asking them to vote with us to repeal SB5, we can win the day," we wrote. "Remember our motto: No regrets on Nov. 9 . . . Let's make Nov. 9th a day we celebrate long into the future."[20]

As the campaign worked into its final days, one of my objectives was to make sure that the University of Cincinnati community, as the state's second-largest university, made a united statement against Senate Bill 5 and in support of a no vote on Issue 2. Paulette Penzvalto, president of the Graduate Student Assembly, shared with me in mid-October that the graduate students had passed a resolution condemning SB 5 and urging a no vote on Issue 2. I was thrilled. Then, on October 13, I learned from Alan Hagerty that the undergraduate Senate had moved as far as they could. They had earlier considered a resolution that would have urged a No vote on Issue 2. But, with no history of political involvement, that became a bridge too far. Instead, the student senators passed a resolution to ask the state legislature and the university to work together to see that shared governance was not destroyed whatever the fate of Senate Bill 5. Since Senate Bill 5 would have undermined shared governance at our universities, I interpreted the Student Senate resolution as yet another voice of opposition.

At about the same time I also learned the Faculty Senate was not going to pass another resolution simply expressing its opposition to Senate Bill 5. Instead, the Faculty Senate Cabinet believed that the resolution would be a more powerful statement if it were voted on at the All University Faculty (AUF) meeting on October 25.

Those final days of the campaign went quickly, as the routine of teaching my classes, grading papers and quizzes, and phone banking and knocking on doors continued, running together now in my memory. When the topic would come up in class, I was honest with my students: "I'm not unbiased about this. I'm president of the faculty union at UC. SB 5 would eliminate the union, and I personally think that is a terrible idea. But investigate, read, make up your own minds about what kind of state you want Ohio to be."

Our defense of collective bargaining rights was getting plenty of national attention. "In dozens of towns across Ohio," *The New York Times* reported on October 15,

> rival sides have set up phone banks and door-knocking efforts. Unions and their allies have created We Are Ohio, a group that is leading the repeal effort, which has 10,000 volunteers and hopes a victory will discourage Republicans in other states from adopting anti-union legislation. Mr. Kasich's allies have created Building a Better Ohio, financed by business and conservative donors, to block repeal.

The story was accurately headlined, "Ohio Wages Fierce Fight on Collective Bargaining," and quoted famed Buckeye football coach Woody Hayes's grandson, Phil Hayes, a public school teacher:

> As someone who set out to serve his students, I don't work on Wall Street; I serve Main Street," Mr. Hayes said. "I didn't cause the economic and financial problems caused by Wall Street, but now public employees like me have to suffer the consequences. We don't sell collateral debt obligations, but we do sell cookies to help keep our schools going.[21]

As we got closer to the All University Faculty (AUF) meeting, I have to admit that I was nervous about the vote on the anti-Issue 2 resolution. Instead of the 45 members at a Senate meeting making the decision, it would instead be the hundreds of university faculty who attend the annual meeting, which features addresses by the university president and the Faculty Senate president. In the course of the meeting, any resolution the Senate wishes to bring to the entire faculty is voted on. At UC, with over 2,000 faculty, there are hundreds of faculty who, for one reason or another, have chosen not to be union members. The AUF, with so many AAUP members and nonmembers, is a difficult situation to predict. But, again, I fell back on my faith in the collective wisdom of the faculty. Our unity had always involved some dissension and disagreement—we are university faculty, after all, and are trained to question authority and consider every angle of an issue, whether it be in biology, a financial plan, the Cold War, or a symphony. Through it all, for more than 40 years, we had hung together. Surely we would this time too.

An especially large group was assembled in the Great Hall in the university center for the 2011 AUF—perhaps to hear what President Williams had to say about an academic master plan that was being developed, or perhaps to hear about the resolution on Issue 2. Early in the meeting, the resolution on Issue 2 was introduced by Faculty Senator Stephena Harmony. She read the proposed resolution aloud for all to hear as a copy of the text was placed on an overhead projector. The resolution condemned Senate Bill 5 in some detail because of its negative impact on the faculty, and then urged faculty to vote no on Issue 2. Then, Faculty President Harknett opened the floor for discussion.

Much to my surprise, Prof. Dale Schaefer, who had written the column in *The Cincinnati Enquirer* back in early May that I had had to correct in detail, got up to speak. He once again made a series of inaccurate and misleading statements and tried instead to introduce a motion of his own, which Harknett, correctly, ruled out of order. Having said his piece and urged a yes vote on Issue 2, Schaefer sat down. Harknett asked whether there was more comment. I could not let Schaefer's misrepresentations pass as reflecting the faculty's view, particularly with the university's trustees sitting in the audience. So I asked for the microphone.

"Almost everything that Dr. Schaefer has just said is not true," I began. I then proceeded to lay out specifically what SB 5 would do to the AAUP at UC, especially that it sought to eliminate the AAUP by making faculty into managers, and thus ineligible for union membership, simply because of doing their normal service role. I emphasized that this was a completely unwarranted attack on the values that the AAUP exists to defend: academic freedom and shared governance. "But this is not just about us," I said, "because it is a broad-based attack against labor all across the state." Even at UC, it attacks the secretaries, the food service workers, and "those employees who set up this big room for us and who will sweep up after we leave." I emphasized that Senate Bill 5 would begin to create an Ohio that none of us would want to be part of, a Mississippi with ice. I urged my colleagues to support the resolution and to vote No on Issue 2, and I sat down.

No one else spoke. Harknett called the question. It was to be a voice vote. The "ayes" rang out in the Great Hall. The "nays" were much quieter. Harknett correctly ruled the motion passed. I was exhilarated. The University of Cincinnati—the faculty, graduate students, and undergraduates—had spoken with one united voice of opposition to Senate Bill 5. At the end of the meeting, Harknett asked whether there was anything further to come before the AUF. I had to speak again. I thanked the faculty for standing together against SB 5. I said that if we had the historic victory that the polls were suggesting on November 8, it would be because of all of them, because of all the big things and the small things that so many faculty had done since the struggle had been forced upon us.

More good news kept coming at us from the pollsters now. A Quinnipiac poll on October 25 showed that we had extended our margin to 57–32. As Columbus's *Business First* newspaper reported, "The campaign to save Senate Bill 5 is taking on water." Gov. Kasich's approval rating had declined by nearly the same ratio, with Ohioans now disapproving of the governor by a 52–36 margin. The Quinnipiac poll had followed closely on the heels of a Public Policy poll that showed that Issue 2/Senate Bill 5 would go down by a crushing 56–36 margin.[22]

"Two weeks before election day," *The Columbus Dispatch* announced, "Ohioans appear ready to stomp Senate Bill 5 out of existence." Opposition to the bill, the *Dispatch* noted, was almost universal, except for Republicans, who still favored the bill 59 percent to 32 percent. The *Dispatch* quoted Peter Brown, executive director of Quinnipiac, that: "Anything is possible in politics, but with such across-the-board support for repealing SB 5, the governor and his team can't be optimistic about the fate of their law." With all this good news, our own leadership was careful to stay focused. "Between now and Election Day," Sara Kilpatrick wrote to the statewide AAUP leadership, "complacency is our greatest opponent." She emphasized to us that the election would still come down to turnout. "Can you imagine if we get 60% or more of the vote? Let's win this big so that we send an unequivocal message to Kasich and his legislative followers that Ohioans will not tolerate any more attacks on workers' rights!"[23]

By late in the campaign, most of the newspapers had weighed in on Issue 2. Since most of them, especially the big dailies, are part of the Republican establishment and local chambers of commerce, they predictably advocated in favor of Senate Bill 5. Even so, most of them found distasteful the way the Republicans had mishandled the process of passing the legislation. Some newspapers were able to reject the misconceptions promoted by Building a Better Ohio. "[Kasich Republicans] used the moment to deal a hammer blow to their political adversaries, Democrats and organized labor," the *Akron Beacon Journal* observed in an editorial, "going after the way unions are structured and function, seeking to diminish their capacity to participate in the political process." The paper, which recommended a no vote on Issue 2, noted that proponents of the bill during the campaign had talked about modest changes and correcting problems: "All of this serves as cover for the partisan power play, Republicans asking the public to approve the sensible so that they can belt the other side . . . Consider the provision eliminating 'fair share,' the required payments to unions from workers who opt out of the bargaining unit. Again, this has nothing to do with tools or savings. Fair share long has reflected that all workers benefit from provisions of a contract."[24]

"Overall," *The Toledo Blade* editorialized, "Issue 2 is primarily a partisan, ideological, and special-interest attack on the ability of union-represented workers—many of whom do difficult and dangerous jobs—to negotiate working conditions as well as pay and benefits. Its net effect would be destructive not only to government employees but also to the taxpayers they serve. It deserves a NO vote." The *Blade* and the *Beacon Journal* were highly critical of the ideologically driven process because they believed that some changes ought to have been made by reaching compromise. "The history of Issue 2," the *Blade* acknowledged, "is a shameful commentary on the partisan polarization of Ohio government. Before they approved Senate Bill 5, Mr. Kasich and GOP lawmakers excluded Democratic legislators and union officials from meaningful participation in its development."[25]

On November 2, a lengthy column written by two of my AAUP colleagues, Marty Kich of Wright State University and Dave Witt of the University of Akron, appeared in *The Chronicle of Higher Education*. Disappointed with a *Chronicle* story that appeared to show Ohio university faculty as being sidelined in the fight to defend collective bargaining, Kich and Witt explained that situation was actually the opposite. Their comments detailed the deep and assertive involvement Ohio's faculty members had engaged in during the campaign. The AAUP, in cooperation with other unions, "has contributed a great deal to the efforts of We Are Ohio," they wrote. They maintained, accurately, that—faced with the complete elimination of collective bargaining at our institutions—the AAUP had "become a more significant, not less significant, factor at the state level." Moreover, they wrote, "We are proud of our collaboration with every union in We Are Ohio, and expect the fruits of our friendships to continue on into the future." They argued that the *Chronicle* had not recognized the "galvanizing effect" the campaign against SB 5 had had on all unions, public and private. "Ohio voters are aware of the political swindle currently underway," Kich and Witt argued, "the anti-union legislation being only one of many patently one-sided schemes designed to favor the far right's corporate sponsors."[26]

In the final days of the campaign, *Inside Higher Ed* did a story focusing on faculty efforts against SB 5. "When faculty members at Ohio public universities mention their governor's quest to end their collective bargaining rights," reporter Kaustuv Basu wrote, "they talk as if they were in a war." Sara Kilpatrick, state executive director of the AAUP, told *Inside Higher Ed* that "The campaign has really placed the Ohio Conference AAUP on the labor map." Previously, the AAUP had not been very involved in the larger labor movement, Kilpatrick explained, noting that the AAUP has both union and nonunion chapters. "But the AAUP in Ohio really stepped up to combat this bad legislation, and even our nonunion members have been active and supportive." David Jackson, president of the Bowling Green chapter and a professor of political science, said that the university presidents had been quiet but were "continuing a trend in backroom-type behavior." Noting the extremist nature of Senate Bill 5, I told Basu that "It is a new thing to be so politically involved, but we have been forced into it. Ohioans recognize the great injustice of this law."[27]

At UC, we issued pleas for more of our faculty to do phone banking and participate in the labor walks. And on the Sunday before the election, I lit a row of candles at St. Peter in Chains Cathedral after Mass in downtown Cincinnati, since by that time the outcome of the vote really was out of our hands.

Cincinnati-area union and political folks appropriately chose the Holy Grail tavern on the Ohio River, downtown, as the site of our viewing party on election night. The AAUP had t-shirts made that explained our efforts over the last several months: "Faculty and Students United for What's Right: No on 2." We had to be confident, given the polls, but it was nevertheless stressful as we waited to receive the results. Early results began to roll in, showing SB 5 being roundly defeated everywhere. Suddenly, at about 9:30 p.m., the Associated Press called the election. Senate Bill 5 was being crushed, working people were being vindicated, and there was joy at the Holy Grail.

"SB 5 was designed to eliminate the AAUP," I told *Inside Higher Ed* that night, "and would have undermined the standards of academic freedom and shared governance that our union has fought for over the decades at more than a dozen Ohio institutions. The result would have been universities with all the academic integrity of a Burger King." I praised the historic coalition to which we belonged, that had assembled to bring this victory for all Ohioans.[28]

"It takes a whole lot to repeal a law, but when you go against the working class and the middle class, this is what happens," Gary Rhoades, former national general secretary of the AAUP and a University of Arizona professor, told *Inside Higher Ed*. He called on college presidents in Ohio to try to reestablish trust with their employees: "They should come to the table and bargain in good faith," Rhoades said. "University presidents should not be behaving like Wall Street executives."[29]

It was only in the next few days that we became fully aware of the sweeping nature of the victory. The final margin was 61.33 percent to 39.67 percent. Only 5 out of Ohio's 88 counties voted in favor of Senate Bill 5. The three most populous counties—where Cincinnati, Cleveland, and Columbus are located—all heavily rejected the legislation. Of the counties that surround Cincinnati in probably the most conservative part of Ohio, only Warren County favored the union-busting bill. Perhaps most important, many more Ohioans voted against Senate Bill 5 (2,148,042) than had voted for Gov. Kasich (1,889,186) back in 2010.

"The overwhelming veto by Ohioans of Senate Bill 5, a GOP plan to crush public-employee unions," political columnist Thomas Suddes wrote in *The Cleveland Plain Dealer*, "was a massive defeat not only for Kasich but also for the blind partisanship of General Assembly Republicans." Suddes went on to describe other historic Republican defeats in Ohio. In 1964, Barry Goldwater won only 5 of 88 counties. In 1958, a union-busting right-to-work initiative pushed by the GOP received the support of only 37 percent of those voting, and, Suddes noted, that number was very close to the 39 percent who had supported Senate Bill 5. Suddes, who doubted Gov. Kasich would learn from the defeat, concluded with a quote from a historian I greatly admire, Gordon S. Wood, about the lessons of history: "History has no lessons . . . except one: that nothing ever quite works out as the participants quite intended or expected. In other words, if history teaches anything, it teaches humility."[30]

CONCLUSION

"A RENDEZVOUS WITH DESTINY"—IF WE CHOOSE

What happened in Ohio in 2011 was an important part of a conflict that has roots in American history about what kind of country the United States should be.

On one side are those who believe that America, its people, and its institutions should be regimented by the free market and private enterprise. Acquisition of money and wealth being the primary social good, society should be molded to allow those with substantial financial resources to operate without restriction in the economic, political, and social life of the nation, imposing whatever values they see fit. After all, the market should be allowed to determine our policies, our values, and our way of life.

On the other side are those who believe that individuals should be able to craft a life for themselves. They value the power of democracy, not the power of wealth. Rather than allowing a small number of plutocrats and corporations to set the course for the nation's economic, political, and social life, they believe that there is room in America for diverse views, and that through cooperative action, life can be made better for the bulk of Americans and their families. Far from surrendering their freedom to the market and the economy, they greatly respect both the strengths and the limitations of free enterprise and believe the economy should be made to serve the people.

To those who believe that this contrast is too sharp, it may be best to return to where we began this story—in the 1930s, with the reaction of the wealthy corporate plutocrats to the New Deal and the campaign they launched, outlined in Chapter 2, to undermine those progressive policy changes that led eventually in 2011 to Senate Bill 5 and the Battle of Ohio.

President Franklin D. Roosevelt was a remarkable individual. Born to wealth, early in his life he operated without a social conscience about the opportunities that were an accident of his birth. But he went through a remarkable transformation while recovering from polio as he struggled against forces that were beyond his control. Through his personal struggle, Roosevelt came to a sophisticated understanding of the plight of ordinary Americans facing an economy that was stacked against them. Consider FDR's perceptive "Rendezvous with Destiny" speech at the 1936 Democratic Party Convention in Philadelphia.

Recognizing the onset of the Great Depression under the Republican administration in 1929, FDR praised the millions of Americans "who have borne disaster bravely and have dared to smile through the storm . . . In our strength we rose together, rallied our energies together, applied the old rules of common sense, and together survived." Although Americans had "conquered fear," he could not tell them that all was now well. "Clouds of suspicion," he noted, "tides of ill-will and intolerance gather darkly in many places." He argued that there were "problems that must be solved if we are to preserve . . . the political and economic freedom for which Washington and Jefferson planned and fought." He urged the people to pledge themselves to "a wider freedom."[1]

Roosevelt argued that the American Revolution had been designed to assure political freedom. "That victory," he said, "gave the business of governing into the hands of the average man, who won the right with his neighbors to make and order his own destiny through his own Government." Since that time, however, the industrial revolution and changes in the nature of the economy have created new problems for those "who seek to remain free":

> For out of this modern civilization economic royalists carved new dynasties. New kingdoms were built upon concentration of control over material things. Through new uses of corporations, banks and securities, new machinery of industry and agriculture, of labor and capital—all undreamed of by the fathers—the whole structure of modern life was impressed into this royal service . . .
>
> It was natural and perhaps human that the privileged princes of these new economic dynasties, thirsting for power, reached out for control over Government itself. They created a new despotism and wrapped it in the robes of legal sanction. In its service new mercenaries sought to regiment the people, their labor, and their property . . .
>
> The hours men and women worked, the wages they received, the conditions of their labor—these had passed beyond the control of the people, and were imposed by this new industrial dictatorship.

> The savings of the average family, the capital of the small business man, the investments set aside for old age—other people's money—these were tools which the new economic royalty used to dig itself in.
>
> For too many of us the political equality we once had won was meaningless in the face of economic inequality. A small group had concentrated into their own hands an almost complete control over other people's property, other people's money, other people's labor—other people's lives. For too many of us life was no longer free; liberty no longer real; men could no longer follow the pursuit of happiness.
>
> The royalists of the economic order have conceded that political freedom was the business of the Government, but they have maintained that economic slavery was nobody's business. They granted that the Government could protect the citizen in his right to vote, but they denied that the Government could do anything to protect the citizen in his right to work and his right to live.
>
> Today we stand committed to the proposition that freedom is no half-and-half affair. If the average citizen is guaranteed equal opportunity in the polling place, he must have equal opportunity in the market place . . .
>
> These economic royalists complain that we seek to overthrow the institutions of America. What they really complain of is that we seek to take away their power. Our allegiance to American institutions requires the overthrow of this kind of power. In vain they seek to hide behind the Flag and the Constitution. In their blindness they forget what the Flag and the Constitution stand for. Now, as always, they stand for democracy, not tyranny; for freedom, not subjection; and against a dictatorship by mob rule and the over-privileged alike.

These are powerful words. Clearly, we can see why FDR's right-wing critics at the Heritage Foundation and elsewhere are so eager to attack him and his legacy: Is he not describing our own day? Given the attacks that working people have faced in Ohio, Wisconsin, Indiana, and Michigan by conservatives in power in those states, backed by corporate money and plutocrats of great wealth, the unavoidable conclusion is that Roosevelt was right then and still is now. The concentration of unprecedented wealth in the hands of a few, and their influence on our political system today, is a threat to American democracy, American workers, and the American way of life. As Michael J. Sandel points out in his powerful book *What Money Can't Buy*, there are moral limits to markets. "The most fateful change in the last three decades," Sandel argues, "was the expansion of markets, and market values, into spheres of life where they don't belong." He argues that it is a very different thing to have a "market economy," in which markets are "a tool for organizing productive activity," or a "market society," which is a way of life where "market activity seeps into every aspect of human endeavor." Americans have an obligation to question the change in values such a transformation imposes.[2]

Roosevelt and the New Deal created a safety net for the poor, imposed regulations on a rapacious economy in order to prevent its worst abuses, gave working men and women some control over their lives and livelihoods, and, in FDR's own words, established a government that was not "indifferent" to the fate of its people.

The movement to undermine the spirit of the New Deal came to power in the person of Ronald Reagan; we've already discussed his transformation from union president to union buster through the efforts of GE's Lemuel Boulware. But to fully understand Reagan and the damaging impact he and his ideology have had on America, it is necessary to understand the work of Kevin Phillips. Phillips was a Republican strategist who played a role in the conservative campaign that helped turn the Old South from a Democratic to a Republican bastion rooted in resistance to civil rights. In 1969, Phillips authored the important book *The Emerging Republican Majority*, which outlined how this electoral shift was going to take place in the South and West.[3] The book—which explained that racial divisions were long-lasting, that Republicans were exploiting these divisions, and that this was leading to an enduring Republican majority—had a tremendous impact on the political world. Strategists and politicians were simultaneously repelled and fascinated by the argument. Nixon, of course, had ridden this Southern strategy to victory in 1968, but it was not yet clear to most observers—as it would become clear later—that this was a long-term realignment, generated by Southern resistance to the civil rights and voting rights acts, and that the Republican Party's Operation Dixie was, in fact, working.[4]

What this meant was that the right-wing economic ideology rooted in the Austrian economists was going to be carried to power on the back of American racial politics. But Nixon was too complicated and independent to be blindly devoted to this new economic ideology, and his abuse of presidential power brought his presidency to an early end. Jimmy Carter won the presidency because of his morality and his Georgia roots, but he was an interruption in the march to power of those who would try to reshape the American economy.[5] The victory of Republican standard-bearer Ronald Reagan in 1980 ushered in the new ideology.

President Reagan and his Republican allies began early on to attack the legacy of the New Deal. Phillips, who gradually became aware of the destructive impact this had on American society, came to criticize the Reagan era in another powerful book, *The Politics of Rich and Poor*, published in 1990.[6] Phillips documents the enormous shift of wealth to the top one percent of the population. "The 1980s were the triumph of upper America," Phillips wrote, "an ostentatious celebration of wealth, the political ascendancy of the richest third of the population, and a glorification of capitalism, free markets, and finance." But hardly anyone asked why. "Despite the armies of homeless sleeping on grates," Phillips notes, "political leaders . . . had little to say about the Republican party's historical role . . . to tilt power, policy, wealth and income toward the richest portions of the population."[7]

Phillips credits several specific actions by the Reagan administration that caused this dramatic shift of wealth to a small percentage of Americans, but it was primarily its advocacy in taking the top tax bracket from 70 percent to 28 percent in only seven years. This was a dramatic windfall for the wealthy. Not surprisingly, in addition to vast deficits, a shocking disparity developed between CEOs and rank-and-file workers. In 1979, CEOs made 29 times the income of the average manufacturing worker. By 1985, CEOs made 40 times more.[8]

It is worth noting that the rhetorical underpinnings of the "Reagan revolution" were often subordinated to a Reagan political reality that led him to compromise on issues like taxes—which he raised 11 times during his presidency. In contrast to today's Republicans, Reagan actually attempted to govern. Today's Reagan devotees, the core of SB 5 advocates and supporters, have forgotten the pragmatic governing Reagan, fixating instead on the rhetorical Reagan, and have taken his extreme rhetoric to even more extreme places. What we often get today is Reagan's extreme rhetoric, devoid of perspective and even devoid of facts. Still, it is necessary to recognize the genuine damage that Reagan's ideology has done to the middle class.

"The presidency of Ronald Reagan," Timothy Noah writes in his important book *The Great Divergence*, "was the first to adopt a public stance that was openly and unapologetically anti-union."[9] And perhaps the most damaging action by President Reagan to the welfare of so many Americans was his decision to crush the Professional Air Traffic Controllers Organization (PATCO). This blatant use of presidential power to crush a white-collar union had severely damaging effects on the labor movement and the income of ordinary Americans for years into the future.[10] The dramatic growth of inequality in America, Britain's *Economist* magazine reported in October 2012, tends to support two beliefs: "First, that a system that works well for the very richest has delivered returns on labor that are disappointing for everyone else. Second, that the people at the top have made out like bandits over the past few decades, and that now everyone else must pick up the bill."[11]

The income inequality that has swept the country since the 1980s has a parallel in academia. In 2009, I lost a close colleague in my department at UC–Blue Ash. Dr. Jim Cebula was a professor of history and had taught at our college for 40 years. He was diagnosed with lung cancer and survived for about a year. He continued to teach until just a few weeks before he died because he loved teaching so much. A historian of labor and Ohio history, his published work included a book on Ohio politician James Cox and several essays about union history. He was one of the organizers who helped bring our AAUP chapter its first collective bargaining contract in 1975. Dr. Cebula served in many positions with the AAUP over four decades, all volunteer, including president of the local chapter, as well as a member of the executive boards of both the state conference and the national organization. He served on several committees over a long period of years at every level at the union and across the university, including the Faculty Senate. Few people have devoted so much effort to promoting the values of the AAUP than did Jim Cebula. He was a fierce defender of the faculty and quality education at UC and elsewhere. His devotion to his students was well known. Jim was, without question, the kind of professor who changed lives. He was awarded the Distinguished Teaching Award at our college in 2007. Jim was known for his demanding teaching style. "He's maddening, irritating, exasperating. He's just wonderful," one student wrote. Hearing of his death, another wrote to me about how Jim had inspired her and her classmates:

> Somewhere along the way, I started really enjoying my new found thirst for knowledge. Being able to speak about a topic and actually have something valuable to contribute to a discussion made me realize what people had been saying all along about the whole "knowledge is power" thing. Professor Cebula made me realize how important it is to know where we came from as a country, and to keep up to date with where we are now. I think he really helped me to become a more well-rounded, less ignorant individual. He caused me many sleepless nights before final exams, but I really learned and knew my stuff.

Shortly after Jim's death, I received an email from a student who had just passed his doctoral dissertation defense at Miami University. He wrote: "Driving home I was struck by how much I would have loved to share the occasion with Dr. Cebula . . . I defended a dissertation . . . that I never would have written had I not registered for

Dr. Cebula's history course. It is safe to say that I would have never developed such an interest in academia w/o Jim's tutelage."[12]

Jim Cebula was doing the real work of the university, educating students, changing lives, contributing in a very real way to the good of society. At the end of Jim's career after 40 years of teaching, his salary amounted to not quite $90,000 a year. A decent salary, certainly, and not one about which Jim would have complained—but, nevertheless, it took a doctorate and four decades to get there.

Obviously, the money in the university is not in faculty salaries. It has become a common joke that the highest-paid person on any campus is the football coach, and that says a great deal about misplaced priorities. But in terms of revenue directed away from a university's primary instructional mission, nothing beats the layers of top administrators.

Gordon Gee, president of Ohio State University, has long been the poster child for presidential pay gone wrong. The *Dayton Daily News* performed an investigation of Gee's compensation that showed that since he took the job in 2007 through 2012 he has drawn more than $8.6 million in salary and compensation. And, shockingly, that does not include his expenses of $7.7 million over the same period. All of this funds an extraordinarily lavish lifestyle. "Records show," the *Daily News* reported, "that Gee stays in luxury hotels, dines at country clubs and swank restaurants, throws lavish parties, flies on private jets and hands out thousands of gifts—all at public expense." Since 2007, Ohio State has spent more than $64,000 on bow ties, bow tie cookies, and O-H and bow tie pins for Gee and others to distribute, the newspaper found. Meanwhile, OSU's endowment has slipped relative to its peers, and student tuition has increased 13.6 percent. Gee resigned in June 2013, under fire for controversial comments, but it is certain he will get a generous severance package.[13]

While Gee and OSU (which does not have a faculty union) are the outsize examples of irresponsibility by boards of trustees, they certainly are not alone. At the University of Cincinnati, for example, President Gregory Williams resigned in 2012, and nevertheless received a nearly $1.3 million severance package—including, amazingly, as *The Cincinnati Enquirer* reported, "a consulting deal that will pay him $300,000 during the first year and $200,000 the second year." Williams even received a $255,000 teaching salary in the law school for a year, but he did not have to teach. Of course, it was not the first time that UC has been so generous. In 2011, for example, David Stern, dean of the College of Medicine, resigned and walked away with a cool $900,000. At Kent State University, President Lester

Lefton, who is paid $417,799 a year, received a $104,000 bonus in 2013 by Kent trustees. In 2011, when the Kent trustees gave Lefton a $100,000 bonus, while hiking tuition 3.5 percent, a columnist in the *Plain Dealer* accused the trustees of "robbing the poor to pay the rich" and pointed out that Lefton made nearly 10 times the average full-time faculty salary.[14]

This is not to single out these individuals for particular criticism but to focus on the reality that, in Ohio and elsewhere, there is a system in academia where the people who actually do the work of the university, the faculty, get a relatively small cut of the revenue generated while a substantial and growing level of administrators at the top are compensated irresponsibly. All the while, tuition continues to go up, and the state contribution continues to dwindle. It does, in fact, mirror the income disparity problem that has developed more broadly in the United States during the same period of the last 30 years.

It is in this context of runaway salaries for top management that the Ohio legislature chose to try to crush the public employee unions. And, to be consistent, Gov. Kasich gave his own top staffers big pay increases while cutting the jobs of those on the lower rungs of his staff. His chief of staff, for example, started at $170,000, while Strickland's had made $122,000. "I appreciate Gov. Kasich keeping one of his campaign promises to operate the governor's office the way he operated Lehman Brothers," Chris Redfern, head of the Ohio Democratic Party, said wryly.[15]

The dramatic growth in inequality has expanded since the Reagan years, as subsequent politicians have continued to undo the New Deal and even introduce new and more creative ways to reward the wealthy for being wealthy. Newt Gingrich and John Kasich, during their control of Congress in the 1990s, continued the drive to make sure that the political system was captive to this new ideology. The role of the Republican Party as an obstructionist force has been well documented by Norman J. Ornstein and Thomas E. Mann in their book, aptly titled, *It's Even Worse Than It Looks: How the American Constitutional System Collided With the New Politics of Extremism*. The "Republican Party has become an insurgent outlier," they point out, "ideologically extreme; contemptuous of the inherited social and economic policy regime; scornful of compromise; unpersuadable by conventional understanding of facts, evidence and science; and dismissive of the legitimacy of its political opposition." When "one party moves this far from the center of American politics," Mann and Ornstein write, "it is extremely difficult to enact policies responsive to the country's most pressing challenges."[16]

This, of course, aptly describes the Republican Party that Ohio was saddled with in the wake of the 2010 election—a regime that continues to be in a position to do great harm as it attempted to do with Senate Bill 5. Consider the observations of *Columbus Dispatch* columnist Joe Hallett, who wrote in April 2013: "These days, the Republican-dominated Ohio General Assembly might be unmatched for its production of bad legislation, its devotion to fringe groups and their narrow-minded ideology, and its loyalty to the lobbies that larder legislative campaign accounts."[17]

Contrary to the ideological extremism represented by SB 5, many economists are actually more supportive of the positive impact that unions can and do have in American society. "The simple story of America," explains Nobel Prize-winning economist Joseph E. Stiglitz, "is this: the rich are getting richer, the richest of the rich are getting still richer, the poor are becoming poorer and more numerous, and the middle class is being hollowed out." He notes that trickle-down economics, the idea that if the people at the top benefit a lot, everyone will share in the success, "has long been discredited" because "higher inequality has not led to more growth, and most Americans have actually seen their incomes sink or stagnate."[18]

Stiglitz sees a clear explanation for the decline in earnings for most Americans: the decline of unions. "This has created an imbalance of economic power and a political vacuum," he argues. Without the protection of unions, "workers have fared even more poorly than they would have otherwise." In contrast to Franklin Roosevelt and the Wagner Act, which encouraged unions, "Republicans at both state and the federal levels, have worked to weaken them," Stiglitz observes, adding that Reagan's attack on PATCO represented "a critical juncture" in the breaking of union strength.[19]

The conservative movement argues that union busting contributes to economic strength, but Stiglitz disagrees: "I would argue that strong worker protections correct what would otherwise be an imbalance of economic power." Such protection, Stiglitz maintains, "leads to a higher-quality labor force with workers who are more loyal to their firms and more willing to invest in themselves and in their jobs. It also makes for a more cohesive society and better workplaces," as well as more sharing of the wealth generated by economic activity with the people actually doing the work.[20]

Stiglitz argues that this is, at heart, an ideological debate, and the right wing has gotten the best of the argument in recent years, aided by Fox News and wealthy right-wing think tanks. The result is the creation of a series of economic problems the nation now faces. "The

Right wants the 'right' rules of the game," Stiglitz points out, which are "those that advantage the wealthy at the expense of the rest." In the world that conservatives imagine, there is a single set of rules "that would be best for all." But, as Stiglitz notes, "that's just not true." If you listened to conservative arguments, he maintains that, for example, "you would have thought that markets always worked and government always failed," and thus you would not have recognized the consistent failures of the market. Stiglitz emphasizes how conservatives can easily recall examples of government failures, but "the massive failures of our financial system in the run-up to the Great Recession are quickly forgotten, described as an anomaly, or blamed on the government."[21]

"The question," writes economist Richard Thaler, "comes down to whether we want a society in which the rich take an ever-increasing share of the pie, or prefer to return to conditions that allow all classes to anticipate an increasing standard of living." He quotes Warren Buffet: "There's class warfare, all right, but it's my class, the rich class, that's making war, and we're winning."[22]

The damage that union-busting legislation like Senate Bill 5 and so-called right-to-work does to the American workforce is easily documented, and in the last few years there has been a plethora of works published about these facts, many of which have been cited in this book. As unions have declined between 1973 and 2011, wage growth in the United States has been just 10.7 percent for the median worker's real hourly compensation, according to the Economic Policy Institute (EPI). "A major factor driving these trends," EPI has determined, "has been the ongoing erosion of unionization and the declining bargaining power of unions, along with the weakened ability of unions to set norms or labor standards that raise the wages of comparable nonunion workers."[23]

And while corporate profits have soared—including a 171 percent increase after taxes just under Barack Obama's presidency—the corporate titans continue to complain about a lack of advantages. Tom Donohue of the U.S. Chamber and John Engler of the National Business Roundtable have both recently been beating a drum about fears of higher taxes and more regulation, and proclaiming that Obama deserves no credit for the economic rebound. But as Bloomberg News points out, business has never had it so good. "Profits are more than twice as high as their peak during President Ronald Reagan's administration," Bloomberg reports, "and more than 50 percent greater than during the late-1990s Internet boom, measured by the size of the economy."[24] Of course, this takes us back to Mann and Ornstein, and their recognition of the inability of so many in today's Republican Party circles to deal with facts. Longtime Republican figure Bruce Bartlett has gone through a change in his attitude toward those conservatives in charge of the GOP because of their unwillingness to deal with real issues. Writing about the Democratic victories in the 2012 election, Bartlett writes: "All the stupidity and closed-mindedness that right-wingers have displayed over the last 10 years has come back to haunt them."[25]

The impact of this ideologically driven strategy is clear. "No one proposes abolishing large corporations because so many exploit their workers or damage the environment or engage in anticompetitive practices," Stiglitz notes. That's because of a recognition that all human institutions have weaknesses. But the attitude toward unions has been the opposite. "They are vilified," Stiglitz points out, "and in many states there are explicit attempts to undermine them" with "no recognition of the important role they can play in countervailing other special interests and in defending the basic social protections that are necessary if workers are to accept change and to adjust to the changing economic environment."[26]

"On paper," Nobel Prize-winning economist Paul Krugman writes, "we're a one-person-one-vote nation; in reality, we're more than a bit of an oligarchy, in which a handful of wealthy people dominate. Given this reality, it's important to have institutions that can act as counterweights to the power of big money. And unions are among the most important of these institutions."[27]

That, of course, leads us to the Tea Party caucus in Congress, the Ohio legislature, and elsewhere. As a historian, it is particularly difficult to listen to the comic-book history promoted by the Tea Party—a central misconception being that the government has never been involved in the economy until now. The truth is that the government has, from the very beginnings of the republic, been an important part of and guide to the economy. High school history courses must routinely cover such government involvement in—even driving of—the economy as the construction of the Erie Canal, the building of the transcontinental railroads, the interstate highway system, and the internet. The plan originally called the "American Way" and eventually known as the "American System" was championed by both Alexander Hamilton and Henry Clay. It required government involvement in the economy at many levels from 1815 onward, for decades. This government economic activism included high tariffs to generate money for the federal government, the preservation of a national bank, and the development and funding of a system of internal improvements, especially roads and canals. Then, of course, there was the massive government spending during the Civil War that industrialized the country, and then the massive government spending during World War II that transformed the American economy and provided the means to become a global power. Further, historian Alex Fields has pointed out that the "decades of the 1930s, 40s, 50s, and 60s were periods of high productivity increases—higher than the decades before and after—and much of this success had to do with public investments."[28] There is much more that could be added, but the obvious facts of American history contradict the Tea Party narrative that somehow, just recently, the government became involved in the economy for the first time and that it is a bad idea.[29]

It is important to note, as well, that with all the predictions by SB 5 proponents of impending disaster for Ohio if the union movement was not crushed, the state of Ohio in 2013 has a surplus of at least a $1 billion. Certainly, the surplus was generated by irresponsible cuts to public education and municipal governments, but, clearly, crushing the unions was not necessary to put the state budget in the black as was claimed.[30]

"The imbalance of wealth and democracy in the United States is unsustainable," Kevin Phillips points out in a warning for the future. "Market theology and unelected leadership have been displacing politics and elections. Either democracy must be renewed, with politics brought back to life, or wealth is likely to cement a new and less democratic regime—plutocracy by some other name."[31]

Several analysts have suggested a few obvious areas of reform that would serve as a way out of having a government throttled by extremists funded by the corporate elite and as a way to create an economy that works for all the people:[32]

- Repeal some or all of the Taft-Hartley Act and allow unions to begin to really advocate for workers once again.
- Create in Ohio and other states a redistricting system that allows democracy to flourish again. Ohio is a prime example of how to gerrymander a state to ensure political extremism. Under a fair system, Republican moderates might have a chance to influence their party.
- At institutions of higher education, redirect at least 15 percent of the revenue currently going to administration to instructional purposes instead. In the public schools, ask teachers and parents how to improve education, not lobbyists for right-wing corporate-funded educational think tanks.

- Restore a system of taxation and regulation that generates necessary revenue from wealthy individuals as well as from the American corporate community. Deficits manufactured for political purposes should never be used to create phony crises as they were with Senate Bill 5. The "Buffet Rule" should have real meaning, and huge corporations, like Exxon, should not be able to avoid paying taxes.
- In Congress, put real limits on the filibuster so that the people's business can once again proceed unmolested by political extremism or by special interests.

The genius of American politics has been compromise based on real and not imagined issues. If we can manage these simple reforms, America, and Ohio as well, may well be poised for an amazingly positive twenty-first century. As FDR said:

> There is a mysterious cycle in human events. To some generations much is given. Of other generations much is expected. This generation of Americans has a rendezvous with destiny.

Notes

Introduction

1. Reginald Fields, "Ohio Voters Overwhelmingly Reject Issue 2, Dealing a Blow to Gov. Kasich," *The Plain Dealer*, Nov. 8, 2011, accessed May 18, 2012.
2. Amy Davidson, "Remember Montana: The Supreme Court Won't Reexamine Citizens United," *The New Yorker*, June 25, 2012, http://www.newyorker.com/online/blogs/closeread/2012/06/remember-montana-citizens-united.html. *Frontline* has done an excellent investigation of the Montana case, *Big Sky, Big Money*, http://www.pbs.org/wgbh/pages/frontline/big-sky-big-money/. For more on Montana's history of corporate domination, see Laura Mercier, *Anaconda: Labor, Community and Culture in Montana's Smelter City* (Urbana: University of Illinois Press, 2001); Michael P. Malone, *The Battle for Butte: Mining and Politics on the Northern Frontier, 1864–1906* (Seattle: University of Washington Press, 1981); C.B. Glasscock, *The War of the Copper Kings: The Builders of Butte and the Wolves of Wall Street* (New York: Grosset & Dunlap, 1966); C.P. Connolly, *The Devil Learns to Vote: The Story of Montana* (New York: Covici, Friede, 1938).
3. Kent State University, another AAUP-unionized faculty, and UC are about the same size.
4. Reginald Fields, "Republican John Kasich Victorious in Ohio; Jobs Message Overcomes Wall Street Baggage," *The Cleveland Plain Dealer*, Nov. 3, 2010, http://www.cleveland.com/politics/index.ssf/2010/11/republican_john_kasich_headed.html.

Chapter 1

1. When Ohio's economy began to recover in 2011, many perceptive political observers called it the "Strickland recovery," since Gov. Kasich's impact on the economy, however negligible, could not begin to appear until 2012, and by then the national recovery and auto bailouts had begun to drive the state's recovery.
2. Lukens was eventually elected to the U.S. Congress and served until 1990. Criminal sexual charges ended his political career; he was

convicted of the misdemeanor crime of contributing to the delinquency of a minor for paying a 16-year-old female for sex. He refused to resign but lost the 1990 Republican primary to John Boehner. While serving out the remaining months of his term, Lukens was accused of fondling an elevator operator in the Capital building and sentenced to 30 days in jail, psychological counseling, and testing for venereal disease. In 1996, Lukens was convicted of bribery and conspiracy in connection to the House banking scandal during his term in Congress.

3. R.W. Apple, Jr., "A Republican with Rough Edges," *New York Times Magazine*, April 26, 1998, http://www.nytimes.com/1998/04/26/magazine/a-republican-with-rough-edges.html; John Hicks, "Fact Checking the Governor's RNC Speeches," *The Washington Post*, Aug. 30, 2012, http://www.washingtonpost.com/blogs/fact-checker/post/fact-checking-the-governors-rnc-speeches/2012/08/30/8f60562e-f2b5-11e1-adc6-87dfa8eff430_blog.html.
4. Herbert Hoover, "The Consequences of the Proposed New Deal," Madison Square Garden, Oct. 21, 1932, and "The Crisis to Free Men," Republican National Convention, June 10, 1936, both available on the Pepperdine University Law School website, Faculty Research, The New Deal, http://publicpolicy.pepperdine.edu/faculty-research/new-deal/hoover-speeches/hh061036.htm.
5. John Kasich, *Courage Is Contagious: Ordinary People Doing Extraordinary Things to Change the Face of America* (New York: Doubleday, 1995) 12.
6. There have been efforts to redeem Hoover's reputation, too often coming from the right-wing fringe seeking to justify flawed policies today. For a balanced historical effort, see Joan Hoff Wilson, *Herbert Hoover: The Forgotten Progressive* (Boston: Little Brown, 1975).
7. Laura Bischoff and Christopher Mangan, "Deep Cuts, Privatization Fill Kasich's First Budget," *Dayton Daily News*, March 16, 2011, http://www.daytondailynews.com/news/news/state-regional/deep-cuts-privatization-fill-kasichs-first-budge-1/nMp5s/.
8. Staff report, "Schneider to Seek 7th Ohio Seat," *Middletown Journal*, Jan. 6, 2010, http://www.middletownjournal.com/news/news/local/schneider-to-seek-7th-ohio-senate-seat-1/nM72n/.
9. Barry Horstman, "Shannon Jones: The Force Behind Senate Bill 5," *The Cincinnati Enquirer*, March 3, 2011, http://news.cincinnati.com/article/20110303/NEWS0108/103040348/Shannon-Jones-force-behind-Senate-Bill-5.
10. Ibid.
11. Politics blog, "Niehaus, Jones Picked as Senate Leaders," *The Cincinnati Enquirer*, Nov. 30, 2010, http://cincinnati.com/blogs/politics/2010/11/30/niehaus-jones-picked-as-senate-leaders/.

12. Rory Ryan, "Niehaus Sworn in as Ohio Senate President," *The Highland County Press*, Jan. 2, 2011, http://highlandcountypress.com/main.asp?FromHome=1&TypeID=1&ArticleID=6315&SectionID=2&SubSectionID=20.
13. Ibid.
14. Jim Siegel and Darrell Rowland, "House Cozy with Charter School Lobby," *The Columbus Dispatch*, June 5, 2011, http://www.dispatch.com/content/stories/local/2011/06/05/house-cozy-with-charter-schoollobby.html; Joe Guillen, "Ohio House Speaker William Batchelder Won't Apologize for Joke That Obama Should Be Jailed," *The Cleveland Plain Dealer*, Feb. 22, 2012, http://www.cleveland.com/open/index.ssf/2012/02/ohio_house_speaker_refuses_to.html. For more on Speaker Batchelder's financial backers, see the National Institute on Money in State Politics's website, http://www.followthemoney.org/database/StateGlance/candidate.phtml?c=123524, and Christine Jindra, "Ohio Probes Campaign Spending by Charter School Operator David Brennan," *The Dayton Daily News*, April 10, 2008, http://blog.cleveland.com/openers/2008/04/give.html.
15. For more on the doubts surrounding Bush's victory in Ohio in 2004, see Mark Crispin Miller, "None Dare Call It Stolen: Ohio, the Election, and America's Servile Press," *Harper's Magazine*, August 2005, http://www.freepress.org/departments/display/19/2005/1383.
16. Reginald Fields, "McGee Brown Highlights Ohio's Education Ranking, but the State's Grades Are Less Flattering," *The Cleveland Plain Dealer*, July 25, 2010, http://www.cleveland.com/open/index.ssf/2010/07/mcgee_brown_highlights_ohios_e.html.
17. Most of this material is taken nearly verbatim from a Policy Matters Ohio fact sheet, "Policy Matters Testifies on Gov. Taft's Tax Reform Proposal," May 23, 2005, http://www.policymattersohio.org/policy-matters-testifies-on-governor-tafts-tax-reform-proposal.
18. Jim Siegel, "Kasich's Budget Slashes Aid to Local Governments," *The Columbus Dispatch*, March 15, 2011, http://www.dispatch.com/content/stories/local/2011/03/15/kasich-releases-budget.html.
19. There will inevitably be an effort by conservatives to disparage Policy Matters Ohio as a "liberal think tank." I would encourage readers to carefully examine Policy Matters' reports and judge them on their own merits without applying ideological blinders.
20. "Wealthiest Ohioans Gain Most from Proposed Tax Changes," Policy Matters Ohio, March 7, 2005, http://www.policymattersohio.org/wp-content/uploads/2011/10/TaftTaxPlanWhoSaves_2005_0307.pdf.
21. "The Taft Plan for Income Tax Cuts Is Not Good for Ohio Because . . . ," Policy Matters Ohio, http://www.policymattersohio.org/

wp-content/uploads/2011/10/IncomeTaxCutsNotGoodForOhio_2005_051.pdf.

22. Jon P. Honeck, testimony to the Ohio Senate Ways and Means Committee, March 16, 2005, Policy Matters Ohio, http://www.policymattersohio.org/policy-matters-testifies-on-governor-tafts-tax-reform-proposal.
23. "Gov. Taft's Plan to Overhaul Tax System Fails to Resonate with Many Business Execs," *Business First*, April 7, 2005, http://www.bizjournals.com/columbus/stories/2005/04/11/story2.html?page=all.
24. "Tax Policy Shortchanges Public Services; Job Growth Remains Anemic," April 24, 2007, Policy Matters Ohio, http://www.policymattersohio.org/wp-content/uploads/2011/10/PMOHouseBudgetStatement2007_04.pdf.
25. "The 2005 Tax Overhaul and Ohio's Economy," Jan. 15, 2009, Policy Matters Ohio, http://www.policymattersohio.org/the-2005-tax-overhaul-and-ohios-economy.
26. Laurence Mishel, "Tax Cuts Won't Create Jobs," Economic Policy Institute website, July 10, 2009, http://www.epi.org/publication/tax_cuts_wont_create_jobs/; Bill Harris, "Tax Cuts Don't Create Jobs," *Forbes*, Nov. 5, 2012, http://www.forbes.com/sites/billharris/2012/11/05/tax-cuts-dont-create-jobs/ (accessed Jan. 9, 2013).
27. William Grieder, "The Education of David Stockman," Dec. 1981, *The Atlantic*, http://www.theatlantic.com/magazine/archive/1981/12/the-education-of-david-stockman/305760/.
28. Jackie Calmes, "John Kasich Wields the Mighty Budget Axe Granted by Gingrich," *The Wall Street Journal*, Jan. 27, 1995.
29. Ibid.
30. Sam Shawver, "Noble County Solar Farm Still in the Works," *The Marietta Times*, April 2, 2012, http://www.mariettatimes.com/page/content.detail/id/543196.html. Groundbreaking for the project has been put off until the summer of 2013 because of difficulty in getting approval from state agencies. But the cost of the project has actually declined, because solar power equipment is becoming less expensive. Jeff Bell, "Turning Point Solar Ready to Move Ahead on Eastern Ohio Project," *Business First*, Dec. 7, 2012, http://www.bizjournals.com/columbus/print-edition/2012/12/07/light-at-end-of-tunnel-in-eastern-ohio.html?page=all.
31. Jeff Bell, "AEP Setback Dims Prospects for $180M Turning Point Solar Project," *Business First*, Jan. 9, 2013, http://www.bizjournals.com/columbus/news/2013/01/09/aep-setback-dims-prospects-for-180m.html?page=all; Dan Gearino, "PUCO Deals Blow to AEP Solar Project," *The Columbus Dispatch*, Jan. 10, 2013, http://www.dispatch.com/content/stories/business/2013/01/10/puco-deals-blow-to-aep-solar-project.html. The *Dispatch* has also reported that the chair of PUCO, Todd Snitchler, is firmly opposed to green energy.

See Darrell Rowland, "PUCO chief blasts green energy on Twitter," *The Columbus Dispatch*, Jan. 12, 2013, http://www.dispatch.com/content/stories/local/2013/01/12/puco-chief-blasts-green-energy-on-twitter.html.

32. Editorial, "Broken School Funding Program Is Showing Cracks Even in the Most Affluent Districts," *The Cleveland Plain Dealer*, Oct. 29, 2011, http://www.cleveland.com/opinion/index.ssf/2011/10/a_broken_school-funding_system.html.
33. For more information on the evidence-based strategy, see the Ohio Education Matters website.
34. Reginald Fields, "Ohio Gov. Strickland Defends School Funding Plan that Kasich Wants to Scrap," *The Cleveland PlainDealer*, Sept. 22, 2010, http://www.cleveland.com/open/index.ssf/2010/09/post_18.html. Once Kasich's budget was actually announced, we discovered that his principal approach to public schools was to drastically underfund them.
35. Editorial, "Gov.-Elect Kasich Is Wrong on Use of Federal Rail Funds," *The Youngstown Vindicator*, Nov. 27, 2010, http://66.232.150.6/news/2010/nov/27/gov-elect-kasich-is-wrong-on-use-of-fede/.
36. Jonathan Riskind, "Ohio, Wisconsin, High-Speed Rail Money to Go Elsewhere," *The Columbus Dispatch*, Dec. 9, 2010, http://www.dispatch.com/content/stories/local/2010/12/09/09-rail-money.html.
37. Reginald Fields, "Governor-Elect John Kasich Hints at Broader Privatization Plans," *The Cleveland Plain Dealer*, Jan. 7, 2011, http://www.cleveland.com/open/index.ssf/2011/01/governor-elect_john_kasich_hin.html.
38. Bob Ortega, "Arizona Private Prisons Slammed by Report," *The Arizona Republic*, Feb. 15, 2012, http://www.azcentral.com/arizonarepublic/local/articles/20120215arizona-private-prisons-slammed-by-report.html; Bob Ortega, "Arizona Prison Oversight Lacking for Private Facilities," *The Arizona Republic*, Aug. 7, 2011, http://www.azcentral.com/news/articles/2011/08/07/20110807arizona-prison-private-oversight.html.
39. Joe Vardon, "JobsOhio Works Amid Funding Question," *The Columbus Dispatch*, Jan. 2, 2013, http://www.dispatch.com/content/stories/local/2013/01/02/jobsohio-works-amid-funding-question.html; Editorial, "JobsOhio Can't Be Allowed to Hide From the Public," *The Cleveland Plain Dealer*, March 20, 2013, http://www.cleveland.com/opinion/index.ssf/2013/03/jobsohio_cant_be_allowed_to_hi.html.
40. William Hershey, "AG Cordray Blasts Kasich Plan to Privatize Economic Development," *Dayton Daily News*, Aug. 23, 2010, http://mo.daytondailynews.com/blogs/content/shared-gen/blogs/dayton/ohiopolitics/entries/2010/08/23/ag_cordray_blasts_kasich_plan

.html; Jeff Bell, "Michigan Woes Show Limits of Kasich's JobsOhio Plan," *Business First*, Aug. 30, 2010, http://www.bizjournals.com/columbus/stories/2010/08/30/story3.html.

41. "Reality Check: Indiana Job Numbers Don't Add Up," WTHR, March 1, 2010, http://www.wthr.com/story/12066021/reality-check-indiana-job-numbers-dont-add-up.
42. Laura Bischoff, "Kasich Tells Lobbyists, Help or Get Out of the Way," *Dayton Daily News*, Nov. 4, 2010, http://mo.daytondailynews.com/o/content/shared-gen/blogs/dayton/ohiopolitics/entries/2010/11/04/kasich_tells_lobbyists_help_or.html.
43. Mark Kovac, "Senate Bill 5/Issue 2: How Did We Get Here?," *The Youngstown Vindicator*, Oct. 23, 2011, http://www.vindy.com/news/2011/oct/23/senate-bill-5issue-2-how-did-we-get-here/.

Chapter 2

1. Naomi Klein, *The Shock Doctrine: The Rise of Disaster Capitalism* (New York: Picador, 2008).
2. Ibid., 6. As will become clear later in the chapter, it is important to note that the man who called for the attack on public schools was economist Milton Friedman, a devotee of Frederick A. Hayek and the Austrian school of economics.
3. "As Companies Seek Tax Deals, Government Pays High Price," *The New York Times*, Dec. 1, 2012, http://www.nytimes.com/2012/12/02/us/how-local-taxpayers-bankroll-corporations.html?pagewanted=all&_r=0.
4. Amity Shlaes, *The Forgotten Man: A New History of the Great Depression* (New York: Harper, 2007); Paul Krugman, "Amity Shlaes Strikes Again," *The New York Times*, Nov. 19, 2008, http://krugman.blogs.nytimes.com/2008/11/19/amity-shlaes-strikes-again/; Arthur C. Brooks, *TheBattle: How the Fight Between Free Enterprise and Big Government Will Shape America's Future* (New York: Basic Books, 2010); Bryan Caplan, "If Only: A Review of Arthur Brooks' *The Battle*," Library of Economics and Liberty, http://econlog.econlib.org/archives/2010/05/If_only_a_revie.html.
5. William E. Leuchtenburg, *Franklin D. Roosevelt and the New Deal, 1932–1940* (New York: Harper & Row, 1963).
6. For a review of the impact of the Wagner Act, see David Brody, *Labor Embattled: History, Power, Rights* (Urbana: University of Illinois Press, 2005), and Robert Michael Smith, *From Blackjacks to Briefcases: A History of Commercialized Strikebreaking and Unionbusting in the United States* (Athens: Ohio University Press, 2003).
7. Frederick A. Von Hayek, *The Road to Serfdom* (London: Routledge, 1944).

8. Greg Sargent, "Mitt Romney: 'America's Economy Runs on Freedom,'" *The Washington Post*, May 18, 2012, http://www.washingtonpost.com/blogs/plum-line/post/mitt-romney-americas-economy-runs-on-freedom/2012/05/18/gIQAWJ1nYU_blog.html.
9. Nicholas Wapshott, *Keynes-Hayek: The Clash That Defined Modern Economics* (New York: Norton & Co., 2011) 100–101.
10. Daniel Yergin and Joseph Stanislaw, *The Commanding Heights: The Battle for the World Economy* (New York: Simon and Schuster, 2002) 124–125; Jeffrey D. Sachs, "Welfare State Beyond Ideology," *Scientific American*, November 2006, http://www.scientificamerican.com/article.cfm?id=the-social-welfare-state; George Orwell, *The [London] Observer*, April 9, 1944.
11. David Harvey, *A Brief History of Neoliberalism* (Oxford: Oxford University Press, 2007) 3, 20–21.
12. "Special Report: Is Greed Good? Only If It Is Properly Governed," *The Economist*, May 16, 2002, http://www.economist.com/node/1119945.
13. Yergin and Stanislaw, 123–131.
14. Kim Phillips-Fein, *Invisible Hands: The Making of the Conservative Movement from the New Deal to Reagan* (New York: Norton, 2009) 45–52.
15. Ibid., 60.
16. Michael Bowen, *The Roots of Modern Conservatism: Dewey, Taft, and the Battle for the Soul of the Republican Party* (Chapel Hill: University of North Carolina Press, 2011) 6–7; David Farber, *The Rise and Fall of Modern American Conservatism: A Short History* (Princeton: Princeton University Press, 2010) 16–17.
17. Farber, 30–31.
18. Ibid.
19. Ibid., 35.
20. Ibid., 35–36.
21. William Leuchtenburg, *In the Shadow of FDR* (Ithaca, NY: Cornell University Press, 1985) 49.
22. Louis Galambos, ed., *The Papers of Dwight D. Eisenhower* (Baltimore, MD, Johns Hopkins University Press, 1989) 13: 1385: 13: 1357.
23. Philips-Fein, ix–xii.
24. Ibid., 100.
25. Ibid., 100–102.
26. Ibid., 103–105.
27. Kari Frederickson, *The Dixie Revolt and the End of the Solid South, 1932–1968* (Chapel Hill: University of North Carolina Press, 2000); Joseph Crespino, *In Search of Another Country: Mississippi and the Conservative Counterrevolution* (Princeton: Princeton University Press, 2007).

28. Daniel J. Galvin, *Presidential Party Building: Dwight Eisenhower to George W. Bush* (Princeton: Princeton University Press, 2010) 65–66.
29. Ibid., 67.
30. Ibid., 67–68.
31. Crespino, 3.
32. Farber, 89–90.
33. Barry Goldwater, *The Conscience of a Conservative* (New York: Macfadden-Bartell, 1961) 48–49.
34. Geoffrey Kabaservice, *Rule and Ruin: The Downfall of Moderation and the Destruction of the Republican Party from Eisenhower to the Tea Party* (New York: Oxford University Press, 2012) 92–93.
35. Ibid., 93–94.
36. Ibid., 102.
37. Ibid., 103; William A Rusher, "Crossroads for the GOP," *National Review*, Feb. 12, 1963, 109–112.
38. Dan T. Carter, *From George Wallace to Newt Gingrich: Race in the Conservative Counterrevolution, 1963–1994* (Baton Rouge: Louisiana State University Press, 1996) xiv.
39. John Micklethwait and Adrian Wooldridge, *The Right Nation: Conservative Power in America* (New York: Penguin Press, 2004) 76–78. Micklethwait and Wooldridge deserve a great deal of credit in tracing the money behind the right-wing ideology mill.
40. Ibid.
41. Ibid.
42. Ibid., 79.
43. Ibid., 79.
44. Ibid., 79.
45. Jacob Weisberg, "Happy Birthday, Heritage Foundation!" *Slate*, Jan 9, 1998, http://www.slate.com/articles/news_and_politics/strange_bedfellow/1998/01/happy_birthday_heritage_foundation.html. Weisberg is quoting Will Marshall, then president of the New Democrat Progressive Policy Institute.
46. Ibid.
47. Robert Novak, "Father of Supply Side," Sept. 1, 2005, CNN website, http://www.cnn.com/2005/POLITICS/09/01/supply.side/index.html.
48. Arthur Laffer, "The Laffer Curve: Past, Present, and Future," June 1, 2004. Heritage Foundation website, http://www.heritage.org/research/reports/2004/06/the-laffer curve past-present-and-future.
49. Ibid.
50. Jude Wanniski, "Will There Be a Budget?" Memos on the Margin, 1995, Polyconomics website, http://www.polyconomics.com/index.php?option=com_content&view=article&id=542:will-there-be-a-budget&catid=19:1995&Itemid=26.

51. Jude Wanniski, "John Kasich, Presidential Timber," Memos on the Margin, 1998. Polyconomics Institute website, http://www.polyconomics.com/index.php?option=com_content&view=article&id=2349:john-kasich-presidential-timber&catid=37:1998&Itemid=30.
52. Jude Wanniski, "Farrakhan at Our Conference," Polyconomics Institute website, http://www.polyconomics.com/index.php?option=com_content&view=article&id=643:farrakhan-at-our-conferencefed-watch&catid=21:1997&Itemid=26. See also Joyce Price, "Kasich Gets Farrakhan's Praise, Kemp Also Has Minister's Respect," *The Washington Times*, March 2, 1997.
53. Review by Benjamin J. Cohen, *Journal of Interdisciplinary History* 10: 10 (Summer 1979), 359–360.
54. Brian Lamb, "Q and A with David Stockman," *C-Span*, April 2, 2013, http://www.c-spanvideo.org/program/AwithDa.
55. Weisberg, ibid.
56. Harvey, 25.
57. Ibid., 26–27.
58. Jonathan Chait, "2012 or Never," *New York Magazine*, Feb. 26, 2012, http://nymag.com/news/features/gop-primary-chait-2012-3/.
59. Ibid. This well-researched theory was first introduced by John Judas and Ruy Teixeira, *The Emerging Democratic Majority*(New York: Scribner, 2004).
60. E.J. Dionne, "Mitt Romney's Class Problem," *The Washington Post*, Nov. 7, 2012, http://www.washingtonpost.com/blogs/post-partisan/post/mitt-romneys-class-problem/2012/11/07/f082c60e-2897-11e2-b4e0-346287b7e56c_blog.html.
61. Jim DeMint, *Last Chance: Saving American from Economic Collapse* (New York: Center Street, 2012). Since Republican policies are largely responsible for the 2008 economic collapse, it stretches reality for DeMint to suggest that he and his party have something to offer at this point. No surprise that Tea Party favorite Rand Paul wrote an introduction to DeMint's book.
62. Sabrina Eaton, "In Evenly Split Ohio, Redistricting Gives GOP 12–4 Edge in Congressional Seats," *The Cleveland Plain Dealer*, Nov. 11, 2012, http://www.cleveland.com/open/index.ssf/2012/11/in_evenly_split_ohio_redistric.html.
63. National Public Radio interview with Nina Totenberg, aired July 6, 2012. http://www.npr.org/blogs/itsallpolitics/2012/07/05/156319272/federal-judge-richard-posner-the-gop-has-made-me-less-conservative.
64. Bruce Bartlett, "Revenge of the Reality-Based Community: My Life on the Republican Right and How I Saw it All Go Wrong," *The American Conservative*, Nov. 26, 2012, http://www.theamericanconservative.com/articles/revenge-of-the-reality-based-community/.

65. Ibid.
66. For a perceptive analysis of the authoritarian aspects of Republican ideology, see Marc J. Hetherington and Jonathan D. Weiler, *Authoritarianism and Polarization in American Politics* (New York: Cambridge University Press, 2009).

Chapter 3

1. UE is an abbreviation for the United Electrical, Radio, and Machine Workers of America, a union that represents 35,000 workers across the country.
2. At the AAUP's national meeting in June 2012 in Washington DC, Herman and Kilpatrick were jointly given the Georgina M. Smith Award for their important roles in defending the faculty through the defeat of Senate Bill 5. The Smith Award is only occasionally given, and only for truly exceptional service to the profession. For the sake of eliminating any confusion, I should note that Sara Kilpatrick was married on May 21, 2011, and prior to that her name was Sara Kaminski.
3. Joe Guillen, "What's Really in Senate Bill 5?" *The Cleveland Plain Dealer*, March 20, 2011, http://www.cleveland.com/open/index.ssf/2011/03/whats_really_in_senate_5_clear.html.
4. This testimony is taken from the notes of Sara Kilpatrick, AAUP-OC executive director, who was in the room.
5. Staff reports, "Public Unions Ready to Fight GOP Proposals," *The Columbus Dispatch*, Feb. 10, 2011, http://www.dispatch.com/content/stories/local/2011/02/10/unions-in-a-fight.html. OCSEA is an abbreviation for the Ohio Civil Service Employees Association.
6. AFSCME is an abbreviation for the American Federation of State, County, and Municipal Employees.
7. Reginald Fields, "Police and Fire Unions Say They Will Make Republicans Pay for Proposal Limiting Collective Bargaining," *The Cleveland Plain Dealer*, Feb. 24, 2011, http://www.cleveland.com/open/index.ssf/2011/02/police_and_fire_unions_say_the.html; Jim Siegel, "Public Workers Ready to Fight GOP Proposals," *The Columbus Dispatch*, Feb. 10, 2011, http://www.dispatch.com/content/stories/local/2011/02/10/unions-in-a-fight.html; Joe Guillen, Overhaul of State's Collective Bargaining Law Proposed in Ohio Senate," *The Cleveland Plain Dealer*, Feb. 9, 2011, http://www.cleveland.com/open/index.ssf/2011/02/overhaul_of_states_collective.html.
8. Cliff Peale, "Kasich: Higher Ed Must Tighten Belt," *The Cincinnati Enquirer*, Dec. 8, 2010, http://news.cincinnati.com/article/20101208/NEWS0102/12090318/Kasich-Higher-ed-must-tighten-belt.
9. Testimony presented by Hayes can be viewed at http://www.youtube.com/watch?v=sTdquroj8R0.

10. John McNay, "Jones Bill Will Lead to a Race to the Bottom in Ohio," Hamilton *Journal-News*, Feb. 18, 2011, http://www.journal-news.com/news/lifestyles/philosophy/john-mcnay-jones-bill-will-lead-to-a-race-to-the-1/nNXLZ/.
11. A transcript of Grayson's testimony can be found at http://www.akronaaup.org/Grayson-SB5_testimony_oral.pdf.
12. Dr. Fichtenbaum's testimony can be found at http://ouaaup.wordpress.com/2011/02/18/aaups-rudy-fichtenbaum-rocks-testimony-against-s-b-5/.
13. Jeffrey Keefe, "Are Ohio Public Employees Over-Compensated?" Feb. 10, 2011, *Economic Policy Institute,* Briefing Paper #296, http://www.epi.org/publication/bp296/.
14. Joe Guillen, "Union Protesters Locked Out of Statehouse, According to Democrats, Who Call on Kasich to Let Them In," *The Cleveland Plain Dealer*, Feb. 22, 2011, http://www.cleveland.com/open/index.ssf/2011/02/union_protesters_locked_out_of.html. The Ohio Senate Democrats produced some video, and much more can be found on the internet: http://www.youtube.com/watch?v=PZGOdgD8WpI.
15. "Democrats Vow to Put Bargaining Rights on Ballot of Senate Bill 5 OK'd," *Dayton Daily News*, Feb. 23, 2011, http://www.daytondailynews.com/news/news/state-regional/democrats-vow-to-put-bargaining-rights-on-ballot-1/nMpRZ/.
16. "Growth in Administrators Outstrips Growth in Faculty," *The Chronicle of Higher Education*, Aug. 17, 2010, http://chronicle.com/blogs/ticker/growth-in-administrators-outstrips-growth-in-faculty-members/26283; John T. McNay, "Ohio College Plan Left Out the Faculty," *The Cincinnati Enquirer*, Jan. 2, 2013, http://news.cincinnati.com/article/20130102/EDIT02/301020078/Ohio-college-plan-left-out-faculty.

Chapter 4

1. Taft, Stettinius, and Hollister website, http://www.taftlaw.com/recognition/history.
2. Kris Maher and James Hagerty, "Ohio GOP Revises Union Bill," *The Wall Street Journal*, March 26, 2011, http://online.wsj.com/article/SB10001424052748703696704576222894142133456.html; Julie Kent, "Ohio Republicans Reconfigure Senate Committee to Ensure Passage of SB5," *The Cleveland Leader,* March 3, 2012, http://www.clevelandleader.com/node/16104.
3. "Senate Bill 5 Pits Housemates Against Each Other," *The Cincinnati Enquirer*, March 4, 2011, http://news.cincinnati.com/article/20110304/NEWS0108/103050327/SB-5-pits-Senate-housemates-against-each-other.

4. The Ohio Senate debate and final vote on Senate Bill 5 occurred on March 2, 2011. Video of the testimony is available at www.ohiochannel.org, and the material for this chapter has been taken from that original source.
5. Deborah Herman and John McNay, "Senate Bill 5 Passes—Amended Version Worse Than the Original Bill," *AAUP Works,* AAUP-UC Chapter Bulletin, March 2, 2011, http://www.aaupuc.org/newsletter-archive/works-2011/18Works4_2March11.pdf.
6. Mark Bousquet, *How the University Works: Higher Education and the Low-Wage Nation* (New York: New York University Press, 2008) 211–223.
7. Sheldon Gelman, "Adopting Ohio Senate Bill 5: The Role of the University Presidents," *Albany Law Review*, 75:1, 2011/2012; Benjamin Ginsberg, *The Fall of the Faculty: The Rise of the All-Administrative University and Why It Matters* (New York: Oxford University Press, 2011). Ginsberg is also the co-author of *We the People: An Introduction to American Politics* (New York: WW Norton & Co., 2011), the most widely used textbook in introductory courses on American government and politics in the nation's colleges and universities.
8. Ginsberg, 2.
9. Ibid.
10. Gelman, 512, 533.
11. Ibid., 518.
12. Ibid., 519.
13. Ibid.
14. "By a Wide Margin, Bowling Green Faculty Vote for AAUP Union," AAUP website, Oct. 20, 2010, http://www.aaup.org/AAUP/newsroom/prarchives/2010/BGSUvote.htm.
15. Gelman, 524–525.
16. Ibid., 527–528; Tom Troy, "BGSU Officials Linked to Role in SB 5 Draft," *The Toledo Blade*, Sept. 22, 2011, accessed July 21, 2012.
17. Ibid.
18. Ida Liezkovszky, "Higher Ed Unions Say Issue 2 Would Be a Death Sentence," *State Impact,* Oct. 21, 2011, https://stateimpact.npr.org/ohio/2011/10/21/higher-ed-unions-say-issue-2-would-be-a-death-sentence.

Chapter 5

1. William J. Cronon, "Wisconsin's Radical Break," *The New York Times,* March 21, 2011, www.nytimes.com/2011/03/22/opinion/22cronon.html.
2. William Cronon's blog, www.scholarascitizen.williamcronon.net, contains a detailed chronology as well as many links to the national news coverage of the attack he faced.

3. Editorial, "A Shabby Crusade in Wisconsin," *The New York Times*, March 25, 2011, www.nytimes.com/2011/03/28/opinion/28mon3.html; Greg Sargent, "Wisconsin GOP: You're Damn Right We Requested Walker Critic's Email," *The Washington Post*, March 25, 2011, www.washingtonpost.com/.../post/wisconsin-gop.../AFytRNWB_blog ; James Fallows, "'Have You No Sense of Decency?': The William Cronon Story," *The Atlantic*, March 25, 2011, http://www.theatlantic.com/national/archive/2011/03/have-you-no-sense-of-decency-the-wm-cronon-story/73010/.
4. Chancellor Martin's response can be found on Cronon's blog, Scholar as Citizen, http://scholarcitizen.williamcronon.net/.
5. For more on Cronon's experience see, Todd Finkelmeyer, "UW's Cronon Sees 'Intimidation' in GOP Request," *The Capital Times*, April 7, 2011, http://host.madison.com/news/local/education/university/uw-s-cronon-sees-intimidation-in-gop-request/article_474631d2-6068-11e0-b25d-001cc4c002e0.html.
6. I've reconstructed much of this from memory, since I was in contact with the organizers and attended the protest. But I also owe much to the Center for Media and Democracy (CMD) website. On the one-year anniversary of the Cincinnati protest, on April 27, 2012, CMD marked the date with a detailed story that recapped much of the event and recognized its historic importance. Importantly, CMD also provides online a copy of the letter the protest team submitted to ALEC, http://www.prwatch.org/news/2012/04/11418/one-year-later-first-alec-protest-cincinnati.
7. Fabien Tepper, "Getting Deep Inside ALEC: Local Activist Exposes Decades of Secret Legislation," *City Beat*, Aug. 3, 2011, http://www.citybeat.com/cincinnati/article-23835-getting_deep_inside_alec.html.
8. Beau Hodal, "Quid pro Status Quo: ALEC & State-Sanctioned Corruption in Ohio," *Center for Media and Democracy*, http://www.prwatch.org/NODE/11498.
9. Ibid.
10. Ibid.
11. Ibid.
12. Joel Rogers and Laure Dresser, "ALEC Exposed: Business Domination, Inc.," *The Nation*, July 12, 2011, www.thenation.com/article/161977/business-domination-inc.
13. "ALEC in Ohio: The Corporate Special Interests That Help Write Ohio's Laws,"People for the American Way, http://www.pfaw.org/ALEC-in-Ohio.
14. *The Nation*, Ibid.
15. Laura A. Bischoff, William Hershey, and Cornelius Frolik, "Democrats Vow to Put Bargaining Rights on Ballot if Senate Bill 5 OK'd," *Dayton Daily News*, Feb. 23, 2011, http://

www.daytondailynews.com/news/news/state-regional/democrats-vow-to-put-bargaining-rights-on-ballot-1/nMpRZ/.

16. IBEW is an abbreviation for the International Brotherhood of Electrical Workers.
17. Bruce Bostick, "Ohio Fight Back Drive Announced at Town Hall Meeting," *The Free Press* (Columbus), April 1, 2011, http://www.freepress.org/departments/display/18/2011/4127.
18. A.J. Stokes, a consultant for Jonathan Varner and Associates, was formerly majority chief of staff for the Democrats in the Ohio House. Before his legislative involvement, he worked for the Teamsters.
19. Ironically, 2011 was the anniversary of the Triangle Shirtwaist Factory fire in New York City, in which 146 women—mostly immigrants and members of the International Lady Garment Workers Union—were killed on March 25, 1911. The Ludlow Massacre took place when Colorado National Guard and guards from a Rockefeller mining company attacked a camp of striking miners on April 20, 1914, killing between 19 and 25 people. The Anaconda Road Massacre was an incident in which Anaconda Copper Mining Co. guards fired on striking miners in Butte, Montana, on April 21, 1920. The guards hit 17 miners in the back as they tried to flee, wounding 16 and killing 1.

Chapter 6

1. As a postscript to the free speech zone issue, a libertarian student group, Young Americans for Liberty, with the help of the nonpartisan Foundation for Individual Rights in Education (FIRE) filed a federal lawsuit against UC because of the zone and related regulations. A federal judge later ruled that the zone was unconstitutional, and no such restrictions on free speech exist at UC today. Further, I argued at the time that Gov. Kasich's visit could not be deemed a private meeting because the news media had been invited. As a former journalist, I know that, by definition, any meeting where there is a blanket invitation to the news media is a public meeting, and thus we had a right to be there. I later confirmed this with David Marburger, a Cleveland attorney specializing in open-meetings law. He wrote, "In my view, you are correct. Once the officials allow the journalism community to attend, only the logistics of physical space could justify discriminating against the rest of the public. The journalists are there—not b/c of some special interest that they have that's distinct from the public's interest—but b/c they are conduits to the gen'l public. So, absent space limitations that would justify allowing only reporters to attend, the decision to exclude others seems to me to violate the First Amendment, which bars gov'tal decisions from arbitrarily denying the public access to information about their gov't."

2. The Ohio House debate and final vote on Senate Bill 5 occurred on March 30, 2011. Video of the testimony is available at www.ohiochannel.org, and the material for this chapter has been taken from that source.
3. Laura Bischoff, "Kasich to Lobbyists: Get on the Bus," *Springfield News-Sun*, Nov. 5, 2010, http://www.springfieldnewssun.com/news/news/national-govt-politics/kasich-to-lobbyists-get-on-the-bus-1/nNJWW/.
4. *The Toledo Blade* pointed out an interesting conflict for Wachtmann: "State Rep. Lynn Wachtmann (R-Napoleon) owns a bottling company that gets its water from Napoleon, which draws from the Lake Erie watershed. He also sits on the board of directors of the International Bottled Water Association. Yet neither he nor—apparently—the Office of the Legislative Inspector General thought that should stop him from sponsoring legislation to significantly increase the volume of water that companies—such as his—are allowed to draw from that same watershed." Editorial, "Political Ethics," *The Toledo Blade*, Jan. 11, 2013, http://www.toledoblade.com/Editorials/2013/01/11/Political-ethics.html.
5. Rachel Lloyd, "Meet the Candidates: Six Introduce Themselves at Town Hall Meeting," *Sidney Daily News*, Feb. 27, 2012.
6. Mary McCleary, "Editorial: Control Compensation to Solve School Funding Crisis in Sidney," Buckeye Institute website, http://www.buckeyeinstitute.org/news-from-the-statehouse?id=74. McCleary is identified as a "policy analyst."
7. Not surprisingly, McCleary was a 2009 magna cum laude graduate of Hillsdale College, an incubator for right-wing extremism, where she majored in economics. According to the Buckeye Institute, McCleary received "Department Honors for her outstanding work as an undergraduate." She was also awarded a "prestigious" Koch Foundation Fellowship. Hillsdale College has been on the AAUP's censure list since 1988. This is a list of academic bad actors that typically make the list by showing a lack of respect for shared governance or, in Hillsdale's case, academic freedom. While a statement on the Hillsdale College webpage says that today the college is a "very different place," it states that it has never worked to remove the AAUP designation because it does not respect the right of the national faculty-driven organization to be an arbiter of such an issue.
8. Reginald Fields, "Ohio Gov. Kasich Using Collective Bargaining Bill as Fundraising Tool Even Before He Signs It," *The Cleveland Plain-Dealer*, March 31, 2011, http://www.cleveland.com/open/index.ssf/2011/03/ohio_gov_kasich_already_using.html.
9. The ceremonial signing of Senate Bill 5 can be viewed at www.ohiochannel.org.

Chapter 7

1. Speech at April 4, 2011, rally in Dayton by Rudy Fichtenbaum. Copy in possession of the author.
2. Sen. John F. Kennedy, "Labor Speaks for Public Interest," *Federation News* (Chicago Federation of Labor), Sept. 5, 1960, papers of John F. Kennedy, pre-presidential papers, presidential campaign files, 196, 03 September 1959–20 September 1960, undated, John F. Kennedy Library, Boston, MA.
3. Letter in possession of the author.
4. Ohio Catholic Conference website, accessed Sept. 23, 2012.
5. Rachel Richardson, "Ohio NAACP, Faith Leaders, Call on Better Ohio to Denounce Huckabee SB 5 Comments," *The Cincinnati Enquirer*, Oct. 18, 2011, http://masonbuzz.com/2011/10/14/huckabee-defends-issue-2-to-crowd-in-mason/.
6. Dale Schaefer, "Unions Playing Hardball on Ohio Campuses," *The Cincinnati Enquirer*, May 6, 2011, http://news.cincinnati.com/article/20110508/EDIT02/105080319/Guest-column-Unions-playing-hardball-Ohio-college-campuses; see also: http://www.washingtontimes.com/news/2011/apr/5/unions-playing-hardball-on-ohio-campuses/.
7. John T. McNay, "Faculty Integrally Involved in AAUP at UC, and in Contracts," *The Cincinnati Enquirer*, May 15, 2011, http://news.cincinnati.com/article/20110515/EDIT02/105150318/Guest-column-Faculty-integrally-involved-AAUP-UC-contracts.
8. Note in possession of the author.
9. Darrell Rowland, "Poll Shows Senate Bill 5 Could Be Repealed," *The Columbus Dispatch*, May 18, 2011, http://www.dispatch.com/content/stories/local/2011/05/18/poll-shows-senate-bill-5-would-be-repealed.html.
10. Jim Provance, "Labor Law's Defenders Gear Up to Fight Repeal: Battle Lines Drawn Over Senate Bill 5," *The Toledo Blade*, May 31, 2011, http://www.toledoblade.com/State/2011/05/31/Labor-law-s-defenders-gear-up-to-fight-repeal.html.
11. James Sprague, "Political Email Petitioning,"*The News-Record*, June 3, 2011, http://www.newsrecord.org/article_0e75df01-292a-518f-b4a2-4f2a0e03fad6.html; Red State blog, June 3, 2011.
12. Deborah Herman and John McNay, "SB 5 Repeal Petition Signatures Hit Astounding Number: 714,137," *Insights* member newsletter, June 17, 2011.
13. "Ohio Secretary of State Determines SB 5 Referendum Can't Be Split Up," *The Columbus Dispatch*, June 23, 2011, http://www.dispatch.com/content/stories/local/2011/06/23/husted-says-sb5-referendum-cant-be-split.html.
14. Joe Vardon, "SB 5 Opponents Make a Statement in a Big Way," *The Columbus Dispatch*, June 30, 2011, http://www.dispatch.com/

content/stories/local/2011/06/30/sb-5-opponents-make-a-statement-in-a-big-way.html.

15. Jim Provance, "Record 1.3 Million Back Vote to Torpedo Senate Bill 5," *The Toledo Blade*, June 30, 2011, http://www.toledoblade.com/State/2011/06/30/Record-1-3M-back-vote-to-torpedo-Senate-Bill-5-2.html.
16. Mark Kovac, "1.3 Million Seek Vote on SB 5," *The Youngstown Vindicator*, June 30, 2011, http://www.vindy.com/news/2011/jun/30/13m-seek-vote-on-sb-5/.
17. Joe Guillen, "Group Opposed to Senate Bill 5 Says It Has Enough Signatures for a Voter Referendum," *The Cleveland PlainDealer*, June 17, 2011, http://www.cleveland.com/open/index.ssf/2011/06/group_opposed_to_senate_bill_5.html.

Chapter 8

1. Andrew J. Tobias, "ALEC Helps Companies Write Ohio Laws," *Dayton Daily News*, May 26, 2012, http://www.daytondailynews.com/news/news/alec-helps-companies-write-ohio-laws/nPSfm/.
2. Cliff Peale, "Kasich Touting Plan for Charter Universities," *The Cincinnati Enquirer*, Feb. 24, 2011, http://news.cincinnati.com/article/20110224/NEWS0102/302240049/Kasich-touts-charter-universities-?odyssey=tab|topnews|text|FRONTPAGE.
3. Plunderbund, "Because Charter Schools Worked Out So Well, Kasich Says 'Let's Try Charter Universities,'" Feb. 28, 2011, http://www.plunderbund.com/2011/02/28/because-charter-schools-worked-out-so-well-kasich-says-lets-try-charter-universities/.
4. Carol Bliczky, "Petro Revisits Charter Universities," *Akron Beacon Journal*, March 2, 2011, http://www.ohio.com/news/petro-revisits-charter-universities-1.200131.
5. Ibid.
6. Encarnacion Pyle, "Charter College Idea Has Appeal," *The Columbus Dispatch*, March 6, 2011, http://www.dispatch.com/content/stories/local/2011/03/06/charter-college-idea-has-appeal.html.
7. Sara Kaminski, "Charter Universities Would Be Bad for Students, Taxpayers," *The Columbus Dispatch*, March 12, 2011, http://www.dispatch.com/content/stories/editorials/2011/03/12/charter-universities-would-be-bad-for-students-taxpayers.html.
8. Ibid.
9. Mark Niquette, "Kasich Takes to Airwaves to Pitch Ohio Budget That May Sell State Prisons," Bloomberg news, March 15, 2011, http://www.bloomberg.com/news/2011-03-15/kasich-takes-to-airwaves-to-pitch-ohio-budget-that-may-sell-state-prisons.html.
10. Laura Bischoff and Christopher Magan, "Deep Cuts, Privatization Fill Kasich's First Budget," *Springfield News-Sun*, March 16, 2011,

http://www.springfieldnewssun.com/news/news/state-regional/deep-cuts-privatization-fill-kasichs-first-budge-1/nMp5s/.

11. Ibid.
12. State of Ohio Executive Budget, *Book Five: The Reforms Book*, p. 16. www.ohio.gov.
13. Report in possession of the author.
14. A transcript of Petro's testimony can be found here: http://www.aaupuc.org/storage/charter-university/Petro%20Testimony%204.4.11.pdf.
15. Gongwer News Service, "Budget Panelists Question Charter University Plan," April 4, 2011, http://www.wright.edu/budget/panelists.html.
16. John McNay, "Charter Universities in Ohio Are Not the Solution," Hamilton *Journal-News*, May 13, 2011, http://www.journal-news.com/news/lifestyles/philosophy/john-mcnay-charter-universities-in-ohio-are-not--1/nNXsx. I have to credit my colleague, Deborah Herman, for the Trojan horse metaphor. When articles appeared in the *Journal-News*, they might also appear in other Cox Media newspapers in southwest Ohio, such as the *Dayton Daily News* (the flagship of the group), the *Middletown Journal*, or the *Springfield News-Sun*.
17. In Washington state, the University of Washington did increase tuition in 2011 by 20 percent and also approved a 16 percent hike in 2012. Washington State University increased tuition 16 percent each year. In Texas, after a more than 130 percent increase in the last 10 years, the Board of Regents have tried to slow down tuition increases.
18. Many of the videos can still be found on the internet by searching for "charter university UC" and similar terms.
19. An example of the failure of shared governance in a non-AAUP institution occurred at Miami in 2011. Essentially, a new regional campus "division" (Miami's term for colleges and schools) was created, disconnecting the regional campus faculty from Miami's main campus in Oxford, a division based solely on geography rather than academic discipline. The change was imposed despite overwhelming opposition not only from the faculty at the Hamilton and Middletown campuses but also from faculty on the main Oxford Campus. The University Senate opposed the move when it came up for a vote. In spite of all this committed opposition to a bad idea, the administration simply imposed the change. "This was an egregious affront to the notion of shared governance," a Miami faculty member told me.
20. Laura Bischoff, "Ohio Plans to Create Charter Universities That Would Take Less State Money," *Dayton Daily News*, Aug. 10, 2011, http://www.daytondailynews.com/news/news/local/ohio-plans-to-create-charter-universities-that-wou/nMtKj/.
21. Ibid.

22. The DAIR report maybe found here: http://www.uc.edu/content/dam/uc/facultysenate/senate/docs/alluniversityfacultymeeting/DAIR_report_052011.pdf.
23. Karen Farkas, "Plan to Create 'Enterprise Universities' in Ohio Remains Stalled," *The Cleveland PlainDealer*, April 22, 2012, http://www.cleveland.com/metro/index.ssf/2012/04/plan_to_create_enterprise_univ.html.

Chapter 9

1. German Lopez, "Jon Husted: Secretary of Suppression,"*City Beat* (Cincinnati), Nov. 7, 2012, http://www.citybeat.com/cincinnati/article-26541-jon_husted_secretary.html.
2. Mark Crispin Miller, "None Dare Call It Stolen: Ohio, the Election, and America's Servile Press," *Harper's Magazine,* August 2005, http://www.freepress.org/departments/display/19/2005/1383.
3. John Caniglia, "Congressional Democrats Bash Voting Law as State Lawmakers Eye Repeal," *The Cleveland Plain Dealer*, May 7, 2012, http://www.cleveland.com/metro/index.ssf/2012/05/congressional_democrats_bash_v.html.
4. Testimony on House Bill 194 can be viewed on www.ohiochannel.org.
5. "Anti-SB 5 and Anti-HB 194 Groups Rally at UT," *The Toledo Blade*, Oct. 12, 2011, http://www.toledoblade.com/Politics/2011/09/12/Anti-S-B-5-and-anti-H-B-194-group-rallies.html.
6. Joe Guillen, "Another Voter Referendum: Ohio Secretary of State Certifies Signatures to Put Elections Law on Next Year's Ballot," *The Cleveland Plain Dealer*, Dec. 9, 2011, http://www.cleveland.com/open/index.ssf/2011/12/another_voter_referendum_ohio.html.
7. "Sneak Attack," *Akron Beacon Journal*, March 27, 2012. Accessed Dec. 9, 2012.
8. Joe Guillen, "Ohio House Votes to Repeal Controversial Election Law," *The Cleveland Plain Dealer*, May 8, 2012, http://www.cleveland.com/open/index.ssf/2012/05/ohio_house_votes_to_repeal_con.html.
9. Darrell Rowland, "Ohio Lawmaker Quits After Drunken-Driving Scandal," *The Columbus Dispatch*, July 18, 2011, http://www.dispatch.com/content/stories/local/2011/07/18/lawmaker-quits-after-drunken-driving-scandal.html. As the *Dispatch* reported: "An embattled Cincinnati-area state representative quit yesterday afternoon, caught up in controversy after being arrested for drunken driving in Indiana with a stripper in his car and Viagra in his system."
10. Connie Schultz, "An Anti-Abortion Ohio Legislator's Embarrassing Night Out," *The Cleveland Plain Dealer*, July 3, 2011, http://www

.cleveland.com/schultz/index.ssf/2011/07/an_anti-abortion_ohio_legislat.html.

Chapter 10

1. Letter in possession of the author.
2. "SB 5 Makes Ballot; Stage Is Set for Battle," *The Columbus Dispatch*, July 22, 2011, http://www.dispatch.com/content/stories/local/2011/07/22/sb-5-makes-the-ballot-stage-is-set-for-battle.html; Joe Guillen, "Ohio's Collective Bargaining Law Will Be on the November Ballot," *The Cleveland Plain Dealer*, July 21, 2011, http://www.cleveland.com/open/index.ssf/2011/07/ohio_elections_chief_announces.html.
3. Mark Naymik, "Newt Gingrich Endorses Ohio's New Collective Bargaining Law," *The Cleveland Plain Dealer*, July 14, 2011, http://www.cleveland.com/naymik/index.ssf/2011/07/newt_gingrich_endorses_ohios_n.html.
4. Brent Larkin, "Cut Ohio's Losses by Cutting a Deal on SB 5," *The Cleveland Plain Dealer*, June 25, 2011, http://www.cleveland.com/opinion/index.ssf/2011/06/cut_ohios_losses_by_cutting_a.html; "Meet in the Middle," *The Columbus Dispatch*, Aug. 7, 2011, http://www.dispatch.com/content/stories/editorials/2011/08/07/meet-in-the-middle.html.
5. Jim Provance, "Kasich Offers to Tone Down SB 5 Language if Referendum is Pulled From the Ballot," *The Toledo Blade*, Aug. 17, 2011, http://www.toledoblade.com/State/2011/08/17/Kasich-offers-to-tone-down-SB-5-language-if-referendum-is-pulled-from-ballot.html.
6. Reginald Fields, "Gov. John Kasich Asks Union Leaders to Compromise on SB 5; Union Group Says Repeal it, Then We'll Talk," *The Cleveland Plain Dealer*, Aug. 17, 2011, http://www.cleveland.com/open/index.ssf/2011/08/ohio_governor_aks_union_leader.html.
7. Ibid.
8. Joe Guillen, "Senate Bill 5 Compromise Unlikely in Coming Days, but Another Version of the Bill Could Re-Emerge in the Future," *The Cleveland Plain Dealer*, Aug. 19, 2011, http://www.cleveland.com/open/index.ssf/2011/08/senate_bill_5_compromise_unlik.html.
9. "Kasich Stages 'Talks,' Assails No-Show Unions," *The Columbus Dispatch*, Aug. 19, 2011, http://www.dispatch.com/content/stories/local/2011/08/20/kasich-stages-talks-assails-no-show-unions.html; Reginald Fields, "Unions No-Shows at Gov. John Kasich's Compromise Meeting on Collective Bargaining Law," *The Cleveland Plain Dealer*, Aug. 19, 2011, http://www.cleveland.com/open/index.ssf/2011/08/unions_stand_together_no-shows.html.

10. Phillip Morris, "Gov. John Kasich, You Asked for the Fight, Now Fight," *The Cleveland Plain Dealer*, Aug. 19, 2011, http://www.cleveland.com/morris/index.ssf/2011/08/gov_john_kasich_you_asked_for.html.
11. Ohio Conference AAUP Communications Committee, Aug. 22, 2011, in possession of the author.
12. Cary Nelson, message to national AAUP members, Aug. 25, 2011, in possession of the author.
13. Joe Guillen, "Pro-Senate Bill 5 Campaign Chooses to Shield Donors' Contribution Amounts," *The Cleveland Plain Dealer*, Sept. 17, 2011, http://www.cleveland.com/open/index.ssf/2011/09/pro-senate_bill_5_campaign_cho.html.
14. Laura Bischoff, "Pro-Issue 2 Group Keeps Trail of Money Hidden," *Dayton Daily News*, Oct. 25, 2011, http://www.springfieldnewssun.com/news/news/national-govt-politics/pro-issue-2-group-keeps-trail-of-money-hidden-1/nMwn6/.
15. Truth-O-Meter, "Alliance for America's Future Says Ohio Can't Afford to Pay 100 Percent of Employees Benefits," *The Cleveland Plain Dealer*, Oct. 11, 2011, http://www.politifact.com/ohio/statements/2011/oct/12/alliance-americas-future/alliance-americas-future-says-government-cant-affo/; Laura Bischoff, "$38M Raised in Issue 2 Battle," *Dayton Daily News*, Oct. 27, 2011, http://www.daytondailynews.com/news/news/national-govt-politics/38m-raised-in-issue-2-battle-1/nMwsQ/; John Nichols, "How Liz Cheney Is Funding the War on Labor Rights in Ohio," *The Nation*, Oct. 18, 2011, http://www.thenation.com/blog/164037/how-liz-cheney-funding-war-labor-rights-ohio.
16. Staff, "Cincinnati Chamber Comes Out Against SB 5 Repeal," *Business Courier*, July 19, 2011, http://www.bizjournals.com/cincinnati/news/2011/07/19/cincinnati-chamber-comes-out-against.html.
17. Mark Naymik, "Gov. Ted Strickland and Challenger John Kasich Figure Out Strategies, Must Sell Them to Voters," *The Cleveland Plain Dealer*, April 2, 2010.
18. David Osborne, Beverly Stein, Jim Chrisinger, "Crisis as Opportunity," Public Strategies Group website, accessed Jan. 15, 2013. Much more on BFO can be found in David Osborne and Peter Hutchinson, *The Price of Government: Getting the Results We Need in an Age of Permanent Fiscal Crisis* (New York: Basic Books, 2004).
19. Ohio Chamber of Commerce, "Redesigning Ohio: Transforming Government into a 21st Century Institution," http://www.ohiochamber.com/mx/hm.asp?id=RedisigningOhio. See also ALEC's State Toolkit, http://www.alec.org/publications/state-budget-reform-toolkit/.

20. Mark Kovac, "House Panel OKs SB 5," *The Youngstown Vindicator*, March 30, 2011, http://www.vindy.com/news/2011/mar/30/house-panel-oks-sb-5/.
21. "The Chamber of Commerce Has Been Transformed into One of the Most Powerful Political Forces in Washington," *The Economist*, April 23, 2012, http://articles.businessinsider.com/2012-04-23/politics/31385442_1_political-spending-chamber-labour.
22. Tom Hamburger, "Chamber of Commerce Vows to Punish Anti-Business Candidates," *Los Angeles Times*, Jan. 8, 2008, http://www.latimes.com/entertainment/la-na-chamber8jan08,0,454295.story.
23. Ibid.
24. Erik Lipton, Mike McIntire, and Don Van Natta Jr., "Top Corporations Aid US Chamber of Commerce Campaign,"*The New York Times*, Oct. 21, 2010, http://www.nytimes.com/2010/10/22/us/politics/22chamber.html?pagewanted=all&_r=0.
25. Rachel Richardson, "Same Old Arguments Heard at Last Night's SB 5 Debate," *Cincinnati Enquirer*, Sept. 23, 2011, http://masonbuzz.com/2011/09/23/same-old-arguments-heard-at-last-nights-sb5-debate/.
26. "Debate Overview: Yes or No on Issue 2?", WKYC Television, Cleveland, Oct. 26, 2011, http://www.wkyc.com/news/state/article/211315/23/Issue-2-debate-to-air-tonight-on-WKYC-at-7-pm.

Chapter 11

1. Document in possession of the author.
2. Letter in possession of the author.
3. John T. McNay, "The War on Higher Education," *Passport*, 42:2, (Sept. 2011) 40–41. See also "The War on Higher Education," History News Network, Sept. 11, 2011, http://hnn.us/articles/9-12-11/war-on-higher-education.html.
4. Editorial, "Youngstown State University Cannot Afford Faculty Strike," *Youngstown Vindicator*, Aug. 14, 2011, http://www.vindy.com/news/2011/aug/14/youngstown-state-university-cannot-affor/.
5. Staff, "YSU Faculty Calls Off Planned Strike," *Youngstown Vindicator*, Aug. 25, 2011, http://www.vindy.com/news/2011/aug/25/ysu-responds-to-faculty-strike-vote/.
6. Cliff Peale, "Cincinnati State Teachers Go on Strike," *The Cincinnati Enquirer*, Sept. 24, 2011, http://news.cincinnati.com/article/20110923/NEWS0102/309240003/Cincinnati-State-teachers-go-strike.
7. Note in possession of the author.
8. All of the advertisements can easily be found on YouTube.

9. It is true that some language in the bill's amendments was intended to include safety equipment as a subject on which the union could negotiate. But the overall impact of the bill, by sharply curtailing negotiated subjects and by eliminating binding arbitration, made it so that even if the union completely disagreed with equipment and staffing levels, management could simply impose what it wanted. So, in reality, the Republicans had inserted a verbiage change without substantive meaning.
10. Jason Guillen, "Anti-Senate Bill 5 Group Debuts First TV Commercial in Campaign to Repeal Law," *The Cleveland Plain Dealer*, Sept. 2, 2011, http://www.cleveland.com/open/index.ssf/2011/09/anti-senate_bill_5_group_debut.html. Jim Provance, "Senate Bill 5 Backer Defends Bell Ad Timing," *The Toledo Blade*, Sept. 8, 2011, http://www.toledoblade.com/Politics/2011/09/08/Senate-Bill-5-backers-defend-Bell-ad-timing.html. As of this writing (December 2012), Mauk is executive director of the Ohio Republican Party.
11. PolitiFact Ohio, "We Are Ohio Claims SB 5 Would Make it Harder for Nurses to Care for Patients," *The Cleveland Plain Dealer*, Sept. 27, 2011, http://www.politifact.com/ohio/statements/2011/oct/10/we-are-ohio/we-are-ohio-claims-sb-5-would/.
12. Jim Siegel, "Recut Television Ad Makes SB 5 Opponent Look Like Supporter," *The Columbus Dispatch*, Oct. 14, 2011, http://www.dispatch.com/content/stories/local/2011/10/12/recut-television-ad-turns-sb-5-opponent-into-backer.html.
13. Ibid.
14. Henry J. Gomez, "SB 5 Ad War Heats Up as Grandmother Complains about Her Inclusion in Supporters' Commercial," *The Cleveland Plain Dealer*, Oct. 11, 2011, http://www.cleveland.com/open/index.ssf/2011/10/sb_5_ad_war_heats_up_as_grandm.html.
15. Siegel, ibid.
16. Gomez, ibid.
17. Editorial, "Issue 2 Ad Treats Opponent Unfairly," *The Cleveland Plain Dealer*, Oct. 13, 2011, http://www.cleveland.com/opinion/index.ssf/2011/10/issue_2_ad_treats_opponent_unf.html.
18. Joe Vardon, "Kasich Backers Join SB 5 TV Ad War," *The Columbus Dispatch*, Sept. 7, 2011, http://www.dispatch.com/content/stories/local/2011/09/07/kasich-backers-join-sb5-tv-ad-war.html; Campaign Ad Watch, "Reasonable, Make Ohio Great," *The Columbus Dispatch*, Sept. 30, 2011, http://www.dispatch.com/content/stories/local/2011/09/30/kasich-rga-ad-watch-g5lebela-1.html.
19. Truth-o-Meter, "Building a Better Ohio Says Public Workers Make 43 Percent More in Wages and Benefits than Private Sector Workers," *The Cleveland Plain Dealer*, Oct. 14, 2011, http://www.politifact.com/ohio/statements/2011/nov/04/building-better-ohio/building-better-ohio-says-public-workers-make-43-p/.

20. Newsletter in possession of author.
21. Steven Greenhouse, "Ohio Wages Fierce Fight on Collective Bargaining," *The New York Times*, Oct. 15, 2011, http://www.nytimes.com/2011/10/16/us/in-ohio-a-battle-over-public-employees-bargaining-rights.html?pagewanted=all&_r=0.
22. Jeff Bell, "SB 5 Support Fading, Along With Kasich's Approval," *Business First*, Oct. 25, 2011, http://www.bizjournals.com/columbus/news/2011/10/25/sb-5-support-fading-along-with.html.
23. Darrell Rowland, "Poll Shows Voters Still Sour on Issue 2," *The Columbus Dispatch*, Oct. 25, 2011, http://www.dispatch.com/content/stories/local/2011/10/25/poll-shows-voters-still-sour-on-issue-2.html; Kilpatrick letter in possession of author.
24. Editorial, "No on Issue 2," *Akron Beacon Journal*, Oct. 22, 2011, http://www.ohio.com/editorial/editorials/no-on-issue-2-1.241623.
25. Editorial, "No on Issue 2 But . . . ," *The Toledo Blade*, Oct. 30, 2011, http://www.toledoblade.com/Editorials/2011/10/30/No-on-Issue-2-but.html.
26. Marty Kich and Dave Witt, "Ohio's Faculty Unions: Front and Center," *The Chronicle of Higher Education*, letter to the editor, Nov. 2, 2011.
27. Kaustuv Basu, "Battle for Survival," *Inside Higher Ed*, Oct. 27, 2011, http://www.insidehighered.com/news/2011/10/27/ohio-faculty-unions-fights-measure-end-collective-bargaining.
28. Kaustuv Basu, "Solidarity in Ohio," *Inside Higher Ed*, Nov. 8, 2011, http://www.insidehighered.com/news/2011/11/08/ohio-rejects-bill-kill-public-unions.
29. Ibid.
30. Thomas Suddes, "The People of Ohio Spoke on Senate Bill 5, but Gov. John Kasich Isn't a Listener," *The Cleveland Plain Dealer*, Nov. 12, 2011, http://www.cleveland.com/opinion/index.ssf/2011/11/the_people_spoke_but_kasich_is.html. For more on Wood, see http://www.nytimes.com/2011/07/24/books/review/the-idea-of-america-by-gordon-s-wood-book-review.html?pagewanted=all

Conclusion

1. Frank Freidel, *Franklin D. Roosevelt: A Rendezvous with Destiny* (Boston: Little Brown, 1990) 202–203. There is, of course, a massive historiography on Roosevelt and the New Deal, but of particular value are H. W. Brands, *Traitor to His Class: The Privileged Life and Radical Presidency of Franklin Delano Roosevelt* (New York: Anchor Books, 2008) and Arthur Schlesinger Jr., *The Age of Roosevelt* (Boston: Houghton Mifflin, 1957). Albert Fried, *FDR and His Enemies* (New York: Palgrave Macmillan, 2001) also offers a valuable perspective.

2. Michael J. Sandel, *What Money Can't Buy: The Moral Limits of Markets* (New York: Farrar, Straus, and Giroux, 2012).
3. Kevin Phillips, *The Emerging Republican Majority* (New York: Arlington House, 1969). See also Daniel Bell, ed., *The Radical Right* (London: Transaction Publishers, 2002).
4. Warren Weaver Jr., "Prejudice and the Presidential Election," *The New York Times*, Sept. 21, 1969, accessed Jan 17, 2013.
5. Peter G. Bourne, *Jimmy Carter: A Comprehensive Biography from Plains to the Post-Presidency* (New York: Scribner, 1997).
6. Kevin Phillips, *The Politics of Rich and Poor: Wealth and the American Electorate in the Reagan Aftermath* (New York: Random House, 1990).
7. Ibid., xvii.
8. Ibid., 76–115, 179–181.
9. Timothy Noah, *The Great Divergence: America's Growing Inequality Crisis and What We Can Do About It* (New York: Bloomsbury Press, 2012) 142–143. See also Steve Fraser and Gary Gerstle, eds., *Ruling America: A History of Wealth and Power in a Democracy* (Cambridge: Harvard University Press, 2005).
10. Joseph McCartin, *Collision Course: Ronald Reagan, the Air Traffic Controllers, and the Strike that Changed America* (New York: Oxford University Press, 2011).
11. Staff, "Income Inequality in America: The 99 percent," *The Economist*, Oct. 28, 2012, http://www.economist.com/blogs/dailychart/2011/10/income-inequality-america.
12. All the student letters and more are in the author's possession.
13. Laura Bischoff, "OSU President Expenses in the Millions," *Dayton Daily News*, Sept. 22, 2012, http://www.daytondailynews.com/news/news/state-regional-govt-politics/expenses-of-osu-president-run-into-millions-for-tr/nSGkK/. In November of 2012, the trustees gave Gee a 3 percent raise and a bonus totaling $333,812, to bring his total yearly compensation to $2.14 million: http://www.daytondailynews.com/news/news/state-regional-govt-politics/osu-trustees-award-president-gee-a-3-percent-pay-r/nS3BJ/.
14. Cliff Peale, "Williams to Get $1.267M Severance from UC," *The Cincinnati Enquirer*, Sept. 24, 2012, http://news.cincinnati.com/article/20120912/NEWS0102/309120056/Williams-get-1-267M-severance-from-UC. Of course, much but not all of the wealth showered on Williams and others is required by contract. But that certainly begs the question of why these arrangements are agreed to and then unnecessarily enhanced. For more on Williams, see Matthew Nordin, "Fox 19 Investigates: Former UC President's Extravagant Lifestyle," *Fox 19 Action News*, Nov. 20, 2012, http://www.19actionnews.com/story/20153066/fox19-investigates-former-uc-presidents-extravagant-lifestyle; Daniel Burnett, "KSU

Trustees Betray Students by Boosting President's Pay," *The Cleveland Plain Dealer*, Aug. 13, 2011.

15. Aaron Marshall, "Gov. John Kasich's Top Staffers Earn More Than Gov. Ted Strickland's, but Overall Budget Less," *The Cleveland Plain Dealer*, Jan. 12, 2011, http://www.cleveland.com/open/index.ssf/2011/01/kasich_top_staffers_earn_more.html.
16. Thomas E. Mann and Norman J. Ornstein, *It's Even Worse Than It Looks: How the American Constitutional System Collided with the New Politics of Extremism* (New York: Basic Books, 2012) xiv.
17. Joe Hallett, "State Lawmakers Stray Far from Their Constituents," *The Columbus Dispatch*, April 21, 2013.
18. Joseph E. Stiglitz, *The Price of Inequality: How Today's Divided Society Endangers Our Future* (New York: Norton, 2012) 6–7.
19. Ibid, 64–65.
20. Ibid.
21. Ibid., 175.
22. Richard Thaler, "What the Rich Don't Need," *The New York Times*, Sept. 25, 2010, http://www.nytimes.com/2010/09/26/business/26view.html?_r=0.
23. Lawrence Mishel, "Unions, Inequality, and Faltering Middle Class Wages," Economic Policy Institute website, Aug. 29, 2012, http://www.epi.org/publication/ib342-unions-inequality-faltering-middle-class/.
24. David J. Lynch, "Corporate Profits Soar as Executives Attack Obama Policy," Bloomberg News, Jan 17, 2013, http://www.bloomberg.com/news/2013-01-17/corporate-profits-soar-as-executives-attack-obama-policy.html.
25. Bruce Bartlett, "Revenge of the Reality-Based Community: My Life on the Republican Right and How I Saw It All Go Wrong," *The American Conservative*, Nov. 26, 2012, http://www.theamericanconservative.com/articles/revenge-of-the-reality-based-community/.
26. Stiglitz, 281–282.
27. Paul Krugman, "Wisconsin Power Play," *The New York Times*, Feb. 20, 2011, http://www.nytimes.com/2011/02/21/opinion/21krugman.html?src=tptw&_r=0.
28. Stiglitz, 283; Alexander J. Field, *A Great Leap Forward: 1930s Depression and U.S. Economic Growth* (New Haven: Yale University Press, 2011).
29. Jill Lepore, *The Whites of Their Eyes: The Tea Party's Revolution and the Battle over American History* (Princeton: Princeton University Press, 2010).
30. Paul Kostyu, "Kasich Says 2-Year Budget Has $1 Billion Surplus," *The Cincinnati Enquirer*, Jan. 30, 2013, http://news.cincinnati.com/article/20130129/NEWS010801/301290148/EXCLUSIVE-Kasich-says-2-year-budget-has-1B-surplus.

31. Kevin Phillips, *Wealth and Democracy: A Political History of the American Rich* (New York: Broadway Books, 2002) 422.
32. For sources of these and other needed reforms, see Stiglitz, 265–290; Noah, 179–195; Mann and Ornstein, 107–201; Ginsberg, 201–219, Phillips, *Wealth and Democracy*, 405–422.

Bibliography

Newspapers

Akron Beacon-Journal
The Arizona Republic
Business First (Columbus)
The Capital Times (WI)
The Chronicle of Higher Education
The Cincinnati Enquirer
The Cleveland Leader
The Cleveland Plain Dealer
The Columbus Dispatch
Dayton Daily News
Hamilton Journal-News
The Highland County Press
Inside Higher Ed
Los Angeles Times
Middletown Journal
The New York Times
Sidney Daily News
Springfield News-Sun
The Toledo Blade
The Wall Street Journal
The Washington Post
The Washington Times
The Youngstown Vindicator

Books

Bell, Daniel, ed. *The Radical Right*. London: Transaction Publishers, 2002.

Bourne, Peter G. *Jimmy Carter: A Comprehensive Biography from Plains to the Post-Presidency*. New York: Scribners, 1997.

Bousquet, Mark. *How the University Works: Higher Education and the Low Wage Nation*. New York: New York University Press, 2008.

Bowen, Michael. *The Roots of Modern Conservatism: Dewey, Taft, and the Battle for the Soul of the Republican Party.* Chapel Hill: University of North Carolina Press, 2011.

Brands, H. W. *Traitor to His Class: The Privileged Life and Radical Presidency of Franklin Delano Roosevelt.* New York: Anchor Books, 2008.

Brennan, Mary C. *Turning Right in the Sixties: The Conservative Capture of the GOP.* Chapel Hill: University of North Carolina Press, 1995.

Brody, David.*Labor Embattled: History, Power, Rights.* Urbana: University of Illinois Press, 2005.

Brooks, Arthur C. *The Battle: How the Fight Between Free Enterprise and Big Government Will Shape America's Future.* New York: Basic Books, 2010.

Cannon, Lou. *President Reagan: The Role of a Lifetime.* New York, Simon & Schuster, 1991.

Carter, Dan T. *From George Wallace to Newt Gingrich: Race in the Conservative Counterrevolution, 1963–1994.* Baton Rouge: Louisiana State University Press, 1996.

Connolly, C. P. *The Devil Learns to Vote: The Story of Montana.* New York: Covici, Friede, 1938.

Crespino, Joseph. *In Search of Another Country: Mississippi and the Conservative Counterrevolution.* Princeton: Princeton University Press, 2007.

———. *Strom Thurmond's America.* New York: Hill and Wang, 2012.

DeMint, Jim. *Last Chance: Saving America from Economic Collapse.* New York: Center Street, 2012.

Edwards, Lee. *The Conservative Revolution: The Movement that Remade America.* New York: The Free Press, 1999.

Farber, David. *The Rise and Fall of Modern American Conservatism: A Short History.* Princeton: Princeton University Press, 2010.

Field, Alexander J. *A Great Leap Forward: 1930s Depression and U.S. Economic Growth.* New Haven: Yale University Press, 2011.

Fraser, Steve, and Gary Gerstle, eds. *Ruling America: A History of Wealth and Power in a Democracy.* Cambridge: Harvard University Press, 2005.

Fried, Albert. *FDR and His Enemies.* New York: Palgrave Macmillan, 2001.

Frederickson, Kari. *The Dixie Revolt and the End of the Solid South, 1932–1968.* Chapel Hill: University of North Carolina Press, 2000.

Freidel, Frank. *Franklin D. Roosevelt: A Rendezvous with Destiny.* Boston: Little Brown, 1990.

Galambos, Louis, ed. *The Papers of Dwight D. Eisenhower.* Baltimore: Johns Hopkins University Press, 1989.

Galvin, Daniel J. *Presidential Party Building: Dwight Eisenhower to George W. Bush.* Princeton: Princeton University Press, 2010.

Ginsberg, Benjamin. *The Fall of the Faculty: The Rise of the All Administrative University and Why It Matters.* New York: Oxford University Press, 2011.

Glasscock, C. B. *The War of the Copper Kings: The Builders of Butte and the Wolves of Wall Street.* New York: Grosset & Dunlap, 1966.

Goldwater, Barry. *The Conscience of a Conservative.* New York: Mcfadden-Bartell, 1961.

Harvey, David. *A Brief History of Neoliberalism.* New York: Oxford University Press, 2007.

von Hayek, Frederick A. *The Road to Serfdom.* London: Routledge, 1944.

Hetherington, Mark J., and Jonathan D. Weiler.*Authoritarianism and Polarization in American Politics.* New York: Cambridge University Press, 2009.

Hoff Wilson, Joan. *Herbert Hoover: The Forgotten Progressive.* Boston: Little Brown, 1975.

Hofstader, Richard. *The Paranoid Style in American Politics.* New York, Knopf, 1965.

Judas, John, and Ruy Teixeira.*The Emerging Democratic Majority.* New York: Scribner, 2004.

Judt, Tony. *Ill Fares The Land.* New York: Penguin Press, 2009.

Kabaservice, Geoffrey. *Rule and Ruin: The Downfall of Moderation and the Destruction of the Republican Party from Eisenhower to the Tea Party.* New York: Oxford University Press, 2012.

Kasich, John. *Courage Is Contagious: Ordinary People Doing Extraordinary Things to Change the Face of America.* New York: Doubleday, 1995.

Klein, Naomi. *The Shock Doctrine: The Rise of Disaster Capitalism.* New York: Picador, 2008.

Krugman, Paul. *The Conscience of a Liberal.* New York: Norton, 2007.

Lepore, Jill. *The Whites of Their Eyes: The Tea Party's Revolution and the Battle over American History.* Princeton: Princeton University Press, 2010.

Leuchtenburg, William E. *Franklin D. Roosevelt and the New Deal, 1932–1940.* New York: Harper & Row, 1963.

———. *The FDR Years: On Roosevelt and His Legacy.* New York: Columbia University Press, 1995.

———. *In the Shadow of FDR: From Harry Truman to Barack Obama.* Ithaca, NY: Cornell University Press, 1985, 2009.

Malone, Michael P. *The Battle for Butte: Mining and Politics on the Northern Frontier, 1864–1906.* Seattle: University of Washington Press, 1981.

Mann, Thomas E., and Norman J. Ornstein. *It's Even Worse Than It Looks: How the American Constitutional System Collided with the New Politics of Extremism.* New York: Basic Books, 2012.

McCartin, Joseph. *Collision Course: Ronald Reagan, the Air Traffic Controllers, and the Strike that Changed America.* New York: Oxford University Press, 2011.

Mercier, Laura. *Anaconda: Labor, Community, and Culture in Montana's Smelter City.* Urbana: University of Illinois Press, 2001.

Micklethwait, John, and Adrian Wooldridge. *The Right Nation: Conservative Power in America.* New York: Penguin Press, 2004.

Noah, Timothy. *The Great Divergence: America's Growing Inequality Crisis and What We Can Do About It.* New York: Bloomsbury Press, 2012.

Osborne, David, and Peter Hutchinson, *The Price of Government: Getting the Results We Need in an Age of Permanent Fiscal Crisis*. New York: Basic Books, 2004.

Parmet, Herbert S. *Richard Nixon and His America*. Boston: Little, Brown, 1990.

Phillips, Kevin. *The Emerging Republican Majority*. New York: Arlington House, 1969.

———. *The Politics of Rich and Poor: Wealth and the American Electorate in the Reagan Aftermath*. New York: Random House, 1990.

———. *Wealth and Democracy: A Political History of the American Rich*. New York: Broadway Books, 2002.

———. *Bad Money: Reckless Finance, Failed Politics, and the Global Crisis of American Capitalism*. New York: Viking, 2008.

Phillips-Fein, Kim. *Invisible Hands: The Making of the Conservative Movement from the New Deal to Reagan*. New York: Norton, 2009.

Sandel, Michael J. *What Money Can't Buy: The Moral Limits of Markets*. New York: Farrar, Straus, and Giroux, 2012.

Schlesinger Jr., Arthur. *The Age of Roosevelt*. Boston: Houghton Mifflin, 1957.

Schwartz, Jordan. *The New Dealers: Power Politics in the Age of Roosevelt*. New York: Knopf, 1993.

Screpanti, Ernesto, and Stephano Zamagni. *An Outline of the History of Economic Thought*. New York: Oxford University Press, 2005.

Shlaes, Amity. *The Forgotten Man: A New History of the Great Depression*. New York: Harper, 2007.

Smith, Robert Michael. *From Blackjacks to Briefcases: A History of Commercialized Strikebreaking and Unionbusting in the United States*. Athens: Ohio University Press, 2003.

Stiglitz, Joseph E. *The Price of Inequality: How Today's Divided Society Endangers Our Future*. New York: Norton, 2012.

Wapshott, Nicholas. *Keynes-Hayek: The Clash That Defined Modern Economics*. New York: Norton, 2011.

Yergin, Daniel, and Joseph Stanislaw. *The Commanding Heights: The Battle for the World Economy*. New York: Simon and Schuster, 2002.

ARTICLES

Apple Jr., R. W. "A Republican with Rough Edges." *New York Times Magazine*, April 26, 1998, http://www.nytimes.com/1998/04/26/magazine/a-republican-with-rough-edges.html.

Bartlett, Bruce. "Revenge of the Reality-Based Community: My Life on the Republican Right and How I Saw It All Go Wrong." *The American Conservative*, Nov. 26, 2012, http://www.theamericanconservative.com/articles/revenge-of-the-reality-based-community.

Chait, Jonathan. "2012 or Never," *New York Magazine*. Feb. 26, 2012, http://nymag.com/news/features/gop-primary-chait-2012-3/.

Davidson, Amy. "Remember Montana: The Supreme Court Won't Reexamine Citizens United." *The New Yorker*, June 25, 2012, http://www.newyorker.com/online/blogs/closeread/2012/06/remember-montana-citizens-united.html.

Fallows, James. "'Have You No Sense of Decency??': The Wiliam Cronon Story." *The Atlantic*, March 25, 2011, http://www.theatlantic.com/national/archive/2011/03/have-you-no-sense-of-decency-the-wm-cronon-story/73010/.

Gelman, Sheldon. "Adopting Ohio Senate Bill 5: The Role of the University Presidents." *Albany Law Review*, 75:1, 2011/2012.

Grieder, William. "The Education of David Stockman." *The Atlantic*, Dec. 1981, http://www.theatlantic.com/magazine/archive/1981/12/the-education-of-david-stockman/305760/.

Harris, Bill. "Tax Cuts Don't Create Jobs." *Forbes*, Nov. 5, 2012, http://www.forbes.com/sites/billharris/2012/11/05/tax-cuts-dont-create-jobs/Accessed on Jan. 9, 2013.

McNay, John T. "The War on Higher Education." *Passport*, 42:2, (Sept. 2011) 40–41.

Miller, Mark Crispin. "None Dare Call It Stolen: Ohio, the Election, and America's Servile Press." *Harper's Magazine*, August 2005, http://www.freepress.org/departments/display/19/2005/1383.

Rogers, Joel, and Laure Dresser. "ALEC Exposed: Business Domination, Inc." *The Nation*, July 12, 2011,www.thenation.com/article/161977/business-domination-inc.

Rusher, William A. "Crossroads for the GOP," *National Review*, Feb. 12, 1963, 109–12.

Sachs, Jeffrey D. "Welfare State Beyond Ideology." *Scientific American*, November 2006, http://www.scientificamerican.com/article.cfm?id=the-social-welfare-state.

Index

Printed in the United States of America